B   Mays, Willie
Mays Say hey
C.2

                            17.95

B
Mays
C.2

Mays, Willie
    Say hey; the autobiography of
Willie Mays. Willie Mays with Lou
Sahadi.   Simon and Schuster, 1988.
    286 p.   photos.

1. Mays, Willie. 2. Baseball -
Biography. I. Title.

Say Hey

The Autobiography of Willie Mays

Willie Mays
with *Lou Sahadi*

SIMON AND SCHUSTER
New York   London   Toronto   Sydney   Tokyo

Simon and Schuster
Simon & Schuster Building
Rockefeller Center
1230 Avenue of the Americas
New York, New York 10020

Designed by Gilda Hannah
Manufactured in the United States of America

10   9   8   7   6   5   4   3   2   1

Library of Congress Cataloging-in-Publication Data
Mays, Willie, 1931–
   Say hey: the autobiography of Willie Mays/Willie Mays with Lou
Sahadi.
      p.   cm.
   Includes index.
   1. Mays, Willie, 1931- . 2. Baseball players—United States—
Biography.   I. Sahadi, Lou.   II. Title.
GV865.M38A3   1988
796.357′092′4—dc19
[B]
ISBN 0-671-63292-2   88-6699
                                                        CIP

To my father, who was there at the start;
to Leo, who was there when it counted;
and to Mae, who was there when it mattered most.

Acknowledgments

The author would be remiss in not signifying special
thanks to the following:
Allen Peacock, an editor with patience, sensitivity, and
professionalism;
Jay Acton, who made it all happen;
and to Mae Mays, Carl Kiesler, Sy Berger, and Piper Davis.

Say Hey

The Autobiography of Willie Mays

1

I NEVER BECAME A CLEANER or a presser in a laundry.
That was the job they trained me for at the Fairfield Industrial High School in Fairfield, Alabama. Don't laugh. That
was a big job for most of us young boys then, back in the
late 1940's, in that part of the South. This country could
always use another hard-working, earnest young man who
knew how to wash a shirt or press a pair of pants. And let's
face it, there just weren't that many other opportunities for
a young black kid living in the Deep South almost twenty
years before the coming of the civil rights movement.

No, they wound up writing a song about me instead,
about me and some other guys you may know of: "Willie,
Mickey, and the Duke."

No matter where I go, people still ask me about those
great days in New York, when three centerfielders who
everyone knew were future Hall of Famers all played at the
same time.

Who was better, they ask. Was there fierce competition
among us—a rivalry among superstars inspiring greater and
more daring feats on the playing field? The questions and
comparisons are inescapable, and they bring back a flood
of memories from the spring of 1951, when I arrived in
New York as a twenty-year-old rookie with the Giants and
found I was the Number 3 centerfielder in a town that

seemed to have room for only two. Duke Snider was already established. The Dook of Flatbush, hitting those high drives over the rightfield wall in Ebbets Field for the Dodgers. Mantle? He was only a Yankee rookie then, but he was already marked for greatness.

He had come up in spring training and quickly hit a ball that they measured at more than 500 feet. Everyone knew the 1951 season was going to be Joe DiMaggio's last year, and Mickey very quickly became DiMaggio's heir apparent. The player who would replace Joltin' Joe would have to show his abilities quickly.

So everything that Mantle did, he was watched. Funny, as a kid I had always thought I'd be the one to replace DiMaggio. He was my idol. He could do things so easily and so well. All the hours I spent catching a ball or throwing it or hitting it—in my mind, it wasn't me, it was the great DiMaggio.

No matter what happened after that brief stretch of time when all three of us played in the Big Apple—it surprises people when I tell them I played there only four full seasons —most fans still recall most vividly those days when on any given summer night they could watch me and the Giants play at the Polo Grounds, Mickey and the Yankees across the river in the House that Ruth Built, or Duke and the Dodgers out in Brooklyn at Ebbets Field. It's interesting, come to think of it, to note that each of the three of us wound up playing in the park that was best suited to our particular talents.

Duke liked to hammer the ball to right center, and he would bang up these high drives—high enough to clear that 40-foot fence at Ebbets Field. Duke was only thirty-one years old when the Dodgers moved to Los Angeles in 1958, but his home-run total fell from 40 to 15. I think you'll agree the Duke was tailor-made for Flatbush.

Then there was Mickey, and Yankee Stadium. It was a big, deep park, with those monuments in centerfield about

450 feet away. With his power he could actually reach the bleachers in right center or left center—420-foot shots. More important, when he batted left-handed he had that short porch in right, which did not curve away as sharply or as deeply as leftfield did. Remember, the two highest home-run totals for one year—61 for Roger Maris, and 60 for Babe Ruth—were hit by left-handed sluggers playing in Yankee Stadium.

I played in the weirdest park of all. It seemed bent out of shape. Yet for me it became a challenge that I overcame and used to my advantage, at bat and in the field.

Here's the thing about the Polo Grounds: It was 475 feet to straightaway center from home plate. Now you can either let that mess with your mind, or you can capitalize on it.

Because I hit the ball to all parts of the field, and with power, I was able to use those incredible alleys in right center and left center. It was 425 feet to the fence in left center, 450 to right center. Forget about homers there. You also had to forget about homers down the line, as inviting as they were. Imagine a place where it is less than 90 yards —258 feet—to the rightfield foul pole. It was only 280 feet to the left. But if you thought about that, you'd be trying to pull everything and you wouldn't hit anything. I learned. A lot of my liners would go for doubles and triples that would bounce past the outfielders. But it was a double-edged sword, of course. A lot of those 400-footers I hit were outs.

The field was like my backyard, though. As I was a fielder, it gave me all the room I needed. I knew its dimensions by heart. If you hit the ball up in the air, you were playing in my place, my territory, and the ball was mine. I had great anticipation when I went after a fly ball. So if you hit the ball with all your might and stroked it a good 420 feet, the chances were that I could run it down.

Not only that, because I was pretty good at getting ground balls, I could run to my left or right to cut off "tweeners"—balls that were hit into the gaps in left or right center. I was able to hold down extra bases because I could spear the ball backhanded.

Yep, no question about it. I was made for the Polo Grounds, just the way Mickey and the Duke were made for their parks.

But if you want to know the honest truth, I never got caught up in the competition that so captivated the fans and the press. I never compared myself to Mickey Mantle or Duke Snider or wondered who was a better ball player. We all had great respect for one another and never wasted any time comparing batting averages and on-base percentages.

One thing, though, makes me proud to this day: A lot of the photographs of me don't show me swinging a bat. They show me making a catch, or a throw, or sliding safe into third base. And usually my cap isn't even in the picture. I hope what I'm about to say doesn't disappoint the people who thought I was running so fast that I just ran out from under the hat, like someone in a cartoon. I lost my cap on purpose. When I first came up to the Giants in 1951, I never lost my cap. How could I? It fit perfectly. It was the right size. But after a while I started thinking about what I could do to give the fans a show, generate a little more excitement. So I came up with a gimmick: I started wearing a cap that was too big for me. And sure enough, every time I ran from first to second and wheeled to my left, that cap would simply fly off just as if I'd been running so fast I'd run out from under it. The cap would fly off when I stole a base, and so after dusting myself off I'd have to go back to pick it up. The moment's delay would keep the fans worked up and make the opposing pitcher think a bit more about the spot I'd got him in, which was fine by me. Sometimes the hat would even go sailing off when I chased a fly ball.

But wait a second. I wasn't out there plotting and scheming, doing everything I could to win a ball game back in 1951. I was a scared rookie, so scared that when Bobby

Thomson stepped into the batter's box and belted his historic, pennant-winning home run against the Dodgers at the Polo Grounds, I was crouched in the on-deck circle praying to God: *Please don't let it be me. Don't make me come to bat now, God.*

Times changed, of course. As the years went by, those clutch situations were what I prayed for. *Please, God, let it be me up at bat when we need the hit.* After a while I developed a special intuition in the clutch, a sense that I was meant to win the game. I wound up hitting more home runs in extra innings than anyone else who ever played—22, to be exact. That is six more than Babe Ruth hit after the ninth inning, and seven more than another clutch player, Frank Robinson, managed in his career.

But that first season was different. All I wanted to do was stay out of trouble. I didn't know what the future held for me. What's more, none of us knew then that sports fans and historians alike would regard the 1951 season as one of baseball's greatest years. Who knows, if I had come to bat one more time that year, there might not have been as much history to write about after all.

2

MY FATHER TOLD ME that I was able to walk when I was only six months old. And wouldn't you know it, he got me walking after a baseball. Getting a baseball was just about the first thing I was able to do. He put two chairs close to each other and then put a baseball on one. I was clinging to the other. He walked me through two or three times. "See the ball," he said. "See the ball." Then he turned me loose—and I went for the ball myself. When he knew I could chase a ball, he gave me batting lessons. He handed me a rubber ball and a little stick maybe two feet long, and sat me in the middle of the floor. I'd play with the ball all day long, hitting it with the stick, then crawling or toddling after it across the room. My dad was determined that if I wanted to, I would become a baseball player and not end up in the steel mills the way he did—although he was an outstanding player for the mill teams.

He was never too tired to play. When I was five years old he'd take me outside and bounce the ball on the sidewalk to me and yell, "Catch it," and we'd do that for hours. He was a very good baseball player. He was quick, really quick, and got the nickname Cat. He played in Birmingham's In-dustrial League, which often attracted six thousand fans a game. He took me to as many games as he could, and I was allowed to sit on the bench next to the grown-ups. There,

I'd hear them discuss strategy—how you'd play a right-handed pull hitter who was batting against a guy with a slow curve. Or how big a lead you could afford to take off first when you had a southpaw with a quick delivery on the mound. So baseball really came naturally to me, more so than to most other kids. My father never pushed me into becoming a baseball player. He just exposed me to it and it happened all by itself from there. How many kids would have a chance before a game to be out on the field? I would run to first and slide, run to second and slide, then to third, then home. Sliding was simply a natural effort to me. I had seen my father do it many times and I had practiced it often. I thought my father was so good, I copied everything he did. I was just a kid, but I had the style, and some of the knowledge, of a grown-up ball player. I knew how to do things the right way.

Even though my father didn't push me into baseball, it was the only thing that made sense. "Don't work in the mills," he would tell me. "You don't make any money there."

But my father waited for me to ask about playing base-ball.

"Willie, remember the time I asked you if you wanted a trumpet?" he likes to remind me. "You said no, that you didn't want it. Well, that's why I waited for you to tell me what you wanted and never gave you a glove until you asked for one. It's like what happened to Joe Louis when he was young. His mother bought him a banjo and he ended up in the gym and became a fighter. You had to do it for yourself. I could only show you the baseball when you were little. I couldn't make you play with it."

Both my parents were eighteen years old when I was born on May 6, 1931, in Westfield, Alabama. My mother, Ann, had been a high-school track star. My father, William Howard Mays, wound up working in the toolroom of a steel mill.

Sadly, my dad and mother separated when I was only three years old. My mother remarried. My stepfather's name was Frank McMorris, and my mother had ten more children—eight girls and two boys. In fact, she died in 1953 giving birth to her eleventh child.

My father was then a porter on the train from Birmingham to Detroit, so he was away a lot at first. At about that time an untimely death left two young girls in the neighborhood orphaned. My father moved the girls, Sarah and Ernestine, in with us to help raise me. I called each of them "Aunt" out of respect and love. After a couple of years Dad quit and went to work in the mills so he could be closer to home. He made good money as a porter and saved most of it for the day when we could move away from the mills in Westfield and live in Fairfield.

I called Otis Brooks my uncle, though he wasn't my real uncle. He was from Mobile, and when we moved to Fairfield, he helped out around the house. Back then in the South, whenever someone like Otis helped out with the chores, you'd always call him uncle. Fortunately, he helped me out all the time. Whenever any of my chores took away time from playing baseball or any of the other sports I played, like football or basketball, he'd cover for me. He was the first person who said to me, "Willie, you're going to be a ball player." I never forgot that.

Sarah was older than Ernestine and she ran the household. When I say older, I don't mean she was a grown-up woman. Both girls were barely teenagers. We lived in a neat little white house that was always clean. Sarah made sure we kept it that way, too. She'd tell me to wash the dishes before I went out, but Otis would give me a wink. I knew he'd do them for me. Sarah, meanwhile, hovered over me all the time, making sure that I went to school every day and always finding chores for me—chopping firewood, cleaning up the yard—that Otis ended up doing. If it hadn't been for Otis, I wouldn't have had the time to play ball as much as I did.

There were times when I went to school without any shoes. But I knew that by Friday I'd get a pair. Friday was payday at the mill—or maybe it should be called chip day, because the workers were paid in chips. Otis would take the chips my father gave him, go to the commissary at the mill, and buy me a pair of shoes. Other than the shoes, I always had clean clothes to wear. Sarah saw to that. Not only did we shop at a company store, we also lived in a company house. My father's dream was not of going to the big leagues himself. His dream was to own his own house, one that wasn't owned by the company—to be his own man.

When she got old enough, Ernestine—we called her Steen —began working as a night waitress in the Owl Club, a bar in Westfield, to earn some extra money. We were one big family, and everyone pulled together, Dad at the mills, Otis with the chores, Sarah in the house, and Steen working at the club. At least one night a week after work she'd come into my bedroom and leave ten dollars on top of my dresser, so I could have lunch money for school.

You'd think ten dollars would go far for school lunch, but a lot of my friends at school didn't have any lunch money, so I helped them out. When we had our lunch period, we'd leave school and head for the grocery store. I'd buy lunch meat, a couple of big loaves of bread, tomatoes, mayonnaise, and some cake, and pretty soon ten or twelve of us would be sitting down to lunch in an empty lot. We shared a great deal in those days. Some of my friends even came home with me at dinnertime, and Aunt Sarah would tell them to sit down and eat.

I was ten years old when we finally moved from the company houses in Westfield to a section of Fairfield called the Heights. One of my closest friends that first year was Charlie Willis, a black kid who lived just up the street. When we weren't playing ball, we were at each other's house. We shared whatever we had.

This is not easy to explain, but I always enjoyed playing ball, and it didn't matter to me whether I played with white kids or black. I never understood why an issue was made of who I played with, and I never felt comfortable, when I grew up, telling other people how to act. Over the years, a lot of organizations have asked me to be their spokesman, or have wanted me to make speeches about my experiences as a black athlete, or to talk to Congressmen about racial issues in sports. But see, I never recall trouble. I believe I had a happy childhood. Besides playing school sports, we'd play football against the white kids. And we thought nothing of it, neither the blacks nor the whites. It was the grown-ups who got upset. If they saw black kids playing on the same team with white kids, they'd call the cops, and the cops would make up stop. I never got into a fight that was started because of racism. To me, it was the adults who caused the problems. I still believe that. Kids could always work things out and find a way to get along.

Football was a game I really loved playing. On Saturdays I'd watch Miles College play. I'd walk over to the field, climb a tree—I didn't have money to get in—and watch my hero, Cap Brown, run up and down the field. One Saturday —I was about twelve years old at the time—I got careless. I fell out of the tree and broke my arm. Of course, I didn't tell anyone I had climbed a tree and I didn't even know the arm was broken. But after I got home I tried to pick up a bucket of coal, and pain shot through my arm.

But my arm only got stronger after that. In fact, right after I recovered I played with the Gray Sox, a semipro team based in Fairfield, against guys who were a couple of years older than I. Cap Brown was one. Before I broke my arm, I used to throw underhand—actually about three quarters underhand, like a submarine pitcher. Now I noticed I was throwing overhand with a great deal of speed. Brown was playing second and I started out at short, but I threw the ball so hard to first that the first baseman complained all the time. So the manager made me a pitcher. I really could hum the ball. My father put a stop to that, though. He felt that if a pitcher hurt his arm, then it was all over, he had nothing else if he wasn't trained to field or to hit. And that's how I became an outfielder.

Throwing was always natural to me and I always had a strong arm. When we first started playing baseball, I was the pitcher and Charlie Willis was the catcher. I threw harder than any of the other kids on the block, and everyone was afraid to catch my balls except Charlie. We respected each other for what we could do and our nicknames showed that. I called him Cool, and he called me Buck.

Every morning we'd go to Robinson Elementary School together. I'd throw a rubber ball against the sidewalk in front of his house while I waited for him to come out. As soon as he did, we'd play catch all the way to school. Thinking back now, I'd guess that I always had a ball in my hand. When I try to remember events as a kid, in my memories somehow a ball always winds up in my hands. I was forever hitting one or throwing one or catching one. Playing ball was an obsession we shared. Charlie shared another obsession with me: comic books. I loved to read them. His dad used to give us each a dime so we could go to Doc Pomran's drugstore and buy comic books.

But there weren't many dimes around. Life was rough for blacks in those days, and you were lucky to have a dime to take to church on Sunday. Even so, I don't think I ever felt poor. I seemed to have the things I needed, and I even tried to help out. One time when I was eight, I sold some moonshine on the weekend and made three dollars. My father found out and got angry. I quickly realized why. He told me that when I was three, my mother used to sell moonshine. When the police found out, they put my father in jail for the night and let my mother stay home with me. He said he didn't want to spend any more nights in jail, especially since he didn't approve of either drinking or smoking.

He was able to get his point across. One day he saw me with another kid who was drinking and smoking. My father made me leave the street corner, took me home, and took care of things in his own way.

"You want to smoke?" And he gave me a cigar, a White Owl, saying, "Smoke it."

I thought I would die from that cigar smoke.

"You want to drink?" my father asked. And he gave me a glass filled with Old Crow. "Drink it."

It was nasty. I never had a drink or even thought about smoking after that.

Although I had done plenty of chores in my time, and even made a quick, short buck selling moonshine, working wasn't for me. The only time I recall I ever worked was the night when I helped a friend of mine wash dishes in a restaurant. I didn't get home until six in the morning. My dad was having breakfast before going to work. He warned me never to come in that late again without telling him or Aunt Sarah.

If I managed to become a ball player, though, I knew I wouldn't have to worry about coming in late or getting stuck at the job. Maybe that's one of the reasons I loved playing baseball so.

I was fifteen, and baseball had come to mean more to me than just about anything else. That summer I played in the Industrial League with my father. He was slowing down by then, and they put him in leftfield while I was in center. My father had always been a symbol of strength to me, strength and ability. I measured my own talent by his. But one day you grow up and you surpass your father. I know now that it's a fact of life, even though it made me feel strange at the time. I would run over and catch every ball hit his way.

The actual break—the game in which he knew and I

knew that I had gone beyond being the kid he was teaching
—remains fixed in my mind. I still look back with sadness
at the last game we played together. I should have let him
catch most of the balls that day. It was his last game in the
league and I was about ready for the Birmingham Black
Barons, the Negro League team that I had dreamed of playing on all my life. I waved him off a deep shot to left center,
a ball he would have caught easily in other years, a ball I
never would have dared to try for, knowing that it was his.

Dad knew what was up, too. You didn't have to tell him;
it was an unspoken thing between us. So one day he took
me with him to meet Piper Davis. Dad had a great amount
of respect for Piper.

Piper Davis, the manager of the Barons, was like a second
father to me. He gave me the chance to play for the Barons
when I was only sixteen. He was a warm man, fatherly, and
all the players respected him. Nobody even knew that his
real name was Lorenzo. He came from a small mining town
called Piper Coleanor. So he became Piper.

I was a kid when I first met him. He used to play ball
with my father in the Industrial League around Birmingham. Late one summer, after my tenth-grade year, I saw
Piper in Chattanooga, where the Gray Sox, with whom I
played occasionally, had a game. Of course, we all stayed
in the only hotel for blacks in the town. So he spotted me
in the lobby.

"Boy, what are you doing up here?"

"Playing for the Grays."

That got him angry. "You know, if they catch you playing out here you won't be able to play high-school sports."

I told him I didn't care: The money was good. While
everyone else at Fairfield High was making eight or ten
dollars a week with part-time jobs, I was making about a
hundred dollars a month.

A few weeks after we'd met, I saw Piper again in Fairfield.

"You still playing out there?" he asked.

I nodded.

"Playing for money?"

I nodded again.

"If you want to play ball for money, have your daddy call me."

I ran home and waited for my father to come in from the mills. I told him what Piper said and he immediately called him. Then he hung up and looked at me.

"Piper says to come to the field at eleven-thirty Sunday."

If you're from a really big city that has a major league team, it may be hard to imagine that somewhere else, a minor league player or manager is great shakes—but believe me, he is, and the Black Barons were a big thing around Birmingham. My dad finally was ready to admit that I could play ball for the Black Barons, something that my friends had encouraged me to do for some time.

"Buck," one of them told me, "you have to do what you have to do." Now my father agreed, and he took me to see about playing Negro League ball.

"Hey, Piper, he thinks he's Joe DiMaggio, but he can't hit a curveball none," my dad said.

"Well, he's got to learn by next season if he's gonna play with us," Piper replied, "but I promise you, I'll give him a chance then."

Meanwhile there was football. Who knows? If times had been different, I might have wound up as a quarterback someplace. During the fall I played football at Fairfield. I loved to throw the ball. I tried to make it a simple game, and I had the arm to do it.

"You run here and you run there," I'd tell my teammates, "and don't stop, because I'll get the ball to you."

I had big hands and could easily grip a football and throw it 50 yards—without even winding up. Quick release, they'd call it now. I was also a pretty good runner, but my dad was always afraid I'd get hurt playing football. When the football season ended, I played on the basketball team and was the leading scorer. No matter the sport, I just loved playing, as long as there was a ball I could do things with.

Well, not always with a ball, either. I was pretty handy with a peach, too. I became the best peach player in town. Fairfield had a great many peach trees, and since I had the strongest arm, I was the one elected to sneak into the orchards, pluck the peaches off the trees, and throw them over the fence to my waiting friends. I'd fill up a big bag in no time.

These truly were fun times for all of us. You kept your friends for a long time then. It's easy to remember their names: Herman Boykin, Jimmy McCall, Robert Taylor, Dusty McGinnis, and Bo Weavil. All of us were close, and never once did we get into serious trouble, although we did some foolish things, as all kids do. Herman was just about the biggest fourteen-year-old I ever saw, and he was the ringleader.

Fourteen, and driving a truck, no less. He drove a panel truck for Stephenson's Dry Cleaners. He'd let us ride in the back with the doors open. Every now and then he'd make a sharp turn, and the door would shut and we'd end up rolling around the floor, laughing. Since he was the only one who could drive, or even had something to drive, Herman helped out with our sandlot team whenever we played out of town. We'd climb into an open dump truck, rain or shine. Sometimes we'd rag passing drivers. One time we started to make faces at the driver of a big truck behind us. After a few minutes he had had enough. He speeded up and passed us, and almost ran us off the road as he cut in front of the surprised Herman and made him stop short. But Herman found out what we had done. When he came to the ball field, he got even with us by raising the dumper— and we all tumbled out of the truck onto the field.

Those were also the days of the pool hall. I always thought pool playing had a bad rap. In the movies you'd always see wiseguys and gangsters shooting pool between

drags of a cigarette as they discussed some heist. But at Big
Tony's pool hall, where we hung out, it wasn't like that. In
fact, Tony was good to us. He wouldn't let us in until four
o'clock in the afternoon. This way he'd be sure we weren't
cutting school to play. He used to talk to us about getting
an education and felt that we should go home after school
to study before he would let us in. And when he did, he
very often let us play for free over one of the old, torn tables
in the back of the room.

The following spring, 1947, my education as a baseball
player took on a new dimension under Piper. He taught me
two key lessons, one about fielding and the other about
hitting. It may seem that everything I did on the field was
natural because in so many of the throws I made or the
balls I caught I followed my instincts. But I also learned.
For example, Piper insisted that I charge a ball hit through
the infield, especially with a runner on second base. This
way I would be in position to throw the ball home or dis-
courage the hitter from reaching second. Throwing was important. He didn't want me to throw it all the way on the
fly because the ball doesn't pick up any speed. A throw is
fastest the moment it leaves your hand. From that point on
it slows down. So now, you've got to try to help it pick up
speed.

"Bounce it," Piper said. "When the ball skips off the
ground it picks up speed." With my big hands, I didn't have
any trouble charging the ball at full speed and picking it up
with my bare hand. Having big hands made it easier for me
than for other outfielders to pick up a ball barehanded, and
it allowed me to get rid of it quicker and to throw it harder.
Most base runners do what they do as a result of their
success in the past against other outfielders. But if they come
against a ball player who's got something they haven't seen
before . . . well, that's when they get fooled, and that's
when they get cut down.

Once in a Barons game against the Kansas City Monarchs, I threw out two base runners. One was trying to make it from first to third on a single past the shortstop. The other tried to score from second on a hit to right center. The third time, Buck O'Neill, the Monarchs' manager, who was coaching at third, held up a runner there on a hit to center. Buck yelled, "Whoa, whoa, that man's got a shotgun."

What I remember mostly about that game, though, was my first meeting with Satchel Paige. Now, you've got to remember that this was in the late 1940's—and he already had been famous *since the 1920's*. The man was the most interesting player I had ever come up against. He stood six four and weighed about 170 pounds. His rules for staying out of trouble and in shape hadn't become famous yet. The one I like the best went: "Don't look back, something might be gaining on you." Fame was to come when he joined the Cleveland Indians in 1948 and helped them win their first pennant since 1920. He was about forty when the Indians brought him up as a rookie, but he was no rookie to me. He showed me the darnedest stuff I ever saw, along with some of the screwiest motions and combinations of different speeds. Old Satchel could really drive you crazy.

He had a knuckleball, a screwball, an assortment of curves—and his hesitation pitch. He'd pump his arm around like a windmill, and bring it over his head, and you expected to see the ball coming down, because that's the point at which a pitcher would throw. But nothing happened. He would be almost in his follow-through when all of a sudden the darn ball would appear and you would be swinging way in front of it.

Yet during this first meeting with the legend, I got a double off Paige my very first time up. I stood on second, dusting myself off, feeling pretty good. Paige walked toward me.

"That's it, kid," he muttered.

I didn't know what he meant—was he angry? Did he mean I had had it for the day?

It didn't take long to find out. My next three times up I went *whoosh, whoosh,* and *whoosh.* I never saw a fastball from him, only those crazy curves and his other soft stuff.

But I soon learned to hit the curveball. I had trouble with it until Piper corrected a problem with my stance. I had a habit of turning my shoulder toward home plate as I crouched. I would get hit quite often, since my body was leaning toward the plate when I was ready to swing. Piper made me turn more to the pitcher, and to stand straighter. I could see the ball better.

Those were the days when no one had a videotape machine and we never watched films of ourselves, certainly not the way Ted Williams had done from the time he was a young ball player. Piper just knew from observing, even though the whole affair—from delivery to swing—had to be over in less than half a second.

"You're knifin' in when the ball's coming in, and that causes you to fight two things—the ball, and the way you go after it," Piper explained. "Straighten up a little more and turn yourself around a little and you'll do a whole lot better."

I can say for sure he was right: The curveball didn't worry me after that. If it had, I don't think I would have hit more than 600 home runs. I adopted the stance that I stayed with for my career. Piper could see a lot in the flash of an instant.

3

WHEN I WAS SIXTEEN, in 1947, Jackie Robinson broke into the major leagues, and that was the first time most baseball fans ever heard of him. But we all knew who Jackie was. In fact, to us black ball players it seemed like a bigger breakthrough when, in 1946, he signed to play with the Dodgers' farm team in Montreal. That was organized ball. I mean, forget about the majors. No Negroes—at least, none who admitted they were Negroes—had ever even been in the minor leagues, had ever played any organized ball.

I wouldn't say that Robinson was my idol. My father had always been that. But it was Jackie Robinson who paved the way for all those black ball players who would eventually make it to the majors. I had not met Jackie then, but his name was special to me and probably to any other black kid who had dreams of becoming a pro. I didn't have any heroes who folded underwear in a laundry.

My own introduction to black baseball didn't arrive with much fanfare. Piper never said much, and he wasn't any different on that particular Sabbath morning. He gave me a worn-out uniform with "Barons" printed across the chest.

The Barons ... actually, I should call them the Black Barons, for there was another Barons team in Alabama then. But people just called that other team the Barons. That meant they were the white team. Funny thing about that white Barons team. I used to listen to them on the radio all the time. You know who their announcer was at one time? His name was Bull Connors. We knew about him in Alabama. But he became better known as Sheriff Bull Connors during the civil rights movement, especially over an integration incident in Selma. But I recall him doing the Barons games. Pretty good announcer, too, although I think he used to get too excited.

Both Barons teams were popular, and we always wondered which was the better club. The white Barons were in the Southern Association—the last minor league to be integrated. Birmingham even had a city law that banned blacks and whites from competing.

Anyway, the Barons—my Barons—always played a doubleheader at Rickwood Field on Sunday. That's where I showed up for my first game, sixteen years old, not realizing that I was going to be part of a chapter of history that was about to end. When I retired twenty-five years later, I was the last ball player except for Hank Aaron who had been in the Negro Leagues.

"Go shag some flies," Piper told me, and so I went to the outfield and spent most of batting practice there. Then, when the first game began, I sat on the bench. These guys were bigger than the kids I had been playing with, stronger, more powerful. And they also were good. Very good. How good I didn't appreciate until years later when going into organized ball was almost easy for me because I actually had been playing at a higher level with the Barons.

Now, though, I just sat.

"Watch," said Piper, "watch what's going on."

Between games we sat in the clubhouse. The guys who had played were cooling off with soft drinks, in a good mood and talking about the opener, which we had won— or I should say, which they had won. I was sitting by myself in the back, a kid about ten years younger than most of them, and an outsider. Then Piper came over to me.

"I'm gonna let you play the second game," he said in a whisper. "I don't know how you're gonna do. Play left field and give it your best shot."

Before we took the field, Piper called over to Roosevelt Atkins and handed him a slip of paper. Atkins was in charge of the equipment, but he also wore a uniform and could play if we needed an extra man. This was not, remember, the major leagues. The equipment man was a body, and sometimes you just needed an extra body to suit up.

"Roo," said Piper to Atkins, "pin this lineup in the dugout."

Piper looked at me and winked. When the rest of the players reached the dugout and looked at the lineup for the second game, they all started to mumble to one another. Piper, sitting on the bench, picked up what they were saying.

"How's the lineup to you, fellas?" he shouted. "Anybody doesn't like that lineup, well, there's the clubhouse—and you can go in and take off the uniform if you want to."

He got no takers.

There it was: "Mays, LF," batting seventh. None of the other players was leaving, even though a sixteen-year-old was about to play in his first Negro League game. But still, I knew I had to show them I could play. First I had to get the butterflies out of my stomach. When I had done that I got two hits off Chet Brewer, who was one of the best pitchers in the league, and when that game was over I was just so excited, I couldn't wait to see what Piper had to say. I was hired, he told me. Come back next week, he said. Not only was I going to play with the Birmingham Black Barons. I was getting $250 a month.

I was still in high school that first year, and Piper wouldn't let me make any road trips until school was out. He wanted to make sure I didn't fall behind in my schoolwork, pointing out that it was important for me to graduate from high school. Still, my playing for the Barons created an uproar at Fairfield Industrial. The principal, E. T. Oliver, didn't like it at all—and neither did my classmates. They felt I was letting them down. I was not permitted to play any high-school athletics while I was getting paid by the Barons. The kids at the school felt I had sold them out. I guess maybe I had. But look at the chance I had been given —to play baseball, and to get paid for doing it.

Mr. Oliver didn't fool around. If he caught you doing something wrong, you were punished. He seemed to know everything that his students did, so if you played hookey you'd better not stay home. He'd find you there. Even if you were sick at home, you worried that he'd think you were faking it. He always sent somebody to check. "Get educated," he would tell us. Athletics were not important, at least not so important that you could spend more time on the field than studying.

He was very proud that his students graduated. I think that's why he got so upset when he found out I was playing for the Barons. He even threatened to suspend me from school. He was sure that my ball playing would keep me out of the classroom. But Piper and my father assured him that I wouldn't miss any days of school by playing baseball. And I didn't, either.

I have always been proud of the fact that I graduated from high school. That was tremendously important to me, especially since I was juggling athletics and studying. Maybe it's no big deal for today's athletes to say they've got a high-school diploma, but it wouldn't surprise me to find that I was in the minority of ball players in my time who actually finished school.

Still, I couldn't wait for the summer to come, for that's when I was allowed to travel with the Barons. It would be easy for me to look back now and say, boy, it was tough. I've gotten used to a certain style in travel, in hotels, in eating, to having things done for me. But it's funny, isn't it, how I look back on those days in the bus and think that it was just about the finest thing that could ever happen to a kid.

I learned many things about my baseball heritage on those rides. I learned, for example, that Jackie Robinson wasn't the first black ball player to wear a big-league uniform. He was just the first who didn't pretend not to be black. For years, players had "passed" or were described as "Indian" or "Cuban." Back in 1872, a Negro named Bud Fowler broke into organized ball. And in 1884, two brothers, Welday and Moses Fleetwood Walker, played with Toledo of the American Association.

Since blacks and whites weren't allowed to compete on the same field in most places in America—although a black jockey did win the Kentucky Derby—a group of waiters at a Babylon, Long Island, restaurant passed themselves off as Cubans and played semipro white teams. They became the noted Cuban Giants, the first outstanding black team in America. Their Spanish probably was limited to "no." I wound up playing a Cuban Giants team in New York myself.

But there were always "situations." The most noted ball player of the 1880's was Adrian (Cap) Anson of the Chicago White Sox. In an exhibition game with Newark of the Eastern League he simply walked off the field rather than perform on the same field with Newark's light-skinned pitcher.

John McGraw, in 1902, tried to sneak a black in when he was managing the Orioles. The player's name was Charley Grant, but McGraw called him Chief Tokahoma. The plot failed, and Grant was forced to leave the team.

Ty Cobb, whose .367 career batting average remains untouched by any other ball player, toured Cuba in 1910, and some of the players on his team were blacks. He came back disgruntled that three of them had outhit him. We would laugh about that on the rides, all right: good ole Ty—the Georgia peach—miffed at being outhit.

Meanwhile, New York was developing into the capital of
black baseball, as tens of thousands of Southern blacks
made the migration north to settle in the major cities. Harlem quickly became the political, cultural, and residential
capital of New York blacks. When World War I ended, a
Negro National League was formed, joined by an Eastern
Colored League. Teams in both leagues played white teams
every fall after the World Series was over.

But this caused some embarrassment to major league
baseball when the black teams won. So Commissioner Kenesaw Mountain Landis ruled that if any of his major
league teams played a black team, that major league team
had better not wear its regular uniform—instead, they had
to call themselves all stars. This way, it wasn't the Yankees
or Giants or White Sox getting beaten by Negro ball players, it was just some collection of white ball players.

My team, the Black Barons, joined the Negro National
League in 1917, along with their rookie pitcher, Satchel
Paige, but it had been formed some years earlier. By the
time the Depression rolled around, the players were grateful
for a chance to play two and three games a day, even though
they traveled in buses.

World War II changed attitudes. Perhaps the first stirrings
of blacks concerning big-league baseball actually happened
during the war. Bill Veeck, who was to do some unpopular
things as an owner—such as make Larry Doby the American League's first black ball player, and put a midget up to
bat—had been aware of the existence of great black players
for decades. It went back to his years with the Chicago
Cubs, when his father was president of the club. During the
war, Veeck owned the Milwaukee Brewers of the American
Association. But as he did with most things in life, he got
tired of them after they had some success and he had made
some money.

In 1945, the war was about to end and Veeck was searching for a team. Now, Veeck took off on his most outrageous

plan of all. The Philadelphia Phillies were for sale. Veeck planned not only to buy those losers—but to stock the team with black baseball stars. After all, there was no law preventing an owner from hiring a black ball player. When Landis got wind of Veeck's plans, the old judge quickly found a more conservative buyer for the team.

While I was growing up, a way of life and a cast of characters with a wonderful history evolved in the black leagues that rivaled anything organized ball could muster. Goose Tatum played first base for the Indianapolis Clowns, for example, before becoming the star attraction of the Harlem Globetrotters.

Players used to recall the days of two-dollar meal money. The problem even with the two bucks was that they couldn't always find a place to spend it. They ate out of grocery stores in the South because often they couldn't find a restaurant that would serve them.

What ironies they must have appreciated. They would go to the Polo Grounds and draw thirty thousand fans. The annual East-West game in Chicago between the black teams attracted as many as fifty thousand fans. The blacks played in South America, Puerto Rico, Cuba—they were America's ambassadors. Did fans know the reason the players were traveling men, going so far from home?

They used a Wilson ball, a store-bought item. Their bats came off the shelves, and were not customized in Louisville by Hillerich and Bradsby. The ball wasn't as lively as the major league ball, the bats not as solid, and certainly not tailor made. In 1948, though, Artie Wilson of Birmingham led everyone, black and white, with a .402 batting average.

Teams would travel in baggage cars. If they were playing in Pittsburgh on Saturday night, why they'd play a doubleheader in Washington on Sunday. If they were staying overnight someplace, they might rent three rooms and squeeze in all nine players.

But what if you got hurt?

"We didn't have a paid trainer," Buck Leonard told me. "We rubbed each other."

Night games presented problems. Teams brought along portable lights, and players would string them up over the field before game time. A pitcher on each team was also a scorer, and kept track of runs and hits and errors. But if he had to come in as a relief pitcher, someone else would finish handling the scoring. No wonder Negro League records are hard to come by.

In nonleague exhibition games against a semipro team, the winner would get 60 percent and the loser 40 percent. Since the umpires were local guys, they favored the semipro teams.

This was the game of baseball in America as it was played outside the big-league parks, in the Texas League or in Triple A places or the Sally League. People think that black baseball somehow was like a minor league version of white baseball. No way. It was baseball for the best black ball players in America. And what kind of teams do you think were composed of the best black players in America? What kind of team do you think we'd have today if it contained the best black players? I think we'd have a shot at the pennant. But there have been a lot of myths about those times and leagues and players, as if we were just a bunch of characters flitting around in a sagging old yellow school bus, as if it was unorganized and sort of played just for fun, not following the rules.

That is so far from the truth. I'm not talking now about the exhibition games we played in Yankee Stadium or Comiskey Park in Chicago. We did fine right in Birmingham, too. On Sundays there would be anywhere from six thousand to ten thousand fans at Rickwood Field. It might have been black baseball, but the white fans got the best seats. Maybe five hundred white folks would show up on Sundays. They sat in a special section along the third-base line. The Black Barons were owned by Tom Hayes, an undertaker from Memphis, and we shared the field with the white Barons. They had the first choice of the playing dates, and we scheduled our games when they were on the road.

Despite its seemingly unorganized nature, black baseball did have its organization, and each season was crowned by the Negro World Series. And we felt that we were as good as the other world champions.

We traveled in an old bus that carried eighteen players, the equipment, our luggage, and a driver named Charlie Wood. The windows were open on those hot Alabama summer days. Charlie was a kindhearted man who was able to keep his eyes on the road and the rearview mirror. He knew everything that was going on in the bus, and he seemed to know all about everyone on it. The players would always meet the bus in front of Bob's Savoy, the biggest Negro café in Birmingham. Piper was a stickler for being on time. He always told us that if we had a good reason for being late, just call the Savoy and leave word for him. Sometimes players didn't bother calling, or they had some sort of difficulty and couldn't get to a phone. Charlie Wood seemed to know this. Many times I noticed Charlie stalling for time by cleaning the windshield, wiping the headlights, checking the tires for air. Anything to waste time until some of the players who hadn't called arrived.

One evening I was hoping he'd do the same for me. I had gotten to the bus early, put my suitcase aboard, and gone looking for a pool hall. Now, Piper, who had been around and knew all the angles, had an interesting system for keeping tabs on you. We didn't have a traveling secretary and there were no spies around to tail us. So Piper used a seating arrangement he called pally-wally. He'd pair us off. Two of us would be pally-wallies. And if one of us happened to be missing, then Piper asked the other where his buddy was. Since I was the youngest on the team, I got the worst seat— in the back, over the rear wheel. Nobody ever asked to

change seats with me. But I did have a seat buddy, Jimmy
Newberry, and Piper asked him about me.

"New, you seen Willie?"

"He's around here somewhere, Piper."

"Well, then, you better go look for him."

"Look where, Piper?"

"He likes to shoot pool, that's where."

Jimmy couldn't find me, though, and the bus took off
without me. I grabbed a cab outside the Savoy and caught
up with the bus a few miles out of town.

"You can't leave me!" I shouted to Piper. I guess when I
shouted, my voice, which was always squeaky, sounded as
if I was crying.

"You don't want to be left, get your little chicken butt on
your seat and sit down so we can get going to Kansas City,"
snapped Piper. I was not late again. I knew that if I was,
why, I'd simply be stranded again, and the next time it
might not be in my hometown.

The bus rides gave me a chance to learn, and to dream,
about big-league baseball. All the guys on the bus had
played against the big names and had been in the big sta-
diums. Johnny Britton, our third baseman, would always
take a newspaper with him and study the sports pages. He
would keep me up to date on what my hero, DiMaggio,
was doing. DiMaggio was the reason I had always wanted
to play centerfield. It might seem strange to think that we
who were ball players ourselves—black ball players, kept
to our own leagues, hotels, and restaurants—would be fans.
But we were, just like anyone else. In fact, maybe our interest was more intense than any other fans' because we knew
what it took to get to the major leagues. In our case, for
most of the guys it was too late because it took more than
talent and desire. It took a certain skin color.

But interesting situations developed on those bus rides.
Sometimes the ride wouldn't begin until midnight. We
would drive all night—saving on a hotel bill, of course. We

ate out of a paper bag or stopped at a grocery store along the way. It was hot. We had no air conditioning. And over the back wheel, in my special seat, it was extra bumpy, too.

One night I couldn't sleep because I was getting knocked around from side to side over that wheel. I moved to the front of the bus to sit next to our catcher, Pepper Batson. We called him Rocking Chair because of a particular talent: When he played with the Indianapolis Clowns, he would sit behind home plate in a rocking chair that had had its right arm removed, and would throw out a runner trying to steal second base. He was so strong, he could do it from a sitting position.

Pepper always sat by himself. He was a big guy and liked to stretch his feet, so he sat in the front seat right behind the door. I tried to get him to move over, but he wouldn't. So I asked Piper to get Pepper Batson to make room for me.

Pepper opened his eyes and growled, "You better get away from me." And then he took a swing at me and missed. He hit the overhead rack and banged his hand pretty hard. He yelled with the pain, and in an instant I was back in my old seat. Probably that's where Piper believed I should have been all along. He had ways of looking out for me, only I didn't realize it at the time.

Every night he would have a different player babysit for me, but there were two he would not leave me with—Newberry, who was good enough for bus rides but not to be trusted in the evenings, and Alonzo Perry, our first baseman. No one knew what they would get into after a game. They liked the ladies and they liked their beer. But I couldn't go anywhere unless I was chaperoned. Piper made good and sure of that.

When so much of your time is taken with just getting from place to place, you want to be treated special when you finally do arrive. We played in different cities every night—Kansas City, Chicago, Little Rock, Memphis, Nashville. New Orleans was one of our favorite stops. We could go in the back of the bus station there and eat. They had black cooks and black waitresses and they got to know us and gave us special service when we hit town. One time when a bunch of us were eating in the back, the service must have got a little slow in the front. The customers started to complain and the manager came back where we were eating and yelled at our waitress that she was taking too much time in the back and not enough in the front. She took off her apron, placed it over a chair, and walked out the door without saying a word.

By June 1, 1948, when I was just a few weeks out of high school, I was the regular centerfielder. Norman Robinson, who was very fast, had broken his leg, and Piper told me to take over. Even when Robinson came back later in the season, Piper kept me in center and played Robinson in left. Piper said Robinson was faster, but that I had a stronger arm. He liked to say, "Willie can go get it, and Willie can bring it back." I would run after anything hit to the outfield, left or right. I always had a sense of what was going on around me, but sometimes my running in every direction was dangerous. One time I ran after a ball hit to deep left in Rickwood, and so did Robinson; we got to the ball at the same time and just missed colliding into each other. He missed the ball, but I leaped, stuck out my bare right hand, and caught it. Then I flipped the ball to our shortstop, Artie Wilson, before anyone realized just what had happened. Piper said later that he never knew I had actually caught the ball until he saw Wilson with it.

In so many ways Piper was the most important person in my early baseball years. I learned one thing about him very quickly. He told you something only once, and he expected you to go on from there. That was a big reason why I matured so quickly—in addition to playing against ball players who were so much older. It was also the reason why I wasn't too worried about going to a minor league team in Trenton. I learned fast in the Negro League and I learned hard, often right on the spot. I learned, for example, that you do things on a ball field that your instincts and your upbringing wouldn't let you do anyplace else. And once you've done it, don't feel bad about it.

I still remember that time in Memphis when I tore around third base and headed for home. I banged into the catcher, Casey Jones, who was blocking home plate. I got there at the same time as the ball and really crashed into Jones. My spikes caught him high on his leg and I ripped him up and down his knee. He dropped the ball and I scored the run, but I felt bad that I'd cut him. When I reached the dugout, I headed straight for Piper.

"Piper, I couldn't help it. I didn't have to hit him like that."

He took me aside.

"Willie, that's the man to hit. He's got all that equipment on and he beats up on everyone, so he's the one to tear up. He won't block the plate on you no more."

Piper taught me many lessons. I had hit a home run off Chet Brewer; the next time I got up, Brewer hit me on the arm with a fastball that sent pain all through my body. I was on the ground in tears when Piper bent over me. He never attempted to pick me up, though.

"Don't let this guy show you up. You see first base over there? I want you to get up and I want you to run to first base. And the first chance you get, I want you to steal second and then third."

The pain still was so bad when I got to my feet that I was crying. But I did what Piper told me and stole second. All of a sudden, as I was standing on the base, I realized what was going on. Piper had made me show the pitcher that he couldn't hurt me by hitting me on the arm. Not only couldn't he hurt me, but that if he tried, I would show him up. That's how I learned against one of the best pitchers in the league, one who could make a ball go four different ways.

That old bus saw a lot of miles, and sometimes it broke down. That happened once on the way to Montgomery, and I still laugh when I think about it. The bus couldn't be repaired in time for us to play the game that night. Piper didn't waste any time looking for another bus. Instead, he came back half an hour later and he was driving an ice truck. Charlie Wood couldn't believe his eyes.

"Got to play a game, fellas," said Piper. "Can't go disappointing the people none." We piled into the truck and stood for the next forty miles, with the door open so we wouldn't freeze.

Our good old bus finally met its end in New York. We were going through the Holland Tunnel on the way to the Polo Grounds to play a doubleheader against the New York Cubans, when the bus caught fire. We charged out of the bus and left it in the tunnel, burning. But I remembered that my suitcase was in the back. I had just bought four new suits and I wasn't going to leave them there. I ran back to my seat and came back with my bag, and everybody was laughing. Five minutes later, the bus blew up.

We lost everything—equipment, uniforms, everything except my brand-new suits. When we got to the Polo Grounds, the Cubans' owner, Alex Pompez, gave us his team's road uniforms, along with bats and gloves. We played both games and split the doubleheader in front of twenty thousand fans. I hit a home run in one of the games, but Alonzo Perry smacked three of them. He was big and strong and I was just a little guy compared to him. That was my first day in the Polo Grounds, and I was wearing the Cubans' uniform. I had no idea that three years later I would be back there, wearing the uniform of the New York Giants.

I never wondered if I'd get into the majors. I just knew I wanted to play baseball. No, not for me was cleaning and pressing shirts. I wanted to play baseball. Not just *play* it, you understand. I lived it and studied it. There was something scientific in the way you caught a ball and then got rid of it. They didn't teach me much biology or mathematics in school—well, anyway, I don't remember if they did—but I studied what you could do with a ball.

And once I made it to the Barons, a lot of my studying took place on the bus. The bus was where I spent my weekends in high school, it seemed. Getting on the bus for those long rides to play a game in the Negro Leagues, getting off the bus for a game, sometimes two, then getting back on the bus, going to sleep, getting home, going to sleep again, getting up in the morning to help around the house. Sometimes the bus ride was so long that I'd be riding all night long, get home Monday morning, get something to eat, and go to bed. And I didn't dream about pressing some pants.

I played in the Negro World Series of 1948, the last one ever held. It was the Birmingham Black Barons against the Homestead Grays, whose stars included Luke Easter and Buck Leonard.

"You were just a kid," Buck Leonard recalled to me when we spoke about that time years later. "You could run the fly balls and throw, but your hitting wasn't good because you couldn't hit the curveball. But a seventeen-year-old boy playing in our league was like a boy of seventeen playing in the major leagues. You could run and catch a fly ball and throw, but to think and hit, a kid your age just didn't have it yet."

That was the last Negro World Series. After Negroes got into the big leagues, all the black fans wanted to go see the big-league teams. Ironically, blacks getting into major league baseball cost hundreds of other black players their jobs.

I was the youngest player on the Barons, and I lived through many long bus rides once high school closed for the summer and I was allowed to travel with the team. Those were long, hot summers, tired but happy days.

4

I SIGNED WITH THE GIANTS by accident.

They were looking for a first baseman for their Sioux City farm club in the Western League, Class A. Those were the days of high minors and low minors, of Triple A leagues and Class C leagues. It was in the days before television spoiled Americans by bringing major league baseball to every small town. Until then, minor league baseball was all over the place. I know. I feel as though I played in most of the country's ballparks.

Sioux City's manager, Hugh Poland, called Jack Schwarz in New York. Schwarz was head of the Giants' minor league operations and he could usually deliver players. By now, the Giants had several years' experience with black ball players. So Schwarz called Pompez, the Cubans' owner. He had helped the Giants get Monte Irvin from the Newark Eagles and Hank Thompson from the Kansas City Monarchs. They were the first two black ball players the Giants ever signed.

Pompez then called Schwarz back and recommended Alonzo Perry, my fellow teammate on the Black Barons. So Schwarz phoned the Giants' Southern scout, Eddie Montague, and told him to take a look at Perry immediately. Montague arrived in Birmingham on a Sunday morning, just in time to see the Barons play a doubleheader. I never knew Montague was in the stands. The next day he turned up in Tuscaloosa, the site of our next game. He arrived before we did and was waiting in the parking lot for our bus. When I got off he quietly approached me and asked to talk to me alone.

"Would you like to play professional baseball, Willie?"

"*Yes, sir!*" I exclaimed. I could hardly believe my ears.

"Would you like to play for the Giants?"

"Yes, sir."

"I'll talk to Mr. Hayes about it then."

I was really pumped up that night knowing that a big-league scout was interested in me. I smacked three doubles and made a couple of big plays in the outfield against Tuscaloosa. I couldn't wait to hear what Mr. Montague had to say once the game ended. He didn't want to talk in the clubhouse, which was small and far from private. Instead, he talked to me on the field, with no one around.

"Everything's okay with Mr. Hayes. I saw him during the game and I'm going to talk to him about your contract."

"What contract?" I wanted to know. I had never signed anything.

"Didn't you sign a contract with him?"

"No, sir. I didn't sign any contract with him. I just told him I'd play."

"Whom should I talk to then?"

"My father and Aunt Sarah."

The next night, Montague was in our little white house in Fairfield, and I signed my first professional contract. Since I was a minor, my father signed, too. Aunt Sarah gave me a kiss for good luck. I got a $4,000 signing bonus, and a salary of $250 a month.

But I never got to Sioux City. Racial prejudice actually kept me from my first job with a white team. The Giants hoped I could play Class A ball there, very important in my development, they figured. But Sioux City was not the place for me at that moment. The city was in an uproar because they had buried an Indian in a whites-only cemetery only a few days before. The farm club refused to take me, fearing the consequences and "bad" publicity. I was surprised, but I guess I should have been shocked. I had never heard of anything like that before. Then again, I had never played outside the Negro League, either.

So instead I headed to Trenton in the Class B Interstate League. I gave a friend a few bucks to take my date to the prom so I could catch an earlier train. I did graduate, which pleased Dad, Aunt Sarah, Piper, and, yes, even E. T. Oliver. But Class B ball? Why, the Barons played better baseball than that, probably as good as Triple A. No one really got to know how good the players were in the Negro League, since the press never covered the games. But I knew it was an experience I'd never forget. I was so much richer from it. I didn't realize that my leaving was another nail in the coffin of all-black baseball. Negro League owners had been upset about losing their players as far back as 1947, when Doby joined the Cleveland Indians in midseason to become the first black ball player in the American League. When Doby joined Robinson in the majors, the black owners must have realized that it was only a matter of time before big-league baseball would be able to get all the stars it wanted.

But for me the studying and the work had paid off. The train ride from Birmingham, Alabama, to Hagerstown, Maryland, where I was to meet my new team, seemed like an eternity that spring day in 1950. I kept looking out the window, or fumbling with the bag of sandwiches that Aunt Sarah had made for me, but I was too nervous to eat. Look out the window, look at the bag, look at my hands.

This ride was different. This was taking me to *organized* ball—the first big step in living out my boyhood dream of playing in the majors someday. I couldn't sit still on the train, and kept getting up from my seat, walking from car to car to help pass the time. It helped, I guess. I wondered whether I was leaving the mill town of my youth for good. It was June, and the countryside was lush and green and beautiful. I knew I would miss it. I already did, in fact. But I had just turned nineteen and I was excited about everything. Who wouldn't be? I had a contract with the New York Giants that paid me four thousand dollars. That was all the money in the world to me back then. No one knew that I would have played baseball for nothing just for the chance to be in the big leagues. I had that chance now, and I couldn't wait to play for Trenton—so much so that I even skipped my senior prom so I could get there a day early.

What songs were they playing at my prom? "Till I Waltz Again with You." "On Top of Old Smokey." Kids were holding each other close, or jitterbugging. I didn't have time for that. No, sir. I was going to play baseball.

What lay before me now? How could I know what to expect? I was a wide-eyed black kid entering a white man's world. Okay, not totally a white man's world any longer. Three years before, Jackie Robinson had put on his white uniform with the Brooklyn Dodgers. The color line was broken, but it was certainly not gone for good.

My new team was the Trenton Giants, and we would be playing teams like Wilmington, which was a Phillies farm team and had Bob Miller, who had pitched in the big leagues; Hagerstown, a Boston Braves organization; Allentown, Pennsylvania, a Cardinals team; and Lancaster, Pennsylvania, the Brooklyn Dodgers' farm team. York, Pennsylvania, was in it, too; their general manager was Bill McKechnie, son of the old Bill McKechnie who had been the manager of Cincinnati.

In Trenton, these teams played at Dunn Field. If you mention the B League now, people don't know what you're talking about, but it was a good league. The B League produced people who played in the minors for four or five years.

The Trenton Giants were playing a weekend series in Hagerstown, starting on Friday night and ending with a doubleheader on Sunday. I realized that I was a pioneer, for not only was I the first black player on the team—I was the first in the entire league.

When I got off the train a fellow came over to me and introduced himself as "a right-handed pitcher from Brooklyn." His name was Ed Monahan. He took me to the ballpark, where I met Chick Genovese for the first time. Chick was the manager, and someone who would be important to me in my first experience with so-called organized baseball. He greeted me warmly and made me feel comfortable.

"You're starting in centerfield" were practically the first words out of his mouth.

It didn't take me long to realize that Hagerstown was the only city in our league below the Mason-Dixon Line. When I walked onto the field for the first time, I heard someone shout, "Who's that nigger walking on the field?" But I didn't let it bother me. I was programmed very well from playing with the Barons. I had learned how to be thick-skinned.

What I didn't get over was the long train ride that had brought me there. Although I did feel good during batting practice—I hit six or seven balls over the fence—in the game I just didn't feel right. I didn't get a hit that first game or for the rest of the four-game series. I started my organized baseball career oh-for-Maryland, and in a segregated town, to boot. I wondered whether my showing confirmed some of those rednecks' feelings that I wouldn't do well in the big time. What a way to start. And then after the game I found I couldn't stay with the team at their hotel. The club had already made arrangements for me to spend the weekend in a small hotel for blacks.

That confused me. In Washington, D.C., I could stay anywhere, the same in Baltimore. But here in Hagerstown, located midway between those cities, I couldn't stay with the rest of the team. Some of my teammates couldn't understand it, either. About midnight, about five of my new teammates knocked on my window to check whether I was okay. It made me feel good, and I didn't have any trouble falling asleep.

Chick Genovese took a special interest in me. I couldn't have had a better manager for my first year in organized ball, and since he was a former outfielder, it made the whole thing that much better. When he was playing for the Louisville Colonels he had been a good prospect with the Boston Red Sox but couldn't beat out a better one—Dominick DiMaggio. Chick quickly sized up my problem over the first few games: I was pressing. He made me aware of what I was doing, and told me just to relax and not overswing—the base hits would come.

My teammates started to call me Junior, and I began to relax, even though I was only nineteen years old. I'd often shout back "Say hey!" whenever I wanted their attention. These were all new people to me and I didn't know their names. "Say hey!" was guaranteed to get them to listen to me. Then the base hits started to come, as Chick had said they would. I didn't have a lot of home runs, but I smacked a lot of blue darts, a lot of line drives. Oh, I knew the power was there, all right. One of my teammates, Bob Myers, told me I had the biggest forearms he'd ever seen. "They look like Popeye's," he claimed. But in those days I wasn't getting under the ball enough to drive it. I finished my first year in the minors hitting .353, best in the league.

I wasn't eligible for the batting title because I came to bat only 306 times after joining the team in late June. Although I played in only 81 games, just a little more than half the season, I also led the league's outfielders in assists with 17. This was my batting line in my first campaign of organized ball:

falseSAY HEY

Willie's 1950 Numbers

Games	At Bats	Hits	Doubles	Triples	Home Runs	Runs	Runs Batted In	Batting Average
81	306	108	20	8	4	50	55	.353

Double those figures for a full season and I produced the
sort of numbers I would achieve in the major leagues—
except for home runs. The home-run total projected to only
eight for the season. I had listened so well to Genovese's
advice to make contact that I wound up hitting doubles and
triples all over the place, but few long drives. It is unlikely
that Genovese was worried. Far from it.

Chick was my biggest rooter. He always watched over
me. He knew about the effect that segregation was having
on me, and he also knew there was nothing he could do
about it. But there were things he could do in his own way.
I didn't show it, and I never spoke about it, but maybe he
could sense my loneliness and anxiety. There were times
when he'd eat with me in the kitchen of a restaurant, either
in Hagerstown or Wilmington, so I wouldn't be alone.
Those were moments I still treasure. It was the first time I
had been off by myself somewhere, for even when I was on
the road with the Barons in a segregated situation, at least
all of us were segregated at the same time in the same place.

Once a week, Chick sent glowing reports on my progress
to the Giants. The owner of the Giants, Horace Stoneham,
came to Trenton four or five times during the season to see
me play. Later I found out that he told the Giants' front
office to make room for me, that I'd be their centerfielder in
another year. Mr. Stoneham came from a baseball family.
That was the custom in those days—a father passing the
team down to son or daughter. It was the family's business.
The team wasn't part of another company; it was owned
by someone at the top who cared about the players. If there
were a Class B league somewhere today, I don't think you'd

be seeing the owner of a parent club dropping by as often as Mr. Stoneham did.

Everything settled down—me included—after that first weekend in Hagerstown. I even stayed cool after they threw at my head while I was batting. I knew they were testing me. Heck, they'd thrown at me in Negro ball all the time. This time I just glared back at the pitcher and he got my message that he couldn't intimidate me. As if that wasn't enough, Eric Rodin, the next batter, did something whose message couldn't be mistaken. After I made out, Rodin, a big rightfielder, laid down a bunt toward first base, attempting to run into the pitcher and knock him down when he tried to field it. Luckily the ball rolled foul. Who knows what would have happened? Here I was, the first black ball player in the league's history, and my teammate was ready to start a fight with someone over me. Even though the ball was foul, both benches emptied onto the field. It was a show of strength and support for me by my teammates, and it cleared the air.

Before long, I had a roommate. I lived in a boarding house on Spring Street in Trenton, which was only five blocks from Dunn Field. The room was fine. On the road, though, the Giants, thinking I was lonely by myself, sent Trenton a pitcher named Jose Fernandez. His father was the manager of the New York Cubans. They played their home games in the Polo Grounds. We didn't get along too well. He was a hot dog from New York and I was still a country boy. One evening he didn't wake me up in time to make the team bus and Chick jumped all over him. Fernandez didn't last long. He was gone in a month. I was happy again.

My teammates always made me feel that way. On the bus rides we were loose. Chick used to get us to sing a song, "Clarence the Clocker," and I would start it off. Pretty soon the whole bus would join in. This bus wasn't much better than the one I had traveled in with the Barons. It was an old school bus and was just as uncomfortable as the other one. I made sure I got my rest, though. I had learned that much—and more, much more—from all those other bus rides. I would pile the duffel bags in the back of the bus, lie down on them, and go to sleep.

I always seemed to need rest, even though I was strong and well built. But I think I expended more energy than the average player on worrying and thinking—and certainly on my playing. Sure, my hat was too big for my head, but I might have run out from under it even if it had fit perfectly. I never believed in playing the game in a halfhearted way. And I suppose that because I put so much of myself into every at bat, every fly ball, every throw, every stolen base, that all these exertions took their toll. That first year I played hard, too. Near the end of the season, in fact, I collapsed from fatigue after playing a string of double-headers. One day I was so wiped out that they called for an ambulance. I'd go after every ball hit into the outfield—crashing into fences, falling on the ground, just running my head off—and think nothing of it. The other outfielders didn't mind at all. In fact, Mo Cunningham, our leftfielder, used to kid me. He'd yell, "Plenty of room, Junior! We'll let you know where the fence is."

At least I didn't have to worry about racial curses for the rest of the year. Len Matte, our catcher, told me that he'd take care of any trouble and that I shouldn't get involved. It was good advice. As the season wore on, there were less and less incidents and curses, until I just didn't hear them anymore. I knew, anyway, that I wouldn't be back in this league next year. I would be leaving Trenton for Minneapolis, the Class AAA team in the American Association. Triple A ball was only one step from the majors. Chick's final words to me that season were "Willie, you're going to make a lot of money one day. I hope I helped you."

He did.

5

"HEY, KID, WHAT ARE YOU going to show me today?"

Those were the first words Leo Durocher ever said to me. It was the spring of 1951 in Sanford, Florida. It was nine o'clock in the morning and I was on the field getting ready to play in an exhibition game for the Minneapolis Millers against Ottawa, another one of the Giants' farm teams. I didn't know it then, but Leo had arranged that game specially to see me play. He had driven over from the Giants' training headquarters in Lakeland with Horace Stoneham.

"I've got quite a report on you from Trenton, kid," said Leo. "This guy Chick Genovese thinks you're the greatest he ever saw."

"Oh, really. What did the report say?"

"It said that your hat keeps flying off," laughed Leo.

That was strange. I had never noticed that it did. Maybe I would never have had to bother getting a hat a size too big just to impress the fans.

That first morning of spring training in a Minneapolis uniform, I wanted to impress Durocher. As I got to know him a little better I always called him Mister Leo, a term of respect that always pleased him. Leo, you know, was not a guy whom people confused with the upper crust. He had played for the old Cardinals' Gashouse Gang; he was a tough, mean player, and he managed a team that way.

Tommy Heath, my new manager, started me in leftfield, but
it didn't stay that way for long. In the first inning I chased
a fly ball into deep leftfield but ran out of room. I got to the
wall in time to make a play but stood there helplessly as it
went out high over the fence. Leo wanted to see me run, so
he ordered Heath to put me in centerfield. Leo wanted some
fast answers and I was able to give them to him.

At least I thought I did. I had a good day—a double my
first time up, and later a long home run. It went over the
clubhouse behind the leftfield fence and sailed over the railroad tracks about 450 feet away. In center, I threw out a
couple of base runners and I also stole a base.

I was having a perfect day. If they were giving out MVP
awards for spring-training games, I had just earned one. But
after the seventh inning Durocher and Stoneham left. Just
like that. I was shocked. Had I done something wrong? Was
there a cutoff man I didn't throw to? Was there an extra
base I could have stolen? I never found out. When the game
was over I just sat in front of my locker, so tired I couldn't
even shake my head. I felt like a raw rookie who had just
flunked his only chance. I didn't see or talk to either of them
the rest of the spring.

But they didn't send me away. That was just their style,
that was baseball's style in those days. Players didn't get
coddled or patted on the back. You had a job to do and
you did it. Hey, weren't they paying you good money—
four, five hundred a month? What did you want, a smile as
well?

There weren't many places for blacks to go in Sanford,
even if you were a baseball player. Just because Jackie Robinson had broken the color line in 1947 didn't mean that
integration was in effect here. There were two other blacks
on the team besides me, and we all stayed at a rooming
house away from the rest of the team. It's a good thing that
I liked to go to movies or I might have gone a little stir-
crazy. I could sit in a movie theater for hours, and many

days and nights I went to double features to help pass the time. I had to use a special entrance to the movie theater in Sanford. It was through a side door that led to a seating section on one side of the balcony. I didn't care. I was having a good spring, just counting the days until we'd break camp and start a new season. I was making a big jump from Class B to Triple A.

This seemed almost as important to me as leaving the Negro Leagues for white baseball. Triple A ball was good ball. I soon found that out in spring training. Look, there were only sixteen major league teams. You had to be better than good to make the majors. You had to be great. The players I saw in Triple A looked as good to me as the big-leaguers did. So you can imagine how great it felt when I hit the hell out of the ball the rest of spring training. We'd play some games against the big boys, the Giants, and I was able to whack a few against some of their pitchers, who included Sal Maglie, Larry Jansen, and Dave Koslo. But most of the time, I didn't get close to people from the big club.

As the camp drew to a close, it was obvious I could handle my job. Tommy Heath, the Millers' manager, called me into his office one morning and told me, "Willie, we're taking you with us to Minneapolis. But I kind of have the feeling you're not going to spend the whole summer with us. I think it's only a matter of time before the Giants call you up."

Boy, that raised my spirits, and kept them that way all the way from Florida to Minneapolis.

Heath was an interesting guy. We used to call him the Round Man. When he was a catcher with the St. Louis Browns back in the 1930's, he weighed 215 pounds, even though he was only five ten. Tommy Heath was a deep thinker, and a very good student of the game. I learned how to think baseball when he was around. He had a good sense of logic. Beyond that, he also was very fair, something I appreciated as a kid trying to play among men. Tommy was an excellent manager: Minneapolis had won the pennant the previous year. Spring training with him was an education.

On the way back north from Sanford, I reminisced a lot with Ray Dandridge, an old black player who was a third baseman for us. Monte Irvin used to say that outside of Josh Gibson, Dandridge was the best of them all. Dandridge was talking to me and he said, "You got a great chance. When I played in the black leagues, we were barnstorming most of the time. Sometimes I played three games in one day. We made about thirty-five dollars a week and ate hamburger. You're going to eat steak and you're going to make a lot of money. You just keep it clean and be a good boy."

You'd think I would have had enough sense to appreciate just what was happening to me and where I was and what it took to eat steak. You'd think so, wouldn't you?

Opening Day. I got up early, looked out the window— and for the second time in my life saw snow. I knew they wouldn't be playing in the snow, so I just went back to bed again. But a couple of hours later, the phone rang. It was Heath.

"Why aren't you out here, Willie, we've got a game to play?" he wanted to know.

"It was snowing, Tommy," I replied.

"It's stopped now and we're about to start the game."

"But I never played in snow before."

He explained to me that they had brought in a helicopter to blow the snow off the field.

Did Piper Davis ever play in any snow, I wondered, as I scrambled into my clothes and headed for the ballpark.

There were photographs of the snow in the next day's papers. There were also some photos of me. I hit a homer and a double and we won. Even though it was cold all of that first week, it didn't bother my hitting. I accumulated 12 hits. I kept thinking to myself that maybe playing in cold weather was better than the hot weather I was used to. In just over a month, I was leading the league in hitting with a .477 average.

Some of the pitchers around the league tried to shake me up by pitching me tight. When it got too close, like a knock-down pitch, Heath didn't waste a second before he let everyone know he wouldn't allow them to take target practice at me. In Louisville, a six-foot-five-inch hard thrower named Joe Atkins winged one at me pretty good—a high, fast one that knocked me down. Heath rushed out of the dugout and stopped when he reached the foul line. He pointed his finger at Atkins and screamed, "If you come close to him again, I'll meet you right here." Once again I found someone who was willing to stick up for me, and I never forgot him. He could have taken it easy on himself and let the other teams try to screw up a rookie, as they did with every new kid. But he seemed to be especially protective of me.

One of the Minneapolis sportswriters in spring training had started to pump me up pretty good. He was writing really nice things about me, so when I finally arrived the fans expected some big things of me. In fact, he told me that after his first few stories his editor telephoned him and said he'd better tone down his copy about this kid—me—because it didn't sound believable. The writer told him, "But I have been toning it down." I heard that people were starting to talk about me. Bob Stewart, who had been an umpire for twenty years in the American League, said, "You won't believe what he's doing."

I really did do well. One of my best days was in Columbus. We got into the ninth inning. It was a 1–1 tie, and Luis Arroyo, who had been a top Yankee reliever for a few years, was pitching for Columbus. He led off the last of the ninth with a three-base hit, which was unusual for him. He wasn't known as a hitter. They put in a pinch runner for him, someone who was pretty fast, and then we walked the next two batters. Now they had the bases loaded and none out, so Heath brought the outfield in, because a deep fly would score the man on third anyway. The hitter whacked one to centerfield. A long drive. I went racing back, leaped up, and caught the ball facing slightly away from home plate. But I whirled around in midair, off the ground, and fired the ball to the plate. It was a strike and it almost threw out the runner, who was a fast rookie. After the game Jake Hurley, the catcher, told me, "Willie, you're losing your control. That pitch was on the outside corner. If you had put it on the inside corner, we would have had him."

Now my early games were being played on the road. When we got home, to Nicollet Park in Minneapolis, people were talking about me. That first home stand I went wild. In the sixteen games on the home stand, I was 38 for 63, or .608. I got the collar once, on May 6. That was my twentieth birthday. I went 0 for 3 that night. The rest of the home stand I went 27 for 43, or .643.

The wildest series of all was when Louisville came in. They had Jimmy Piersall, although he hadn't started to create a sensation yet, not the sort of stuff that led Hollywood to make the memorable movie *Fear Strikes Out* about him. Louisville had an outfielder by the name of Taft Wright. He was a really good major league hitter, but he couldn't field. He was big and slow. One game in that series, first time up, Taft hit a home run. The next time he hit a ball to right center. The funny part was, it was only about 280 at the foul line, but was about 400 in dead center. And this shot was well out to the flagpole in center. It looked as though it was going to hit high on the fence. It got quite a ways up, and I had to improvise a way to catch it, so I just got my spikes in the wall, and I sort of walked up the wall. How high, I couldn't estimate, but I caught the ball and threw it back in, and Taft steamed into second base and he stood there. He wiped off his hands and did all the other little straightening-out chores a base runner does. Then he's getting ready to take his lead off second and the umpire says, "You're out."

Taft said, "No I'm not. He didn't catch that. He couldn't." And Taft wouldn't leave the field. Mike Higgins, the manager, had to come out and lead him off the field, but Taft was still protesting. Bob Beebe, the Minneapolis newspaperman who covered me, told me that many years later he saw Taft in Orlando, Florida. Beebe reminded him about that play, and Wright said, "That little son of a bitch never did catch the ball. How could he catch that?" And that was thirty years later.

Because I was twenty, and I used to get so excited, my teammates used to razz me. They'd tell me that when I got so excited that squeaky voice of mine would be at such a high pitch, you could hardly hear me. Yet when I was at the plate my nervousness left me. I would leave it all behind. Same thing when I was in the field. I never stopped to think if something was catchable. I just tried to figure out how to catch it. It didn't seem to matter to me how good the opposition was.

One time, Boo Ferriss, the old Red Sox pitcher, was going against me in Minneapolis. Ferriss was winding up his career in Triple A. He threw me what Beebe said was the greatest knockdown pitch he had ever seen. "Willie, if you had stayed there, God, you would have been wiped out," he told me later. I scattered. I lost my hat. I don't know whether my shoe fell off, but I really got undressed. So what happened? I got back up there, Ferriss threw another pitch, and I hit it so hard it pretty near killed the shortstop. After the game, Beebe congratulated Ferriss on the knockdown pitch, and Ferriss said, "Yeah, I was kind of proud of it myself. But it didn't do me any good. I was just wasting my time."

I stole half a dozen bases on the home stand. I drove in 30 runs altogether in the 35 games I played, but I got 15 RBI's in sixteen home games. I remember while I was doing

all this I had some dental work done, too. I had some bad
teeth.

Nothing was bothering me now, though. We moved on
to Sioux City for an exhibition. I was sitting in a movie
theater, of course, enjoying my day off. I was alone, as
usual. That is something that has carried through over the
years. There are times of the day when I just look forward
to being by myself, either watching a movie or just hanging
out. I didn't get to relax too long on this day, though. About
halfway through the movie, the house lights went on, and a
guy came on stage to make an announcement.

"If Willie Mays is in the audience, would he please report
immediately to his manager at the hotel."

What was wrong? Had something happened to my father
or Aunt Sarah? To someone else back home? I rushed back
to the hotel and headed straight for Heath's room.

"What's up, Skip?" I asked.

What a relief! It was good news.

"Guess what?" said Heath. "I just got off the phone with
New York. Let me be the first to congratulate you."

"What for?"

"The Giants want you right away."

"Who says so?" I wanted to know.

"Leo himself."

I couldn't believe my ears.

I thought for a moment, then I got scared.

"Call him back," I pleaded.

"What for?"

I didn't know what to say. So I just blurted out, "Tell
him I don't want to go to New York. I'm happy here, and
we got a good chance to win the pennant."

Heath was stunned. "Do you realize what you're saying,
Willie? You have a chance to go to the big leagues. It's
something you always wanted. It's something every kid always wanted."

"I know," I told him. "It's just that I'm not ready to go yet."

Heath was beginning to get a little nervous. There was no way he was going to tell Durocher that himself.

"You better talk to Leo yourself," said Heath, and he placed a call to New York.

"Leo, I got Willie here and he's got something to tell you."

There was a loud voice on the other end demanding, "Tell me what?" as Heath handed me the phone.

I said to Leo, "I'm not coming."

He screamed at me for two minutes, starting with "What the hell do you mean you're not coming?"

When he was finished I told him I wasn't ready for the majors yet. I admitted I was scared and I didn't think I could hit big-league pitching.

"What are you hitting now?" he asked.

I told him, "Four seventy-seven."

"Well," he asked, barely containing his anger, "do you think you can hit two-fucking-fifty for me?"

"Sure," I told him. That didn't seem too hard.

"Then get down here on the next plane," he said. "We're playing in Philadelphia tonight and I want you there." And he hung up.

Willie's Minneapolis Numbers (1951)

G	AB	H	2B	3B	HR	R	RBI	BA
35	149	71	18	3	8	38	30	.477

The average might have gone higher. I was riding a 16-game hitting streak in which I was batting .569—41 hits in 72 at bats. The stretch included one 5–5 game and another 4–5. Only two teams had been able to hold me to a .333 average. Against Louisville I hit .563 in seven games and .643 against Milwaukee.

I was hitting the ball so well, and had made such an immediate impact, that the fans in Minneapolis were up in arms about my departure. I can't say I blamed them. I was not only hitting almost a hundred points higher than anyone else in Triple A ball, I was going at a pace that could have seen me slug more than 70 doubles, score more than 150 runs, and drive in more than 120. And now I was adding the home-run stroke, which had been only fair the year before in Class B. At Minneapolis I was going at a 30-homer rate.

To quiet the fans, Stoneham had to take out an ad in the *Sunday Minneapolis Tribune* of May 27, 1951. It read:

We feel that the Minneapolis fans, who have so enthusiastically supported the Minneapolis club, are entitled to an explanation for the player deal that on Friday transferred outfielder Willie Mays from the Millers to the New York Giants. We appreciate his worth to the Millers, but in all fairness, Mays himself must be a factor in these considerations. On the record of his performance since the American Association season started, Mays is entitled to his promotion and the chance to prove he can play major league baseball.

6

WHAT DID THE GIANTS need me for? They were so far behind the Brooklyn Dodgers that I figured they wouldn't catch them until next year.

Durocher told me not to bother packing, just to get to New York immediately. I brought along one Adirondack bat, my glove, my spikes, some underwear, and one golf cap, which I wore.

I didn't think I'd do much good, but there I was on a plane flying from Iowa to New York. I couldn't figure out what Durocher was going to do with me. I worried on the trip: Was he going to make me a leftfielder, a rightfielder? Did he have me pigeonholed as a pinch hitter? How was I going to break into a lineup that had Bobby Thomson and Alvin Dark and Hank Thompson, and that still was in a pennant race, although I didn't really give them much of a chance?

I put my cap and glove on the empty seat next to me. The stewardess looked at them and asked me, "Are you Jackie Robinson?"

I arrived in New York on a Friday. It was May 25, 1951. The Giants' record was 17–19, fifth place, but they seemed to be improving, although the Dodgers were running away with the pennant race. The Giants, though, were getting out of a hole they had fallen into during an eleven-game losing streak.

On the day I arrived, this was what was happening in New York: New Yorkers were very proud of their new five-hundred-siren air-raid warning system, which was being readied for its first test. (Remember, the Russians were a threat because they, too, had an atomic bomb.) The Empire State Building was sold for $50 million. A twenty-six-month dispute involving rail employees was settled. They got a raise of 33¢ an hour. You could buy a cord suit from Saks Fifth Avenue for $41.50. At the Roxy movie theater, *On the Riviera,* starring Danny Kaye, Gene Tierney, and Corinne Calvet, was playing. On Broadway, Robert Alda was starring in *Guys and Dolls,* and *The Happy Time* also was bringing in crowds.

It was also a big weekend for sports. Cal Abrams of the Dodgers was leading the league in hitting, which went over especially well in Brooklyn, since Abrams was Jewish and Brooklyn boasted more Jews than Tel Aviv.

The night of my debut, New Yorkers could listen to the game on the radio or, if they chose, they could tune in to the *Gracie Fields Show* or *Suspense.* If they couldn't make a decision about the radio, then if they had a television set they could watch the *Lilli Palmer Show* or *Stop the Music.*

In all the places I had been up to that time, my team had been the center of attention. New York was different. They had three baseball teams. The Giants were trying to crack the ranks, get up there to the top where the Yankees and Dodgers were. The Yankees had won the pennant and the World Series every year since 1949, when Casey Stengel became their manager. The Dodgers, pennant winners in 1949, had lost to the Philadelphia Phillies, who were known as the Whiz Kids, in 1950, but now were back on top. Look at their lineup. Why, a kid could spend all his teenage years rooting for the same players. At first base there was the quiet but powerful Gil Hodges. Jackie Robinson, baseball's

1

Two shots of good old Rickwood Field, where I played my first game with the Birmingham Black Barons. They're going to tear down the field this May, I'm told.

3

Me and my Barons teammates celebrating after a game in our locker room. Not very fancy, I'm sure you'll agree.

4

Josh Gibson, a Negro League immortal, born too early to play in the majors.

Here are two uniforms you may never have seen me playing in: Santurce of the Puerto Rican League.

5

6

Me with the Minneapolis Millers not long before I joined the Giants.

There I am reading the *Sporting News* the day I got the call from Mister Leo.

7

8

There were plenty of bats to choose from at the Polo Grounds.

9

At this point I still did not know how to drive a car.

10

I wasn't smiling like this in the on-deck circle in those tense moments before Bobby Thomson hit his historic homer against the Dodgers in 1951.

That's Bobby Thomson himself, finishing up his home-run swing.

Bobby Thomson surrounded by Giants at home plate. If you look carefully, you can see that Leo (No. 2) and me (No. 24) were part of the celebration.

11

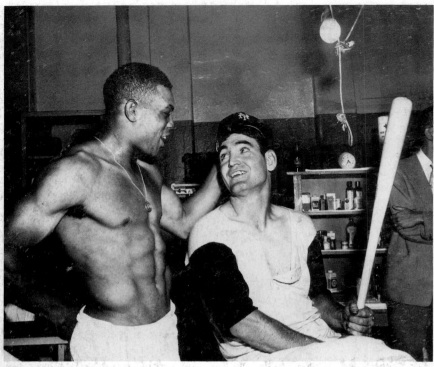

That's me with Dusty Rhodes after the first game of the 1954 World Series.

Not quite stickball, but I liked to play in a pick-up game now and then, too.

I traded in my Giants uniform for an Army outfit for two seasons.

15

We were a close-knit group during those early days in New York.

16

Here's my famous catch against Vic Wertz of the Cleveland Indians in the opener of the 1954 World Series. If you want to know the honest truth, I think I've made better ones.

I traded in my Giants uniform for an Army outfit for two seasons.

We were a close-knit group during those early days in New York.

Here's my famous catch against Vic Wertz of the Cleveland Indians in the opener of the 1954 World Series. If you want to know the honest truth, I think I've made better ones.

most exciting player, was the anchor at second. Pee Wee Reese, the captain, was the shortstop. Billy Cox, an acrobat, was at third. Roy Campanella was baseball's best catcher behind home plate. Abrams, with his .400 start, seemed to fill the leftfield spot that such players as Dick Williams and Marv Rackley and Gene Hermanski had failed to hold. Duke Snider, the graceful left-handed-hitting slugger, was in center. And out in right, the Reading Rifle, Carl Furillo, was in command. I always had a lot of respect for him. He knew all the crazy angles of that awesome rightfield screen and wall, the one that had a promise from the clothier Abe Stark: "Hit Sign Win Suit."

The pitching staff boasted Preacher Roe, the smart old southpaw. We used to say he had two fastball speeds— slow, and slower. Then there was Don Newcombe, one of the best young pitchers in baseball, on his way to a 20-game season, even though he had a dread of flying that forced him to see a hypnotist. Another young right-hander on the staff was Carl Erskine, who had a heck of a change-up. In addition, there was Clyde King, and Ralph Branca, the youngest 20-game winner in baseball history only a few years before.

Leo had his troubles when he took over the Giants from Mel Ott in the middle of the 1948 season. Leo said that it was like General Grant becoming the governor of Georgia.

To every Giants fan and player Durocher was the most-hated Dodger. He had been their manager since 1939. And then he was asked what he thought of replacing Ott, the Giants' onetime hero and such a nice guy.

"Nice guys finish last," said Durocher.

Leo the Lip was one of the nicer things they called Durocher. His big mouth got him suspended for the 1947 season by Commissioner Happy Chandler after Durocher claimed that one of the Yankee owners had gone to Cuba with a mobster friend. By 1948, the president of the Dodgers, Branch Rickey, who liked to quote the Bible, had had enough of Leo. But Rickey couldn't figure out how to get rid of him. Then one day, Stoneham told Rickey he'd like to talk to him about a manager. Rickey said sure. Stoneham had been interested in Burt Shotton, who led the Dodgers to the pennant in 1947 while Durocher was under the one-year suspension. But when Stoneham came to Rickey's office, Rickey suddenly offered him Durocher, and not Shotton. Stoneham took him. Am I glad he did. We were two unalike guys, but we developed a love, a respect, that has never faded.

Part of it was that Durocher molded me. The Giants that he inherited were hardly his kind of team. In 1947 they had set a major league record of 221 home runs—and finished fourth. Those sluggers with elephant feet included Johnny Mize and Walker Cooper and Sid Gordon. Not one player on the team stole more than seven bases, and only one, Bill Rigney, even stole that many. No one else even had as many as five.

Durocher's first full season was 1949. He brought Hank Thompson from the Kansas City Monarchs, acquired Monte Irvin from the Newark Eagles, and got a third black player, Ray Noble, a Latin who pronounced his name "Noblay." Then Durocher put together a new coaching staff: Herman Franks and a pair of ex-Giant heroes, Fred Fitzsimmons and Frankie Frisch.

These changes still didn't win over many Giants fans. Some of them swore they would never set foot in the Polo Grounds as long as the hated Durocher was there.

"I want my kind of guys," Durocher said. And in 1950 he got the nucleus together while he waited for someone to take over centerfield. Over the winter he acquired Sal Maglie—the aging pitcher had been "pardoned" by Chandler for jumping to the Mexican League. Then Durocher made a deal with the Braves in which he sent them Gordon, Cooper, Buddy Kerr, and Willard Marshall and acquired a double-play combination: Eddie Stanky at second and Alvin Dark at short. Stanky? He was another of those hated ex-Dodgers. Early in the 1950 season, Durocher recalled Irvin. And when the season ended, Mel Ott was released from a scouting job. He was the last of "McGraw's Boys." It was Leo's team now.

And that was the team I would be part of for the next twenty-one years as I headed for the Giants offices on Forty-second Street.

Eddie Brannick, the team's traveling secretary, was waiting for me. So was Doc Bowman, the trainer. I signed the contract that Brannick had already filled out. Under salary it read "$5,000." No discussion. I was a Giant, and Bowman accompanied me on the train ride to Philadelphia. I knew a little about the team. Bowman told me Irvin would be my roommate. I had met Monte the year before, when he came through Birmingham on a barnstorming tour. Hank Thompson was on the team now, too, so that meant I knew two Giants. When Thompson and Irvin had come through town, Piper Davis got some of us local players together; I had made more money in these exhibition games than from playing all of the 1950 season for Trenton. One of those barnstorming games was the first time I saw Jackie Robinson. He impressed me with what he was doing. Jackie was in charge of a team that included some of his teammates on the Dodgers—Pee Wee Reese, Ralph Branca, Gil Hodges, Roy Campanella. That told me a lot about Robinson, even though we never had a chance to talk. Campy told me that Jackie had recommended me to the Dodgers long before the Giants signed me. But that wasn't what gave me that special feeling about him. Reese, Hodges, and Branca were white —and as far as I know, they were the first ones ever to play with black teammates in the South.

"Hiya, roomie," Monte said, as he opened the door. "Does Skip know you're here?"

"I don't think anybody knows I'm here," I told him. Actually, I didn't want anybody to know. I just wanted to blend in and hide.

But five minutes later we were in Durocher's room, the first time I had ever seen a hotel suite. I could see that Leo was a fancy dresser. This was only a weekend series, but the closet was stuffed with his clothes and shoes. Leo definitely liked the finer things in life.

"Glad to see you, son," he said. "Glad you're hitting four seventy-seven."

He might have made players nervous with his style, but he made me relaxed right away. I see now what he did. He buttered me up.

"I wanted you to be here all along, from that first day I saw you in Sanford," he said. "But Mr. Stoneham said no. He said you needed some more seasoning, but I could see that you were a natural and only needed to play."

He told me not to worry about a thing but playing ball. He said the only problem the club had was being so far behind the Dodgers. We needed to get a big streak going.

It was a quiet clubhouse. I guess when you're in fifth place, there isn't much to talk about. There was a locker waiting for me next to Monte's. A shirt with a number 24 on it was hanging inside. I looked at the number as Leo came over. He spoke to me in that fatherly way of his, a manner I didn't see him use with other ball players but that I appreciated.

"Son, you're batting third and playing centerfield."

Whew! Third . . . center. That sounded to me like something DiMaggio might be doing. Just to hear him say those words made me feel like a big-leaguer already. You don't put a man up third unless you think he's your best all-around hitter. And centerfield—I guess of all the fielding positions on a team, that has always been the one filled by a player who can lead the team, take charge, make plays.

I just couldn't believe this was happening to me. I tried to stay calm at the thought, even though I gave Leo a big grin. I sat in front of my locker and tried to think of the job I had to do. But it was funny. All of a sudden, I was in the major leagues and doing major league things. Someone passed a ball to me for my signature. That's one of the things you're always doing in locker rooms—autographing a ton of balls. I wrote my name on it: "Willie Mays." And then I added "#24." It looked so . . . real. I wished that my father and aunts could be there to see me in a major league uniform. But at least Leo and Monte were on hand. My heart was racing. I should have realized that the intensity I was feeling was something I would have to deal with for the rest of my career. It didn't happen then, because I wasn't physically exhausted. But those feelings, combined with exhaustion, would lead to some of my collapses years down the road.

Shibe Park, Philadelphia. It was old, full of history. But all I realized as I stepped into the batting cage, to take my pregame cuts, was that this was the majors. I felt loose. I hit some dingers and drove four or five others into the stands. Leo was waiting for me on the top step when I finished.

"I gotta tell you something," he said, shaking his head. "In all the years I've been in baseball, I've never seen the other team's ball players stop what they were doing to watch a guy hit batting practice. Four seven seven, huh? I'm glad you're here."

I wondered whether Leo still was glad after I'd spent a few days in the majors. Did anyone ever have a worse start than I did? That first game I went 0 for 5. In my first at bat I took a third strike against Bubba Church. But we won, and so the next day my debut was written about in passing, just as a part of the whole story. The following day, Saturday afternoon, we got to .500 for the first time all season as Larry Jansen pitched a seven-hitter. But against Robin Roberts I went 0 for 3, even though I walked twice. In the third game, on Sunday, we went over .500—but I went 0 for 4 against Russ Meyer.

I came to New York 0 for 12. And we were returning to the Polo Grounds to face the Braves and Warren Spahn, the best lefty in the business.

The Polo Grounds! What magic the name held for me over the years. I'd been hearing about it from the time when the old Barons ball players used to tell me about their duels with Josh Gibson or Satchel Paige. I had even been in the place once or twice playing for the Barons. Now, I was returning as a Giant.

When I arrived, the Polo Grounds could hold 55,987 people. Not that it did very often, for the Giants had not won a pennant since 1937. The old place was shaped like a horseshoe, but there was nothing lucky about balls being hit to straightaway center. It was 475 feet from home plate. Incredibly, there were 74 feet behind home plate to the backstop. Leo warned me that a runner could advance from first to third on a wild pitch or passed ball. But this was the truly intriguing aspect of the place: The distance to the rightfield foul pole was only 258 feet—less than three times the distance from home to first. And it was only 280 feet to the leftfield foul pole. You could hit a "Chinese" home run that didn't even go 260 feet—and you could hit a 450-foot ball for an out. Even the distances to left center and right center went way beyond the average hitter's abilities: 425 to left center, 450 to right center.

The Polo Grounds was my new home. Although everyone called the three teams New York clubs, the Giants were the only major league team actually based on the island of Manhattan. The Yankees played in The Bronx, and the Dodgers were nestled in Brooklyn. Stoneham loved to talk about the history of his park. He explained to me that no one ever played polo in the Polo Grounds. It got its name from the fact that baseball teams in the 1880's often played in open fields in Manhattan, where there were plenty of pastures. A team named the Giants did play in a polo field at Fifth Avenue and 110th Street, owned by a newspaper publisher, James Gordon Bennett. From then on, wherever the Giants played their home field was automatically called the polo grounds. Bennett, the publisher of the *New York Herald,* never saw the Giants actually play on his field, and so history remembers him more for his financing of Stanley's trip to Africa to find Livingstone than for his activities as a baseball patron.

In 1889 the Giants moved to Coogan's Hollow, on Eighth Avenue between 155th and 157th Streets. The hollow, looking like a giant excavation, was all that remained of a farm granted by the British Crown in the seventeenth century to John Lion Gardiner, whose descendants still live on Gardiner's Island today.

One of Gardiner's descendants, Harriet Gardiner Lynch, married a Bowery upholsterer named James L. Coogan, who also was to be the first borough president of Manhattan. Coogan enjoyed his rise from the Bowery. He held open-air horse shows in the hollow beneath the bluff. He even considered bringing in Shakespearean actors from England to stage plays in the hollow. When the Giants moved into the park, though, the field at Coogan's Bluff became known as the Polo Grounds. When fire destroyed the old wooden structure in 1911, it was rebuilt into the shape that we all came to know. The decks were hung with friezes that depicted scenes from mythology. The Giants had a real-life character, though—John J. McGraw, a.k.a. Muggsy, the battling tyrant who brought the Giants fame and fortune on a scale that neither the Yankees nor the Dodgers were to enjoy until much later. McGraw's successes included pennants from 1921 to 1924, a feat that Bill Terry came close to matching by taking three pennants in the mid-1930's. Still, the Giants didn't attract a million people until 1945, when attendance boomed with the coming of the end of the war. In 1947 the club set a mark of 1.6 million visitors, who witnessed the greatest outpouring of home runs by any team in big-league history—221 by such sluggers as Johnny

Mize, Walker Cooper, Willard Marshall, Sid Gordon, and
a rookie named Bobby Thomson. For all its power, the club
finished fourth. It had no speed and no fielding and poor
pitching. But its home-run record lasted fourteen years,
until a modern Murderers Row of Yankees, led by Maris's
61 and Mantle's 54, busted the home-run mark.

This is the place I was in for the first time as a Giant, and
all I had to worry about was Spahn. He got the first two
hitters in the first inning, and then I was up. What did he
throw me? I don't think I ever knew. All I know is I swung
at it and hit it to the top of the leftfield roof. Finally, my
first major league hit, and a homer at that. My slump was
over.

Oh, no it wasn't. We played a doubleheader the next day.
I went 0 for 3 in the first game and was batting 0 for 2 in
the second, when I got cramps in both legs after sliding into
second and had to leave.

I was in the middle of another hitless streak. The next
game I went hitless against Lew Burdette and left men on
base four times. After that home run against Spahn, I went
0 for 13. I was now 1 for 25. Leo was so mad he kicked
over a chair in the clubhouse and ran upstairs to his office.
After the game, I sat next to my locker and cried.

Someone must have gone and told Leo, because the next
thing I knew he was back in the locker room putting his
arm around me.

"What's the matter, son?" he asked.

"Mister Leo," I bawled, in a high squeaky voice, "I can't
hit up here."

Leo got pretty angry then, I could tell. But he tried not to
show it.

"What do you mean you can't hit? You're going to be a
great ball player!"

"The pitching is just too fast for me here. They're going
to send me back to Minneapolis."

Leo wasn't having any of that kind of talk. No sir. Leo

pointed to his uniform and told me, "Willie, see what's printed across my jersey? It says Giants. As long as I'm the manager of the Giants, you're my centerfielder. You're here to stay. Stop worrying. With your talent you're going to get plenty of hits."

Leo then explained his philosophy. He liked to repeat it often. He believed there were five things a ball player had to be able to do to be great: hit, hit with power, run, field, and throw.

"Willie, you could do all five from the first time I ever saw you," he said. "You're the greatest ball player I ever saw or ever hope to see. But, Willie, you and your damn pull hitting. I don't know why you won't take the ball to rightfield. You can hit it into the bleachers here, over the fence, anywhere you want, yet you're still trying to pull the ball all the time. For you to do something wrong is an absolute disgrace. And I know you don't want to disgrace me, do you, Willie?"

I wiped my eyes and smiled, feeling better. "Get some sleep," he said. "This one's over. It's in the safe and they got it locked up, but tomorrow's another day."

He walked back toward the staircase leading to his office, but stopped suddenly, as if remembering something. "Speaking of tomorrow," he said with a grin, "when you put on your pants pull them up higher. They were so low out there today, the umpires thought the strike zone went all the way down to your ankles."

But besides just trying to butter me up, Leo could see I did need some help with my batting. I was apparently turning my right hand over while swinging. That made me pull everything toward shortstop and third base. But if he could get me to swing straightaway, he said he knew I had enough power to take the ball deep to right center.

What Leo told me worked. He also used some psychology on me. He asked me to bat eighth—something I had never done before. He explained that it was a dead spot in the batting order and he needed someone to spark it. I think he had a master plan for catching the Dodgers, but he needed to keep a winning streak going and he needed to avoid any weak spots that could hurt that. I told him I'd do anything to help out.

My 0-for-13 and 1-for-25 streak ended with a single in a game against Pittsburgh. I went 2 for 4 that game. My other hit was a triple that landed over the "449" sign in right center. This big park wasn't going to hurt me, after all. In fact, I could use it by hitting the ball anyplace, as long as I could drive it. The next game I hit a pair of doubles and went 2 for 3. I broke out of my hitless string by going 9 for 24, and we were above .500 to stay. Now, we thought about the Dodgers for the first time.

My first at bat against the Dodgers, Campanella tried to drive me crazy. He knew he had a twenty-year-old kid coming up, and I was facing their smartest pitcher, Preacher Roe. As usual, Campanella was jawing behind the plate. He used to do that all the time, engage the hitters in conversation, get their minds off the business at hand. Anything to put you at a disadvantage.

"What do you think of him, Willie?" he asked me as I dug in against Roe.

"He's a mighty good pitcher," I said.

"You're lucky today," said Campy. "Wait till you get Don Newcombe tomorrow. He hates colored rookies. He'll blow you down." I was learning, though, not to pay any attention to everything I heard.

As we continued winning, and as I continued hitting, I started to become something of a celebrity. But not only for my exploits at the Polo Grounds. New York has a lot of street games, the kind of games you don't see in other cities. Even with all the traffic and the crowds, the kids play all sorts of ball games, probably because there aren't many parks or fields available. I started to play one of those street games with the neighborhood kids after my home games were over. It's called stickball. You take a broomstick and saw off about six inches. Then you put tape around one end for a handle. And you play.

There are manhole covers all over the streets of New York. You batted at one manhole cover. That was home plate. A pitcher threw a pink rubber ball, which the kids called a "spaldeen," and you just tried to hit it as far and as straight as you could. There were different rules. If you hit it over the next manhole cover down the block, it might be a single. If you hit it two covers away, you were a "two-sewer hitter." That meant you were pretty good. I was a five-sewer hitter. So I was pretty damn good. And I never used to think much of playing with the kids after school, until one day a photographer from one of the papers—I forget which, we had so many in New York back then—took a picture of me playing stickball with kids in the street. That changed my image forever. I guess it made me seem like a grown-up kid. That wasn't too far from the truth back then. I had just turned twenty. I didn't have a heck of a lot to do with my teammates, who were older and already settled in New York. So I played games with neighborhood kids. One night I got so wrapped up in a big stickball game that I forgot to make it to the Polo Grounds. Leo sent Frank Forbes, one of his assistants, to look for me. Sure enough, he found me standing on one of the "sewers."

That first summer in New York was terrific. I stayed with a couple named David and Anna Goosby. They had a house on St. Nicholas Avenue and 151st Street. Forbes had made the arrangements for me to stay with them. He told me he was afraid that if I stayed in an apartment house, I might start running around with a lot of other single people. Mrs. Goosby reminded me of my Aunt Sarah, the way she took care of me. Her husband was a kind man who had retired from the railroad. They made me feel at home. There was lots of home cooking, she washed my clothes, and she made sure I'd be places on time. When it was suppertime, she opened the window and called out to me to come in from the stickball game.

One evening, I played a trick on Leo. I knew he'd be coming by in his new Cadillac to pick me up. We were going to speak at a father-son banquet in Hackensack, New Jersey. I told all the kids and everyone else in the neighborhood that a chauffeur was coming for me in a limousine. This everyone had to see, so all the neighbors went out into the street, and by the time Leo pulled up, there must have been a few dozen people around.

I opened the backdoor, waved to everyone, and shouted to Leo, "Okay, chauffeur, let's go."

"You're pretty smart for a rookie," Leo said. But he went along with it. At least for a few blocks. Then he stopped the car and said, "Okay, now get up here in the front seat with me."

At the dinner, I was shocked when Leo told me that I was expected to say a few words. I had never made a speech before in my life.

"Nothing to it," said Leo, who could speak at the drop of a hat. "Just tell them you're happy to be here. Stuff like that. When I think you've said enough, I'll pull on your coat so you'll know you should sit down."

But I didn't expect to be the first speaker. I was as nervous as can be. Butterflies even worse than before a big game. It was a strange feeling to look out and see all those people in a big room looking straight at me, waiting to hear what I had to say to them. I started.

"Mr. Leo is the main speaker so I'm not going to say much."

Now what?

While I was stammering and trying to think what to say next, a little black boy from the back of the room hollered something at me. I couldn't hear him, and I looked at Leo for help. He told me to ask the youngster to come up front. The boy repeated the question.

"Who's the best centerfielder in baseball?" he asked.

"You're looking at him," I said. Leo pulled on my coat, I sat down, and everyone applauded.

I never met anybody like Leo. Still haven't. Mr. Leo. He was married to Laraine Day at the time, and they had a young son named Chris. He was a cute kid who used to copy Leo by standing in the dugout with his leg on the top step, just as Leo did. Chris spent more time with me that summer than he did with Leo. On many of the road trips we would eat together, room together, and have a catch, and Leo never saw us until we came to the ballpark. I didn't realize it then, but I think Leo actually was using Chris to babysit for me. He'd give me twenty dollars every day and say, "Get the kid something to eat tonight." But it was a guarantee that I'd be with Chris. Leo—did that man ever do anything without a motive?

With that kind of money, I ate pretty well. Most times we'd have dinner at the home of a friend and that twenty-dollar bill stayed in my pocket. We'd go to a movie practically every night, then fall asleep in bed reading comic books. One night in Cincinnati, a cop stopped us on our way back from a movie. He wanted to know what I was doing at that hour with a white boy in my car. He wouldn't let us go until he had called Leo at the hotel and checked my story.

While I learned about stickball on the streets of Harlem, I learned infinitely more about baseball at the Polo Grounds, and not only from Leo. There were many good teachers on the Giants. It was a smart club with many older players, veterans who had studied the game and turned it into a fine art. Eddie Stanky already was thirty-four years old, but he knew how to play second base and he knew how to take advantage of people. Boy, he was smart and tricky. Leo liked to say, "Stanky can't hit, run, or throw, but I wouldn't trade him for a million dollars."

One of Stanky's tricks came in handy when there were

runners on first and second and none out. If there was a ground ball to the shortstop and a throw to second, Stanky would make the putout at second. But instead of throwing to first for the double play, he'd throw to third. Why would he do that? It wasn't for the force play. The runner already had reached the bag. But often, the runner instinctively rounded third figuring Stanky would throw to first. A quick throw would catch the man off third, and now we'd have a runner at first, with two out, instead of the runner on third.

Irvin was also a very smart ball player. He was especially good at base running and figuring out ways to get an extra base. One time he stole home with a left-handed batter up. I asked him how he had the nerve to do that, since the catcher had a clear shot at him.

"You're right, Willie, he had a clean shot," said Monte. "But did you notice how the third baseman was playing very wide because a pull-hitter was at bat? So I could take a big lead."

I also learned about playing centerfield. I watched for the catcher's signs. That gave me a clue to where the ball would be hit. If catcher Wes Westrum signaled for a fastball against a right-handed hitter who had trouble with the pitch, he might swing late. That would send the ball to right. I also learned how balls travel when a certain pitch is hit. When a fastball was hit to me in center, I just knew it would sail. But a liner off a curveball will drop more quickly. We had the biggest centerfield in baseball, and it was a good thing I picked up all those keys. Once I did, having that big area actually helped me because I was able to get to balls that might have been homers in other parks, and at least extra-bases in the Polo Grounds.

This was also a crucial time in my development as a hitter. I started going to rightfield on outside pitches, the way Leo had told me, and the base hits came. When the pitches were inside, I'd pull the ball. I was becoming an inside-outside hitter. Eventually, I could even take an inside pitch and hit it to rightfield easily. But that part of the game didn't come just yet. That took me a couple of years. I learned that there were so many fine points to the game, and Leo knew them all; he was the smartest manager I ever saw. Irvin told me that I had a manager who loved me. "Just keep quiet and play," Monte advised me. "You'll learn more in a day from Leo than from anyone else."

Boy, was Monte right. Leo always was a couple of innings ahead of the other manager. The opposing teams were always looking at our coaches trying to steal the signs. But Leo had already given it to them before the inning began! He told us what to do before the situation even came up.

One of Leo's favorite plays was the hit-and-run. If we had a runner on first and the first pitch to the next batter was a ball, then there would be a hit-and-run on the next pitch. The coaches would be going through all sorts of signs to throw off the other team. But the batter didn't pay attention to the coaches. All he had to do was step out of the box and rub his hands with dirt. That let Leo know that the batter understood that the hit-and-run was on. While all this was going on, the other team would even try looking at Leo in the dugout to see if they could pick up any kind of sign.

But Leo—bless him, the only thing he would pick up in the dugout was a towel. That looked simple enough, as if he just was wiping his hands. But when I was in the field, Leo had told me to be watching him. If he picked up the towel, that was a sign for me to move either right or left, depending on the batter. When Leo dropped the towel, that told me where he wanted me to stop right then. Everyone else on the other clubs thought Leo had a nervous habit of fumbling around with a towel.

The psychology that he used confounded us sometimes. You never could be sure what tactic he was using, or why. In late July of my first season we dropped a Sunday doubleheader to the Cardinals in St. Louis, 10–1, and 11–2. On top of that, we had to play a night game on Monday. When we staggered into the clubhouse, Leo was waiting for us.

"Don't anybody get undressed," he began. "You looked like a bunch of girls out there today. Now I'm giving each one of you an order. I don't want to see any of you until eight o'clock in the morning. You heard me right. Stay out all night, do whatever you want—but don't show your faces at the hotel until eight A.M. If anybody does, I'll fine him two hundred dollars. Do I make myself clear?"

Now I had heard everything, at least up until that point in my rookie season. Nobody said a word, though. I certainly wasn't going back to that hotel. I stayed with friends. The next night, Leo was chipper and he smiled as he greeted us. Most of us were dragging.

"How does everybody feel?" he shouted. I started to think Leo might have outsmarted himself this time. All the starting pitchers looked green around the gills. Leo asked for a volunteer. Would anyone be willing to go out on the mound and throw for him?

"I'll pitch," said Sal Maglie. He had been mostly a relief pitcher up until then, but Leo took him, saying, "Okay, you're my pitcher." And that's the way Sal Maglie became a starting pitcher and went on to win all those games during our pennant drive.

I loved it when Maglie pitched. I knew I was going to get good pitches to hit. Now, how do you figure that, I can just imagine a fan asking. Simple. When Maglie pitched for us, no other pitcher would throw at me. Because they knew Sal would knock down their hitters without thinking about it for a moment. That's how he earned his nickname, the Barber. It wasn't because he never shaved the day he was going to pitch—which he didn't. It was because his pitches came so close to the other guy's head, it was like shaving him. Sal was fearless and looked it, especially with that dark shadow on his face. He never smiled. I used to think of one of those bad guys in a cowboy movie when I looked at Sal.

Another guy Leo revived in the pennant chase was Bobby
Thomson. When Leo called me up, Bobby had been the
centerfielder, but he was batting only .229. Since I had never
played any other position, Leo put me in center and
switched Thomson to third. While I was struggling when I
joined the team, Bobby suddenly got hot. He got five hits in
his next 11 at bats.

On August 11, between games of a doubleheader with
the Boston Braves, the Dodgers achieved their biggest lead
of the season—13½ games. They had stopped Boston in the
first game of their twin bill while we were being shut out by
the Phillies.

This is the way the standings looked at that moment, with
the season two thirds over:

	Won	Lost	Percentage	Games Behind
DODGERS	70	35	.667	—
GIANTS	59	51	.536	13½

Pretty grim statistics.

The Dodgers dropped the second game, to our relief, but
they still had a 13-game edge to carry them through the
season, didn't they? And the Dodgers could possibly increase that huge lead, for in two days we were going to face
them in a three-game series. By the time that series started
in the Polo Grounds we were still 12½ games out, although
we did have a four-game winning streak. Big deal.

We had to keep winning immediately or we could find
ourselves almost 16 games out by the weekend. This was
our batting lineup for our series against the Dodgers:

First base—Whitey Lockman
Second base—Eddie Stanky
Shortstop—Alvin Dark
Third base—Bobby Thomson
Leftfield—Monte Irvin

Centerfield—Willie Mays
Rightfield—Don Mueller
Catcher—Wes Westrum
Pitchers—Sal Maglie, Larry Jansen, Dave Koslo, Jim Hearn

When that series started we didn't concede anything to the Dodgers. This was when Leo was at his best. He honestly believed we could catch the Dodgers. We hadn't started to play our best ball yet, he told us. Leo figured that if we could sweep the Dodgers, we could catch fire.

Boy, did we. We not only swept them, we kept winning as we put together a 16-game winning streak. It was the most consistently spectacular baseball I've ever been a part of.

Remember, we opened that series after having lost six straight games to the Dodgers. But we unloaded for three runs in the first inning against Erv Palica. We got a two-run homer in the first from Don Mueller and also a homer from Whitey Lockman. We might have gotten more. I walked after Whitey's shot, but Campanella, that cagey old pro, picked me off first with a bullet throw when I wasn't paying attention.

Leo didn't have any starters left because he had been manipulating pitchers so heavily for the last week. So he called on a rookie, George Spencer, who normally was a relief pitcher. George held them to only six hits and won, 4–2.

That streak we were riding might never have happened if I hadn't gotten a chance to make a big play the next day. Jim Hearn was pitching against Ralph Branca. We were tied 1–1 in the eighth inning, and the Dodgers looked as if they were going to break open the game. Billy Cox was on third base and Branca was on first with only one out. Carl Furillo was up. Even though he often drilled the ball to right, I was shading him to left center, figuring he was going to pull. Instead, he sent a looping fly ball to right center. I took off as soon as he hit it and was at full speed when I got near it. My instincts told me that even if I caught the ball, I was still in big trouble. I had to worry about Cox tagging from third and scoring the go-ahead run. Still striding at full speed I stretched out my arm, stretched out my glove—and caught the ball. At that same moment I spun around toward the plate and threw as my body was facing home. I got off a heck of a throw. It went right to Westrum and it got there in time. He blocked the plate and tagged out Cox.

I always thought that was one of my best throws. So do a lot of other people. That's one of the plays that thousands of people swore they saw in person. I'm still getting pats on the back from it. I had a job to do just then, though. I got up in the bottom of the inning and hit a single. Ever notice that the man who makes a big fielding play always seems to come to bat immediately? It's true. That started a winning rally. Westrum, who hadn't hit one out of the park in a month, followed with a homer, and we won by 3–1. Those are the kinds of things that happen when you're hot.

But of course Charley Dressen, the Dodgers' manager, wouldn't let me enjoy my big day in the field. I think he was hinting that there was some luck involved. After the game he spoke about that throw and what it did to his team and said, "Mays will have to do it again before I'll believe it."

The next day Maglie went out for us against Newcombe. Both were at their peak. They each had a 16–5 record. But we pecked away a little better and escaped with a 2–1 victory when Monte drove home Stanky with a triple in the eighth. Now we had a six-game winning streak and were only 9½ games out. "Only"—a funny word when you're that far behind a team that has all those great players. But that's how we felt. So did Leo. This was his team, finally, and when he had gotten the players he wanted, he was the best. We really felt nothing could stop us. When we finally did lose, it was only by 2–0 to the Pirates. Our 16-game streak was the best in the National League since 1935.

We met the Dodgers again in the middle of September, and we were only 5½ games behind them. People forget. They think that the Dodgers collapsed after their 13½ game lead in August. But that isn't what happened at all. We just got great. The Dodgers weren't playing .600 ball anymore, but they weren't playing losing ball, either. They were still playing better than .500. In fact, when that September series began in Ebbets Field, they stopped us in the opening game. Newcombe pitched a two-hit shutout. The next day, we came back with Maglie and got a 2–1 victory.

This was a game in which I came to realize what sort of competitor Jackie Robinson truly was. Bobby Morgan lined a shot to left center that I raced over for. It was a low liner and I dived for it, caught it backhanded, and landed on the ground. Actually, looking back on it, I guess I think that that was one of my better catches, too. But at that moment I was stunned. Hitting the field so hard with your arms outstretched, your body absorbs the full force of your landing. When I finally came to myself, Leo and some of my teammates were around me. Through the haze I could see Robinson walking away.

"Jackie was coming out here to see if I was all right?" I asked Leo.

"Are you nuts?" he said. "He only came out here to see if you still had the ball in your glove!"

7

AS LONG AS I LIVE, I'll never forget the finish we put on my rookie year. The Miracle of Coogan's Bluff. We caught the Dodgers on the next-to-last day of the season, and then won it in the last inning of the last playoff game. No thanks to me in that last game. But I had great teammates, and Irvin might have been the best player in the league that year. If he wasn't, the only one better was Robinson. Me? I still had to learn how to deal with the pressure. The numbers showed I had an outstanding rookie season—I even got voted Rookie of the Year. But I wasn't ready to take it on my shoulders.

The Giants and Dodgers went into Sunday, September 30, the last day of the regular season, tied for first. We were riding high with a six-game winning streak, ready to play the Braves in Boston, while the Dodgers were about to square off against the Phillies in Philadelphia. What followed was one of the most dramatic afternoons in baseball history, an afternoon that seemingly could never be topped. But of course it would be one day. That's the beauty of the game.

The Giants got it over with first. Larry Jansen pitched a clutch game for us, at one point retiring twenty-two straight batters. It was a tough afternoon for me, though. Batting seventh, I went 0–4 and struck out at a key moment in the sixth, with Bobby Thomson on first and the Giants nursing a 3–1 lead. Thomson was then doubled up on the hit-and-run.

Jansen took that 3–1 lead into the bottom of the ninth, but almost lost the victory when the Braves scored once and put two runners on base following sloppy fielding on our part. But Jansen grimly collected the third out and we came out with a squeaker, a 3–2 victory.

We also thought it had given us the pennant. For down in Shibe Park the Brooklyns, as they were affectionately called, trailed for most of the game, first by 6–1 and then by 8–5. But they tied it with a stunning three-run splurge in the eighth. Then the game dragged into extra innings—10th, 11th, 12th. Finally, in the bottom of the 12th it seemed to be all over. The Phillies loaded the bases with two out, and Eddie Waitkus came to bat to face Don Newcombe. Waitkus smacked a sure base hit, a low line drive to the right of second base. Robinson raced over, dived, and clutched the ball in his glove just off the ground. Umpire Lon Warneke shot his arm into the air, signaling "out." Robinson, groggy, but ever the hero, fell hard on his shoulder and collapsed. He couldn't get up for a few minutes. Finally, he rose and walked unsteadily to the dugout. He remained in the game he'd just saved long enough to win it.

In the 14th, as fate would have it, Robinson came up with two out and Robin Roberts pitching. Robinson crashed a home run into the upper leftfield stands. It gave the Dodgers a 9–8 victory and forced the second playoff in the 75-year history of the National League. The first, in 1946, involved the Dodgers, as so many zany events in baseball history seem to have. The Dodgers lost that one to the Cardinals in two straight games.

New York went nuts for this one, folks. Five thousand fans were waiting for our ball club when our delayed Merchants Limited train glided into Grand Central Terminal at nine-thirty that night. Another two thousand Dodger fans waited for their heroes.

"The Dodgers are like that every year," one man was overheard saying of the finish. "They always drive everybody crazy."

The final regular-season standings showed, mutely but dramatically, just what the Giants had done under Durocher's inspired leadership.

	Won	Lost	Percentage	Games Behind
DODGERS	96	58	.623	—
GIANTS	96	58	.623	—

We'd won 37 of our last 44 games, including all of our last seven, and 12 of our last 13. The Dodgers hadn't exactly collapsed. They played over .500 ball. But no one ever staged a finish the way we did.

And this miracle finish wasn't over yet. Not by a long shot.

The playoffs, a best-of-three affair, began the next day at Ebbets Field. Whichever team won two games first would play the Yankees in the World Series. The prospect of all three teams in postseason action led Acting Mayor Joseph T. Sharkey to proclaim "Baseball Week in the World's Greatest City." That was baseball fever at its best.

The big blow in the opening playoff game was Thomson's two-run homer off Branca. With Hearn pitching, the Giants captured the game, 3–1. Irvin also starred, scoring on Thomson's home run, then belting one into the stands himself in the eighth inning, after making a great running catch on Andy Pafko to end the seventh.

"I hit a fastball for that homer," Thomson recalled when the game was over.

I went 0 for 3 that day, and struck out twice against Branca. I didn't want to face him again.

Despite the victory, Mister Leo refused to pose for pictures—"Not until this is over," he said.

His superstition was upheld the next day, when the Dodgers, behind Clem Labine, shut out the Giants 10–0. I'm told that during the game, as Wall Street traders looked over the stock ticker, they read, "Dow Jones 2 P.M. Stock Averages 30 indus 274.20 up 1.64 . . . Baseball NY Giants —no runs two hits no errors . . ."

I went 1–4 and committed an error. Thomson struck out with the bases loaded in the third inning when the Dodgers held only a 2–0 edge.

On Wednesday, October 3, 1951, the Dodgers and Giants met for the National League championship: history in the making.

There was much happening in the rest of the United States that day, as well. Indeed, it could almost be described as a historic day for the country in general:

- The first parking meters were installed in Brooklyn, "But their success is held in doubt," ran a headline in the *New York Times*.
- Joe Louis signed to fight Rocky Marciano.
- RCA invited the public to see its color-TV tests.
- Dr. Phillip C. Jessup, ambassador-at-large, decried Senator Joseph McCarthy's charges that he had ties to the Communist Party. The hearings were interrupted to announce the Giants-Dodgers score.
- The papers announced that when the World Series started the next day it would be televised in New York over Channels 4, 9, and 11.
- A newspaper ad for pressers offered "top salary."

The temperature was in the low sixties as Newcombe (20–9) started against Maglie (23–6).

The Dodgers got the first run, but a bonehead running

play by Thomson messed up a potential Giants rally. The Dodgers took a 4–1 lead with a three-run splurge off Maglie in the eighth, and Newcombe, tiring badly, tried to preserve it in the ninth. He had pitched more than 14 innings over Saturday and Sunday, as the Dodgers' manager, Chuck Dressen, was desperate for pitching. Preacher Roe had a sore arm late in the season. Even Campanella, the sturdy catcher who was to win the league's MVP award, was unable to perform against the Giants because of an old injury.

Meanwhile, I'm afraid I might as well have been sidelined. I was 0–3, and struck out once—and this was the biggest game of the season! I went 1 for 10 in the three playoff games, with three strikeouts and a fielding error to boot. Duke Snider, who was to be my opposite number on both coasts for many years to come, wound up 5–10 in the three games. I really had the rookie jitters.

In the bottom of the ninth, Dark opened with a single off Gil Hodges's glove, only the fifth hit off Newcombe. Don Mueller then singled through the right side as Hodges, unaccountably, held Dark close to first. Irvin, though, popped out. Whitey Lockman rammed a double to left, scoring Dark, with Mueller racing to third—but as he slid into the bag, he sprained his left ankle. He was carried off on a stretcher, prolonging the suspense. There was a lull on the field, but not at the phone company. In the course of the day, we learned, it was to receive more than 700,000 phone calls at its special number giving the score of the game.

Dressen called his bullpen. What to do? Carl Erskine, sinker-ball pitcher, was warming up. He could get a grounder, perhaps a double-play ball. Branca, who had tossed the homer in Game 1 to Thomson, also was warming up.

"Erskine's sinker is hanging," came the report to Dressen from the bullpen coach. That meant Branca. There were runners on second and third, and the Dodgers led by 4–2. If Branca walked Thomson, that could set up a force play at the other bases. But that also went against the "book"—

the unwritten set of rules which included the admonition that you never intentionally put the potential winning run on first. Dressen wasn't a book manager, but he went by it this time.

I think I must have been the most scared person in the whole ballpark in the bottom of the ninth inning. As I mentioned in the first chapter, I was the on-deck batter when Bobby Thomson came up. If Bobby made out, it would be my turn at bat. I would have been in a position to become the hero, sure, but the way I was swinging I was more likely to make the last out of the season. Leo came down from the coach's box at third base to talk to Thomson. It was typical Leo. He remembered everything and took every edge. Thomson had hit a home run off Branca on Monday, in the first game. Leo now asked Thomson if that pitch had been a slider. When Thomson, who had forgotten it actually was a fastball, said it was a slider, Leo said, "Then look for a fastball this time.

"He remembers you hit a slider. He won't throw it again. Just be ready for the fastball."

I never saw Leo so sure about anything—and in such a tough situation. Sure enough, the first pitch was a fastball, a called strike. I heard Leo holler down to Bobby, "C'mon, now, he'll come back with one." And sure enough he did. When I looked up the ball was heading for the leftfield stands. It sailed in upstairs, over the 315-foot mark. But it was the kind of drive that didn't seem like a home run when it took off. It never occurred to me at that moment—we had just won the pennant!

What happened next everyone seems to remember: Thomson running around the bases, dancing with joy; Leo running with him from third base on toward home plate; Jackie Robinson watching to make sure Thomson stepped on every base. Me? I was still kneeling in the on-deck circle when Thomson touched second, frozen with excitement and wonder. On the radio, fans were listening to Russ

Hodges screaming over and over, "The Giants win the pennant! The Giants win the pennant!" I didn't hear Hodges's ecstatic five-word chant, of course, but I've heard it on tape many times since, and it is an indelible part of my memory of that great, great day.

We had to run all the way to the center-field clubhouse. We just couldn't believe it. We still were jumping. Once we got inside, I had my first taste of champagne. It was also my last. I didn't like it much. Leo came over to me with a big smile on his face and said he was surprised Dressen didn't walk Thomson and pitch to me with the bases loaded.

"I'm glad he didn't," I told Durocher. "I didn't want the pennant hanging on my shoulders."

Well, enough analysis. We had the pennant, a great feeling. Especially for a rookie like me. I couldn't believe the World Series was starting the next day. For the moment, however, we just tried to enjoy ourselves. Outside the clubhouse we could hear fans shouting "Thomson, Thomson," or "Stanky" or "Leo." Finally, a police official told us we had better go out one by one onto the clubhouse steps and wave to the crowd, or the people would never leave.

Leo couldn't stop chortling. He thought Dressen made some other mistakes besides not walking Thomson. "I don't care if Clem Labine pitched yesterday," he said. "Dressen should have brought him in and with that sinker ball he could have made Thomson hit it on the ground. When he brought in Branca, I looked into the dugout to see if Campanella would catch him. Campy was hurt, sure, but I'd put him in there for Rube Walker. Campy wasn't so hurt that he couldn't catch for one or two batters. Campy is the smartest catcher in the game. Things could have come out different."

Leo was such a good, competitive manager, he spent a lot of time second-guessing his opposite number—never more so than after that game.

     *   *   *

I saw Joe DiMaggio for the first time just before the World Series opened against the Yankees. I spotted him on the field surrounded by reporters, but I was too shy to go up and introduce myself. A photographer came over to me and asked if I would pose with Joe for a photo.

"Why would he want to take a picture with me?" I asked.

The photographer brought me over and introduced us. I got the chance to talk with him for just a few minutes, a dream come true. I didn't realize it then, but the photographs would turn out to be something special. He hadn't announced it, but Joe had decided to retire once the Series ended. That was the only time I got to see my boyhood hero play. And it was the only time we posed for pictures when we both were playing. What a champion, what dignity. He's a great man, to this day.

There was another ball player there, though, with whom I was destined to be compared over the years—Mickey Mantle. We were both rookies, and even though he was the rightfielder in 1951, he was going to be the centerfielder for many years to come. With that team of sluggers, Mickey wasn't even batting third in the lineup. He was the lead-off batter in the series. As luck would have it, I had an effect on his career.

Before the game, Yankee Manager Casey Stengel told Mickey, "Take everything you can get over in center. The Dago's heel is hurting pretty bad." That was Casey's affectionate nickname for Joltin' Joe.

In the fifth inning of the second game I hit a high fly to right center. DiMaggio and Mantle both went for it. It was going to be another out for me. God, I was still looking for my first Series hit. But Mantle, following Stengel's instructions, chased the ball even though it was closer to DiMaggio. When DiMaggio yelled, "I got it," Mantle stopped short. As Joe made the catch, Mickey suddenly fell as if he had been shot. He was on the grass struggling and they had to carry him off on a stretcher.

No one could figure out what had happened. It turned out that he had caught his spikes in the rubber cover of a drainage ditch, and it messed up his right leg, beginning a series of knee problems that would plague him for the rest of his career. From that day on, Mickey seemed to be marked with a sort of pity; people were forever saying, "Just think what he could have done if his knees weren't bad." But Mickey had a great career anyway.

This was the Giants' first World Series in fourteen years, the first time the Yankees and Giants had met in the big one since 1937. We were still riding high and were also a bit spent emotionally after our victory over the Dodgers, but Leo rallied us as best he could.

"Just keep going," Durocher told us.

Sure enough, we won the opener at Yankee Stadium 5–1. Dave Koslo, a left-hander, held those awesome Yankee sluggers to seven hits, while my friend Monte Irvin tied a Series record with four hits in one game, and also became the first man in thirty years to steal home in the Series, after he detected a flaw in Allie Reynolds's pitching rhythm: Reynolds would take the throw back to the mound from Yogi Berra, then look down for an instant.

"When he does that again," Durocher, the third-base coach, told Irvin, "you go."

The Yankees came back to win the second game, 3–1, as Ed Lopat tossed a five hitter. But the victory was tempered by concern over Mantle's future. I felt bad about the accident, too. Still, the powerful Yankees hardly appeared to miss him. Hank Bauer simply took his place in right field. With Lopat throwing his famous "junk"—screwballs, off-speed curves—we were never in the game despite Irvin's three hits.

In Korea, I'm told, some soldiers were complaining. They couldn't hear the game live over armed forces radio because it was being treated as a program and not news. And to compound their anger, they weren't even told the results.

"That would be taking the suspense off it, like revealing the ending of a murder mystery," a major supposedly explained. So the troops didn't know the Series score until twelve hours after the game was over.

The teams moved to the Polo Grounds for Game 3, and this one produced the famous "field goal" by Eddie Stanky that still drives Phil Rizzuto crazy when he talks about it. In the fifth inning, during which five unearned Giants runs crossed the plate to seal the game, Stanky and Rizzuto were involved in a play at second. It keyed the Giants' rally. With one out, Stanky walked. Then he tore for second, attempting to steal the bag. Berra tossed a bullet to Rizzuto, waiting for Stanky, and Rizzuto applied the tag. Instead of being called out, though, Stanky kicked the ball out of Rizzuto's glove with his right foot. While Rizzuto chased the ball, Stanky headed for third. Rizzuto and Stengel were outraged. They charged that Stanky never went for the bag with his foot, but instead aimed for Rizzuto's glove, which should be interference. And anyway, said the excitable Rizzuto, "he never even touched second." The Giants won the game, 6–2, to take a 2–1 lead in the games.

Stengel was concerned about DiMaggio. Three games and no hits. The great centerfielder looked listless, as if just playing was an effort. But Stengel didn't know what to do. He had to make some changes, that was certain. He got a break the next day when rain washed out Game 4. Stengel made a decision. He would rearrange the batting order, moving Bauer from eighth to lead-off, shuttling Gene Woodling from the top spot to sixth. And DiMaggio would remain the cleanup hitter.

DiMaggio came up in the fifth inning the next day with the Yankees leading Maglie 2–1 and Berra on first. DiMaggio blasted the ball into the third deck in left field to increase the edge. Reynolds kept out of trouble by getting me to hit into three double plays—including the final outs of the game.

The Series was now tied at two games apiece. Durocher's manipulating, confidence building, and cajoling had taken us pretty far against a team that was to place four players in the Hall of Fame—DiMaggio, Mantle, Johnny Mize, Berra—not to mention its manager, Casey Stengel, and general manager, George Weiss. Of all the Giants in the Series, on the field and in the front office, I was to be the only one voted into the Hall, although Monte Irwin made it for his play in the Negro League. Durocher didn't make it, nor did Stanky or Dark or Thomson or Jansen or Maglie.

The Yankees of those days also had other outstanding players, people who dominated their positions while their performances often were overshadowed by more famous teammates: Gil McDougald at third, Jerry Coleman at second, Bauer and Woodling in the outfield.

McDougald became the star of Game 5. In the long history of the World Series, there had been only two grand-slam homers—one by the Cleveland Indians' Elmer Smith in 1920, against the Dodgers, of course, and one by the Yankees' Tony Lazzeri in 1936, against the Giants at the Polo Grounds. Bill Terry had been the manager of the Giants back then.

This time, McDougald, a twenty-three-year-old, put the game out of reach in the third inning by slamming one into the seats.

"For a moment," said Terry, a spectator at the game, "I thought it was the same nightmare."

The Yankees went on to crush us 13–1, behind Lopat. DiMaggio went 3–5, driving in three runs. I went 0–2, striking out once against Lopat, even though I did manage a walk. DiMaggio still was the big-game player and I hadn't proved I was. He showed me something in that series, coming back out of a slump when it counted.

While the game was going on, there was a development

in Philadelphia that threatened to change the face of sports in America. The Justice Department was attempting to stop blackouts of televised sports events. The immediate target was the National Football League. The Justice Department's antitrust division filed suit to prevent the N.F.L. from restricting broadcasts of games to certain networks. If the suit succeeded, said a Justice Department official, the Department would go after the N.C.A.A. and all other professional and amateur sports organizations that followed similar practices. "The public should be able to buy what it wants free of any restrictions," the Justice Department contended.

To New Yorkers, however, blessed with being able to watch most of their teams' home games for free, that must have seemed an unnecessary action by the feds.

The Yankees went for the clincher in the Stadium. And this game had overtones—if that was possible—of the great Giants-Dodgers finale of the week before. The Yankees, thanks to Bauer's bases-loaded triple, took a 4–1 lead into the ninth inning. Stengel had been making all the right pitching moves, starting Raschi, then relieving him with Johnny Sain when Raschi faltered. While these moves hinted at the dynasty that Stengel was to command, that game ended an era. In the sixth inning. Stengel sent in a pinch runner for DiMaggio, who trotted off the field to a standing ovation. Somehow, the fans sensed that this was his last appearance on a field. And it was.

Finally the Giants broke through in the ninth. Stanky led off with a single and Dark outraced a bunt. Then Lockman drilled a single to right. The bases were filled and there were none out and Irvin, who had pounded 11 hits—one less than the Series record—was coming to bat.

Stengel then mystified just about everyone in the park by going against that famous "book"—he brought in Bob Kuzava, a left-hander, to face Irvin, a right-handed batter.

"The Negro star," as Irvin was described, immediately blasted a tremendous fly to deep left center. But Woodling ran it down, with Stanky scoring, and the other runners moved up to second and third.

Now, incredibly, Thomson was up in the exact same setting—his team trailing 4–2, two men on, first base open, ninth inning. And Stengel taunted fate by employing the same strategy that had backfired on Dressen.

What had spelled disaster for the Dodgers worked well enough for Old Casey, though. Thomson hit a towering fly to left center. Woodling caught this one, even though it scored a runner. The Giants were down to their last out, and Durocher had just about run out of pinch hitters as the tying run was on second.

He sent up still another right-hander, Sal Yvars, Westrum's perennial backup. Yvars smacked the first pitch on a line toward right. It looked as if it would hit the grass. But Bauer, on a dead run, speared the ball while tumbling to the turf. He held it. The game was over. So was the Series. The on-deck batter, sure enough, was me.

I wish I had a great series. But I was only 4 for 22. No doubles, triples, or homers. One run scored and one run batted in. I had a batting average of .182. I had played like a twenty-year-old.

Even so, I was named the National League's Rookie of the Year for 1951.

Willie's 1951 Numbers

G	AB	H	2B	3B	HR	R	RBI	BB	SO	SB	BA	SA
121	464	127	22	5	20	59	68	56	60	7	.274	.472

While I was producing those numbers, Mantle hit .267 and Snider batted .277. The comparisons were underway.

It's worth mentioning that I was the third straight black player to win the rookie award in the league, and the fourth in the five years since the award had begun with Jackie Robinson. Over in the American League, however, it took sixteen years for the first black player to gain the rookie honor.

8

I TOOK MY World Series paycheck of five thousand dollars—the most ever paid to players on a losing team—back to Fairfield. The day I got home the mail brought a letter to me from the Selective Service Board. I was told to report to my draft board in Birmingham within ten days. There was a war on, even though it wasn't an official war. We were fighting in Korea. I took care of things around the house. I bought some furniture and appliances with the money. I also helped out my mother, who was having a tough time. Her husband wasn't working much, and they had nine kids, my stepbrothers and stepsisters.

I even had enough money after all that to buy a car, even though I didn't know how to drive. My friend Herman Boykin could, and I let him take me all over the place. I might have learned faster if I had had an automatic shift, but the car had a manual transmission. One day I said the heck with it. I was going to drive the thing. So I hopped in and jerked down the streets of Fairfield until I got to Big Tony's pool hall. They all laughed, but I told them I didn't need Herman anymore.

I took my test for the Army a few weeks after the season ended. I asked for an exemption on the basis of the fact I had eleven dependents. I passed the physical, but I failed the aptitude test. Because I was a high-school graduate—and in the top half of my class—they ordered me to take a second test. Meanwhile, other ball players had already been called up. Ted Williams and Jerry Coleman went back to the Marines, and Don Newcombe was taken by the Army. The Army claimed they weren't making a special case out of me, but I don't know of many people with eleven dependents who were being called up then. The Giants figured I'd be going, and they even made a deal to get another outfielder. They got Chuck Diering from the Cardinals in a trade for Stanky when Stanky became the Cardinals' manager.

The following January, I took my second test and passed. They told me I'd be called up in two months. I appealed, but I did not qualify for either of the two requirements the Army had established for consideration as a hardship case: Either you had to be a married man with a child, or you had to be living in the home looking after the people you claimed as dependents. That fact that I was helping my mother and four of my nine stepbrothers and sisters out didn't count. Nor did the fact that my stepfather was out of a job.

I knew I'd be gone for two years, that I would probably be called up early in the season. I tried to keep my mind on business as I joined the Giants for spring training in Phoenix, Arizona. It was a pretty good spring, too. And then it turned terrible. Monte Irvin broke his ankle during an exhibition game in Denver. I cried. It was a horrible thing to see. He was on first base when I hit a single to right. Hustling, even though it was just a spring-training game, he slid into third base, but jammed his ankle on the bag. The bag didn't give and his ankle snapped. He was on the ground in pain, his arms covering his head. I ran over to him, but I had to look away and started to cry. He had been so important to me in my rookie year, when I roomed with him on the road. Leo had told him to look after me, and he did. Now, he was on the ground and suffering and I couldn't do anything for him.

Despite Monte's injury, we had a great start. In fact, we had the best start in baseball as we continued to play the same way we had ended the regular season. I knew now that I'd be going into the Army at the end of May, and we knew we wouldn't have Monte until September. But our pitching was terrific. Maglie won his first nine games, Jansen six of his first seven, Jim Hearn four of his first five. I left for the Army with my Giants holding the best record in baseball—26–8, a perentage of .765, good for a 2½-game lead over the Dodgers.

I hadn't been doing that much. Not much at all. In those 34 games I had a .236 batting average and four home runs. But when I left we had won seven straight games, including two in a row over the Dodgers. I think I was about to start really hitting the ball. In my next-to-last game I got three hits, including a homer, against Brooklyn. Then, in my last game, which was in Ebbets Field, those Dodger fans showed me something. In my last at bat, they stood up for me. I was touched, but not so surprised. It didn't take me long to realize that the New York fans, who hate and love more strongly than any other fans, also show their appreciation better than most others.

The Giants, meanwhile, gave me a portable radio as a going-away present, and Leo and Laraine handed me a jeweled tie clip. I was sorry to leave my teammates behind, but proud all the same to serve my country. The next morning, I was sworn into the Army.

Coincidence? Maybe, or maybe I had really become a cog on the team. After I left, the Giants' record for the rest of the season was 66–54. These were my numbers for 1952:

Willie's 1952 Numbers

G	AB	H	2B	3B	HR	R	RBI	BB	SO	SB	BA	SA
34	127	30	2	4	4	17	23	16	17	4	.236	.409

The Giants wound up second, finishing 4½ games behind the Dodgers.

I reported to Fort Eustis, Virginia. They discovered pretty quickly that I was a ball player. I went through the regular basic training, which didn't bother me, since I was in good shape. We played games against some other Army camps and colleges, and I came across other major-leaguers: Johnny Antonelli of the Braves, Vernon Law of the Pirates, and Lou Skizas of the Yankees. Although there were plenty of photographs showing me marching, they didn't take many of me playing ball, which is how the Army really used me most of the time. Of course, I enjoyed it. I was raised to say "Yes, sir," and I always respected authority, so the Army and I got along very well.

Meanwhile, Leo was looking after me even while I was in the service. Somehow, he would find out things that would disturb him. Once he found out I sprained an ankle while I was playing basketball. He told me, "No more basketball, Willie." Another time he called me over an unnecessary chance I had taken—I tried to steal a base with my team leading. Leo couldn't stand dumb plays, even if he was a few hundred miles away and it wasn't even his team. When he got excited he would scream and talk so fast he sounded like Donald Duck. Leo used to send me a little money now and then, I think just to let me know he still cared.

Besides playing, I was also an instructor—not in how to use a hand grenade, but how to throw and catch and hit. One of the soldiers I was talking to suddenly said to me, "Try it my way," and he held his glove in front of his stomach, but with the palm up. I tried it and it felt more comfortable. My body was aligned correctly. I adopted that style. It came to be called my "basket" catch. What it allowed me to do was to have my hands in the correct position to make a throw instantly. What's wrong with it, though, is that you tend to take your eyes off the ball at the last second. Still, I dropped only a couple of flies in my career that way.

My worst time in the service came the day I heard my mother had died while giving birth to her eleventh child. I now had ten brothers and sisters, the oldest only eighteen. So there were a lot of younger ones to look after. I had always thought of them as my brothers and sisters. Now, certainly, the Army would let me out to be with them and take care of them. I always have believed that if a lesser-known soldier had gone through that ordeal, he would have been free to leave. I don't know whether the Army was concerned because the public thought it would be playing favorites, or whether there was just some technicality. All I knew then was that I was very sad. Even though my aunts had raised me, I had remained close to my mother and her new family. Now, although I wasn't much older than some of my brothers and sisters, I felt responsible for taking care of them. It didn't help my final months in the Army.

I was in the service all of 1953, and didn't play a game for the Giants. They slumped to a 70–84 record, and fell to fifth place, 35 games behind the Dodgers. Finally, I was going back to my old teammates. I had played two seasons of service baseball, and led my team by batting .420 in 1952 and .389 in 1953, but I was eager to get back to the Giants. In my two big-league seasons I had played a mere 155 games, the equivalent of only one complete year in the era of the 154-game season, so I was champing at the bit. Besides, when I left for the Army, the Giants had been a first-place club. While I was away, they were little more than mediocre. I planned to turn things around right away.

It was a cold late-winter day when I was discharged from Fort Eustis on March 1, 1954, and left immediately for the Giants' spring-training site in Phoenix. The Giants sent Frank Forbes from New York to meet me and send me off to Arizona. I didn't have an overcoat, so Frank took his off and gave it to me. It was two sizes too big, but I put it on anyway, probably looking like a scarecrow, or a panhandler. Frank stuffed some newspapers under his sports jacket for insulation. We must have been a sight when we arrived in Washington to catch a train for Phoenix. We had some time to kill, so naturally I suggested we go to the movies. When we got out, we were stopped by two F.B.I. agents. They must have thought they were arresting Dillinger, the way they grabbed us as we left the theater! Thank God, it turned out to be a case of mistaken identity. It turned out that they had been tipped off that two guys they were looking for might be in the same movie theater. I guess we did look sort of suspicious, after all.

I finally made my train, but I didn't stay on it for long. It made a stop in New Orleans, and I got off to get a sandwich and a soda. I didn't do it quickly enough, though, and when I got back to the track, the train had gone. I had to call Leo and tell him I was going to be late.

"Didn't they teach you about trains in the Army?" he said. He sounded exasperated, but I could tell he probably was laughing about the whole thing.

I couldn't wait to see all the guys, to be in the old locker room, to be on the same field again. I had heard that things hadn't been the same. There wasn't much joking around the clubhouse any more. I guess when you finish fifth and aren't even playing .500 ball, there's not much to laugh about, especially when Leo is there every day kicking and screaming when things don't go the way he likes. I hoped that my return would make a difference in terms of morale. I always tried to keep things light, and I know the guys used to enjoy making fun of me and my squeaky voice. Even though I had played part of two seasons with the Giants, I was still three years younger than anyone else on the club.

I finally got to the ballpark. When I went into the clubhouse, Eddie Logan, the equipment manager, was the first person I saw. He didn't say anything to me. I thought maybe he didn't recognize me. I found my locker and changed into my uniform. I was alone. The players were already on the field when I walked onto the Arizona diamond for the first time in two years. Nobody said anything to me, and I was beginning to wonder what was going on. Then I remembered: the silent treatment. It's a way that ball players have of not showing emotion, of doing just the opposite of how they feel. We'd do that after someone hit a home run, say, a player who normally wasn't a long-ball hitter. He'd come back to the bench all excited, and we'd just sit there, yawning, or just looking out into space, and it would drive him crazy because he'd be looking for someone to say something nice, a pat on the back, anything at all.

Just when I was starting to get a little annoyed, someone yelled out, "Hey, Leo, here comes your pennant!" Leo turned around and with a big grin he rushed at me and grabbed me in a bear hug that took the wind out of me. The last time I had seen him do that to someone was when Thomson's homer won the pennant for us against Brooklyn. I couldn't even grab a bat and take some swings, though. Leo explained that I had to sign a contract first.

"Hey, give me a pen," I told him.

"Don't you even want to know how much we're paying you?" he asked.

"I'll sign for whatever they're offering me," I told him.

I trusted Leo, but I also loved playing baseball so much that I hardly cared what my salary was. I guess that always showed through. When I was in the Army, I once saw a tap dancer at a nightclub. He could make his feet fly, he was having so much fun. He'd laugh and say, "It's a shame to take the money." He said it for a laugh, but somehow I could tell that he really meant it. That's just how I always felt about baseball.

The ball club I returned to was pretty much the same as far as the regulars were concerned. But there were a couple of changes. We traded for Johnny Antonelli, a left-hander who had been a bonus baby with the Braves before he went into military service. Sadly, we had to give up Bobby Thomson for him. Leo also got Dusty Rhodes, a funny-looking fellow who wasn't a day-in, day-out player, but could be a pinch hitter. The only thing about Dusty was that he liked —make that loved—to drink. But he could hit, which is all Leo really cared about. Even though Dusty wasn't much of a fielder, he was loose when he got to the plate, and to Leo that meant he would be a perfect pinch hitter. You couldn't be a worrier when you came to pinch-hit. Most of the time, a pinch hitter comes up in clutch situations, where you're either behind or tied. He was a left-handed hitter, and Leo was thinking about that short rightfield of the Polo Grounds.

I was introduced to Rhodes while I was waiting to take my turn in the batting cage. I overheard him talking to another player. He talked about drinking. "You could drink in this weather and you could play ball in this weather," said Rhodes. "Some guys can't do either, but I can do both," he said, bragging. I asked Leo whether this guy was for real.

Leo told me a story about Rhodes. They'd been together on a tour of Japan that winter. Leo had spotted Rhodes early in the morning in the hotel lobby, but he couldn't tell whether Dusty was out all night or whether he was just getting up. Leo finally asked him and Dusty told him, "I went to see my sister."

Now Leo had heard everything. A sister in Japan? He was so annoyed he went up to tell Horace Stoneham in his suite. Who should open the door, with a drink in his hands but Dusty, drinking with the boss. But the funny thing was, Dusty was telling the truth. He did have a sister in Japan— she was married to a sailor.

Dusty didn't seem bothered by Leo's rules. He would borrow money from Leo all the time. Leo was a heck of a good dresser and he was a heck of a spender. He always had a big roll of bills, and he could peel a fifty or a hundred off the top like he was giving change. Dusty would always be asking for a hundred. The thing was, he always paid Leo back. The next day, Leo, maybe wanting to know if his money was well spent, would ask, "Dusty, what time did you get in last night?" And Dusty would tell the truth: four A.M., six A.M., whenever.

But the kind of guy Dusty was also tells you about the kind of guy Leo was. Could you play for him? That was what Leo wanted to know above everything else. And Leo had no beef with Dusty because Dusty was always one of the first in the clubhouse ready to play.

"I'm your man, Skip, if you need me today," Rhodes would tell him.

I really felt good about the team, and I told Leo that I thought we could win it all. I had a great spring. At one point after a month of exhibitions, I was batting .420. When it was time to head back east to the Polo Grounds, I was hitting at a .381 clip and felt ready for anything.

9

JUST BEFORE THE 1954 season began, Leo told the writers in spring training that I was going to bat .300 and hit 30 home runs. "Sure, sure," they said. They had heard Leo praise so many other youngsters that they didn't believe him. I'm told Leo did tend to go out of his way to puff up some of the hitters we had before I joined the club, guys Leo thought could do it all: Hondo Hartung, Tookie Gilbert. So when Leo said to some of the writers, "Willie's the greatest player I ever saw," they weren't buying it.

Besides, during my two full seasons out of baseball, Snider and Mantle had established themselves as the most glamorous centerfielders in baseball. In New York, the question raged—Mantle or Snider? Who was better? Their clubs had won the pennants in '52 and '53, with Mantle's Yankees toppling Snider's Dodgers in the Series each time. The Yankees now had won five in a row.

Mantle, a switch-hitter, was taking on legendary proportions because of the length of his home runs, which he could hit from either side of the plate. Before popping his knee on my 1951 World Series fly to right center, he had been timed going to first base faster than anyone else on the Yankees, and probably faster than anyone in baseball. In 1952, in his first full season, at the age of twenty, he batted .311, stroked 23 homers, drove in 87 runs, and scored 94. He also thrilled opposing teams' fans with a league-leading 111 strikeouts. The next year Mantle batted .295, hit 21 homers, scored 105 runs, and drove home 92.

Snider, meanwhile, was a pleasure to watch. With his sweet swing, he was a left-handed slugger who was able to make hitting look easy. In 1952 he stroked 21 home runs, drove in 92 runs, and scored 80 while batting .303. But in 1953 he was even more productive, waging perhaps the finest campaign in the big leagues: a .336 batting average, a league-leading .627 slugging percentage, and a league-leading 132 runs scored. He crashed 42 home runs and drove in 126 runners.

Besides the blossoming of Snider and Mantle, baseball had changed for the first time in fifty years. The major league baseball I returned to in 1954 was different from the one I had left. The Braves had moved to Milwaukee, and in the American League, the St. Louis Browns had moved to Baltimore and now called themselves the Orioles.

America was changing, too, but it remained optimistic, nestled in the lap of the Eisenhower Administration. In the movie houses, Danny Kaye starred in *Knock on Wood* and Doris Day was in *Lucky Me,* while *The Best Years of Our Lives* was being revived. The comedy *Anniversary Waltz* was packing them in on Broadway, along with such other comedies as *Oh, Men! Oh, Women!* and *The Seven-Year Itch, Wonderful Town,* and *The Solid Gold Cadillac.*

People were laughing even though *Pravda* charged that the United States planned to wage atomic war with China. Closer to home, New Yorkers were shocked when Rudolf Bing, general manager of the Metropolitan Opera, was held up at knifepoint in Central Park while walking his dachshund.

There now was television programming from 7:00 A.M. (*Today,* with Dave Garroway) until 2:45 A.M. (*Give Us This Day*). A new TV show, *The Goldbergs,* premiered on the opening day of the season.

Coming into the 1954 season, I was twenty-three years old, Snider was twenty-seven, and Mantle was twenty-two. On Opening Day—capitalized as if it were a national holiday—which was my first game since I'd returned from the Army, I was facing a Dodgers team that had a new manager named Walter (Smokey) Alston.

Before the game, the splendid weather made Durocher beam. But he was always superstitious.

"I've been so amazed at everything I've seen during spring training, I keep warning myself that things can't be that good—our pitching, our hitting, our fielding, and now even our weather," he said from the dugout steps.

It was a typical New York baseball opener. The players paraded behind Major Francis Sutherland's Seventh Regiment band to the Polo Grounds' centerfield flagpole, where they watched a Marine Corps color guard raise the flag. Then the players marched back. Mayor Robert F. Wagner unfurled a southpaw delivery as he tossed out the first ball.

I broke a 3–all tie against the Dodgers by blasting a Carl Erskine pitch deep into the upper leftfield stands for the winning blow. Now it was my turn to show Mickey and the Duke.

We were all saying that 1954 was going to be our year. From the moment I joined the team that day in Phoenix, that's all we had spoken about, how we were going to get it back. But even though I hit that homer to win the opening game, it was about the only kind of hit I was getting. I helped us win four games with the long ball by the first week in May, but I wasn't hitting for average—about .250 —and we were in fifth place. Leo gave me another one of his hitting lectures. He pointed out that I was back into my old habit of trying to pull every ball to leftfield. He didn't miss a thing. That day—just trying to make contact, to spray the ball to right if that's where it was pitched—I hit a home run and drove a double to rightfield. All Leo said afterward was "I told ya." By the end of May I was hitting better than .300, and we reached second place.

By the end of June we passed the Dodgers and moved into first place, just the way we thought we could. We had a one-game lead when we opened a three-game series in the Polo Grounds. Now was our chance to put them away. We swept them and stretched our lead to four games. I don't believe that the Dodgers ever really recovered from that. In the last game of the series I hit two homers, giving me 30. I was actually way ahead of the pace that Babe Ruth had been at when he hit his 60 homers in 1927, and now people were starting to make the comparison. We were all doing pretty well on the field. By the All-Star break we had a 5½-game lead over the Dodgers.

I played in my first All-Star Game that year, and I never missed another one as long as I played; I made 24 of them and we won 17. At the time I retired I had played in more All-Star Games than anyone else in baseball history. I went 1 for 2 in my first.

I was in St. Louis a few days later when I learned that my Aunt Sarah had died. Going back to Fairfield was very emotional for me, and Frank Forbes was along for support. Frank, also a black man, was a New York State boxing official as well as someone who helped the Giants in the front office, and he was always there when I needed him, whether helping me to find a place to stay in Harlem, or being with me at this sad time. The moment I walked into the house I started to think about the years that Aunt Sarah had raised me, and I started to cry. She was very dear to me, a second mother. Practically the whole time I was there for the funeral I stayed in my bedroom. About five hundred people paid their respects. The church overflowed and the minister gave a sermon that lasted more than an hour. I was too upset, though, to go to the cemetery. I almost fainted from the heat.

It was strange how, over the years, I would pass out after putting a great deal of effort, emotional and physical, into something. Yet, following Aunt Sarah's funeral, baseball revived me and allowed me to bounce back quickly. My first game back, the Giants were in Milwaukee. I beat Warren Spahn with a home run. When we returned to the Polo Grounds five days later I hit two more and was heading for the mid-30's. Every ten years or so someone had a lot of home runs by midseason and was ahead of the pace that Ruth had set. Of course, that was misleading. You couldn't just be ahead of the pace—you had to be way, way ahead, because he hit 17 homers in the last month of the season. Now people started to ask me about the Babe's record. For the first time, I had the feeling that people were going to be disappointed in me if I didn't do something. I felt defensive.

I tried to explain that I never think about records, that all I do is swing where the ball is pitched. For me, the minute I think about hitting a home run is when I stop hitting one. I got up to 36 homers. Frank Forbes was getting busy now taking me to all the television studios for interviews. I made the cover of *Time,* and the *Saturday Evening Post* was writing about me. I was introduced on the *Ed Sullivan Show.*

All the time, though, Leo was thinking.

One night before we played Pittsburgh, he called me into his office at the park and closed the door.

"Willie," he said, "I want you to do something for me and the ball club."

"What's up, Mister Leo?" I asked.

"I want you to stop going for home runs."

He explained his reasoning to me: I hit most of my home runs with nobody on base. But if I got more hits, and got on base more, we'd score more runs because then I'd be on when Monte Irvin, or Dusty Rhodes, or Hank Thompson came up. He also told me I'd have a chance at the batting title. I was down around the middle of the pack, battling with Stan Musial, while Snider and Don Mueller were running away with the batting race.

Leo was very convincing, and I even told him I liked the idea. Besides, I really wasn't into the Babe Ruth thing. I was naive about records and too young to appreciate what they meant. Leo asked me to change my stance. I had been batting with my legs spread wide apart, and I had a slight crouch. Leo got me to bring my feet closer together and stand straighter. I got my thirty-sixth home run off Tom Poholsky of the Cards on July 28. It was our ninety-ninth game, and I was batting .326. I played in 55 more games, but I got only five more homers—and one of those was an inside-the-park job. But I also batted .379 over that stretch.

By August the Dodgers were only two games behind us, and that worried Leo. The rest of the year I hit only five more homers, but I added a total of 19 points to my batting average, just as Leo predicted. With my new stance, I was able to rip outside pitches to right and right center, since the pitchers knew my power had been against high inside deliveries. They had started to keep the ball away from me. He was right about another thing: On the final day of the season, I had a chance to win the batting title.

That Leo. He had set it up for me—or at least given me the opportunity to be in the race. As the season drew to a close, I got my average into the .340's. Leo then moved me up in the batting order, to the third spot. That gave me more at bats and more chances to catch Snider.

Now the three of us, Duke, and Don Mueller, and I, went into the final week just thinking about the title.

We clinched the pennant on the last Monday of the season, at Ebbets Field. I got three hits that game, and for the first time all season, I was in the batting lead.

Duke was a power hitter. Mueller was a good contact hitter who didn't have much power; he hit four home runs that year. Like me, he was in the lineup every day, since Leo had to make sure Mueller had an equal shot at the batting title, even though he wasn't that strong as an outfielder. Before the start of the season, Leo had given me the word to cover everything I could in rightfield. Mueller knew that and didn't like it at all. He'd be miffed whenever a ball was hit just a little to his right and I'd be calling for it. Mueller was one of the few guys on the club who didn't like Leo, but we still played together, and we captured the pennant.

Going into the final game of the season, Mueller held a one-tenth point edge on Snider, and four tenths on me. Mueller was hitting .3426, Snider .3425, and I was at .3422. The odds that last day favored Mueller or Snider. The Giants were going up against the outstanding Robin Roberts in Philadelphia. He had more victories (23), complete games, and strikeouts than anyone else in the National League. Mueller, being a left-handed batter, would have an advantage against him. Snider, meanwhile, was playing in Brooklyn against a Pittsburgh right-hander named Jake Thies who had won three games and lost eight. Alston had been very careful to help preserve Snider's lead by sitting him down when left-handers started.

But when the day was over, it was I who came up with three hits in four official at bats to win the batting championship—the first for a Giant since Bill Terry's .401 in 1930. I wound up at .345; Mueller was 2 for 6 in the 11-inning game to finish second at .342; and Snider went hitless to finish at .341.

Mueller singled in his first time up, then fouled out and twice flied to left. In the 10th he doubled and in the 11th hit into a force play. I also singled my first time up. Then I grounded out, tripled to right center, and doubled in the same spot. As I came to bat in the 10th with Mueller already on second, Roberts intentionally walked me. It was a move to set up a force play, not to guarantee the title for me. But I had the title, and more. In my first full season in the major leagues I also led in triples with 13 and in slugging average with a robust .667.

Willie's 1954 Numbers

G	AB	H	2B	3B	HR	R	RBI	BB	SO	SB	BA	SA
141	565	185	18	13	41	119	110	66	57	8	.345	.667

On the way back to New York, Leo said to me, "I told you so."

That night I was on two different network television shows. Frank Forbes hustled me onto *Ed Sullivan,* and then the *Colgate Comedy Hour.*

Sullivan asked me what it felt like beating out my teammate for the title.

"If I hadn't won it," I said, meaning it, "I would have wanted him to."

But something or somebody was bothering Mueller. The day after the season ended, we had to show up at the Polo Grounds to be photographed for our team picture. Mueller walked past me as I was getting dressed and said, "Hey, Willie, is it true you're the best centerfielder in baseball?"

I knew what he was getting at.

"The best rightfielder, too," I told him. We both got dressed and didn't say another word.

Don was from St. Louis, and he probably didn't approve of the way Leo treated me and the fact that he ordered me to catch anything I could get my hands on in rightfield. But we won the pennant doing what Leo wanted, and that's all I cared about. Leo had asked me to stop going for home runs and I did. He asked me to cover rightfield and I did. Nobody says you have to love the guy next to you, but what's important is to respect the role he's playing. If I was the one that Leo built the club around, then everybody else should play his role, no matter what that might be.

Leo might have seemed to be a wiseguy to many—and he really was in many ways—but he also had his diplomatic side. So when we had a parade down Broadway to celebrate the pennant, he insisted that Alvin Dark, our team captain, should be in the front car with him, along with me.

That was quite a day. When we won the pennant from the Dodgers in 1951 there had been no time for parades. We'd had to start the Series the next day. This time, though, we had New York to ourselves. The Yankees were out of it, and a million people watched us drive through the city in open cars. Then, when we got to City Hall, Leo brought tears to my eyes. He got up on the steps and said into a microphone, "Willie Mays is the greatest player I ever laid eyes on." But the crowd also cheered when each of my teammates was introduced—Maglie, Antonelli, Gomez, Marv Grissom, Hoyt Wilhelm, Westrum, Mueller, Rhodes, Davey Williams, Hank Thompson, Dark.

There was a funny side to what was going on, and you had to be in New York to appreciate it. In any other city, all the politicians would be behind the team that won. But we had three teams in one city back then. Abe Stark, a politician from Brooklyn who also owned the clothing store that gave you a free suit if you hit his sign in Ebbets Field, started to speak to the crowd. He was a Dodger fan.

"Wait till next year," he said.

Everyone booed him and we all looked at each other and laughed. Here we were, celebrating our pennant, and a guy from Brooklyn was crying about his Dodgers.

Now we were going to play the Indians. We had won 97 games and the pennant by five games over the Dodgers. But Cleveland was the heavy favorite. They set an American League record of 111 victories, which meant they lost only 43 games the entire season. The Yankees won more games that season than they ever did under Stengel, 103, and they still finished eight games out of first. No question we were the underdogs. Besides that Cleveland record, there was our own bad World Series background—the Giants had been in the Series thirteen times and won only four.

The Indians had some team, with both pitching and hitting in abundance. Their starters were all righties—Bob Lemon, Early Wynn, Mike Garcia, Bob Feller, Art Houtteman. They had the American League's top home-run hitter in Larry Doby. They had Al Rosen and Vic Wertz and Bobby Avila, who led his league in batting average. Going into the Series, though, I felt sure we would rise to the occasion. And I was glad we had Sal Maglie. He always won the big ones for us.

There are some unforgettable moments in baseball history that define the game: Yogi Berra jumping into Don Larsen's arms at the end of the perfect game; Carlton Fisk waving his drive fair into the seats; Reggie Jackson stopping to watch his third home run in a World Series game sail into the bleachers. But few memories have to do with a catch. Well, I made a catch in the first game of the 1954 World Series that has become the stuff of legend.

Bob Lemon (23–7) started Game 1 against Maglie, who was 14–6, even though Durocher had Antonelli, a 21-game winner. Maglie and Lemon, the old pros, were locked in a 2–2 tie when the eighth inning began.

Doby led off with a walk, and Rosen beat out an infield hit. First and second, none out, and Vic Wertz was up. He was 3 for 3 against Maglie—a triple in the first, a single in the fourth, single in the sixth. He was a left-handed power hitter. Leo had seen enough, and he called for Don Liddle, a left-handed pitcher, to relieve Maglie and face Wertz.

I played Wertz to pull the ball slightly. He had been getting around well all day, and in this situation, two runners on, I figured he'd be likely to try to hit behind them so they could advance. Also, I knew that most hitters like to swing at a relief pitcher's first pitch, and that crossed my mind as Liddle was warming up.

And that's what happened. He swung at Liddle's first pitch. I saw it clearly. As soon as I picked it up in the sky, I knew I had to get over toward straightaway centerfield. I turned and ran at full speed toward center with my back to the plate. But even as I was running, I realized I had to be in stride if I was going to catch it, so about 450 feet away from the plate I looked up over my left shoulder and spotted the ball. I timed it perfectly and it dropped into my glove maybe 10 or 15 feet from the bleacher wall. At that same moment, I wheeled and threw in one motion and fell to the ground. I must have looked like a corkscrew. I could feel my hat flying off, but I saw the ball heading straight to Davey Williams on second. Davey grabbed the relay and threw home. Doby had tagged up at second after the catch. That held Doby to third base, while Rosen had to get back to first very quickly.

Was it the greatest catch I ever made? Some people think it was the greatest catch anyone ever made, but I think that's because it was in a World Series and seen by so many people on television. Also, there is a famous action sequence of the catch by a photographer and it is pretty dramatic.

But I always thought the catch I made in Ebbets Field when I knocked myself out after diving for the ball was more difficult. I also made one in Trenton in 1950 that was even more fun to watch. Lou Haymen of Wilmington hit a shot to dead center, right at the 405-foot sign. I ran back, jumped, and caught it bare-handed just as it was going over. I bounced off the fence and threw the ball on the fly all the way to home plate. Nobody knew about it because it was just another game in a small town. To me, it was still a catch. And what about the catch and throw I made against Carl Furillo in 1951? People still remind me of that one.

Another one I'm proud of came in 1960. We were playing the Cubs in Candlestick Park. Ed Bouchee nailed the ball to right center and I charged to my left, figuring I could cut the ball off before it hit the fence. This way I might hold him to a single. I got to the spot, went down on one knee, and stretched. I actually caught the ball after it went past me.

But while you're doing these things in a game, you don't have a perspective on it at that moment. This was a game we still had to win. We got out of the inning. The game went into extra innings.

I made another play on Wertz that game, but who remembers it? It wasn't for an out, but it might have saved us the game anyway. It was the 10th inning. Marv Grissom now was pitching for us, and who should come up but Wertz? He hit a screwball, Grissom's best pitch, to left center. But once again I had been playing Wertz to pull, so I was in right center. I chased the ball and finally caught up with it after it bounced and I caught it bare-handed in the alley. I held it to a double. There's no doubt it would have been an inside-the-park homer if I hadn't stopped it. We were able to get out of the inning.

Then, in the bottom of the 10th, I got up with Lemon still pitching. I asked Leo if I could steal if I got on and he told me to go ahead. The Indians had put in a new catcher, Mickey Grasso, and during his practice throws I noticed his arm wasn't as strong as Jim Hegan's. I got a walk against Lemon. I had no trouble stealing second. Now, with first base open, the managing game began. Al Lopez decided to walk Hank Thompson. This would set up a double-play possibility with Monte Irvin coming up against Lemon. Like me, Monte had been 0 for 3 against Lemon.

But Leo didn't let Monte get to bat again. Leo called for Dusty Rhodes. He had had a great year pinch-hitting, along with Bobby Hofman. It seemed that whenever he connected, the ball was going places. Dusty had 56 hits that year, but 15 were homers. This could have been a touchy situation, putting up a pinch hitter for one of your leading batters in a clutch situation. But Leo knew Monte's disposition—he was a good-natured guy—and made the move.

Lemon's first pitch was the only one he threw. Dusty jumped on it and pulled it down the rightfield line—a shot maybe 270 feet away—but the ball sailed into the stands.

A three-run home run and we won the opening game of the Series. I knew Dusty would celebrate big that night, but that he'd be there the next day if we needed him.

Dusty took all the kidding about his Chinese home run.

"I measured it off just right," he told us later.

But the next day the Indians came back with their other 23-game winner, Early Wynn. We came back with our super pinch hitter, Dusty. First we had to get by the opening inning, as Antonelli started and got in trouble right away.

Al Smith led off the game with a home run. Then Antonelli walked Rosen and Wertz with two out. Rosen was having some running problems, and I was aware of that when Wally Westlake came up. He hit a single over second, and I thought if I could just get close enough to it, I could keep Rosen from scoring. Normally, you'd never get a runner from second in that situation, with two out. But I charged the ball and fired it immediately to Westrum. Rosen held up at third. We got out of the inning.

It was a good thing, too. Wynn was great that day. But he was no match for Dusty, our instant legend. This time he came up to pinch-hit for Monte in the fifth inning, with the Indians leading 1–0. Wynn had been pitching a perfect game till then. I led off the fifth and I could tell he was pitching around me. That was fine. We had to get something started. I walked. Then I ran to third when Hank Thompson singled for our first hit of the game, and Monte, who was on deck, stepped toward the batter's box. Leo called him back.

Leo wanted Rhodes, even though it was early in the game and there wasn't even anybody out. But Leo remembered that Wynn had struck out Irvin earlier. I was surprised, I'll admit, even though that season Leo always made the right moves.

Dusty came to bat. He hit a high fly to short center. But Doby was playing way back, which was unusual, since you figure he'd be trying to stop me from scoring on a fly ball.

Doby ran and ran for Dusty's ball, but it fell in front of him and I came home. We got another run to take the lead, and Dusty came up with no one on base in the seventh because Leo had left him in the game to play leftfield. This time he belted the ball for a long homer. He didn't need the friendly foul pole.

In the ninth inning that 3–1 lead didn't look too strong. Antonelli had been getting in and out of trouble all day. Now they had two men on base with two out—and Wertz was up. He belted a pair of balls foul. Then he swung again and hit a long shot to left center. When Leo had put Rhodes in left, he told me to get anything hit to left center. So I ran back and got the ball sighted. Suddenly, Rhodes appeared in front of me. He waved me off. The guy made the catch to end the game. Just like that. He kept running and ran up the clubhouse steps—in the Polo Grounds the clubhouse was in centerfield—and Dusty was just waiting for Leo to follow. We won the game 3–1, as the Indians left thirteen runners on base.

When Leo showed up after his 500-foot walk from the dugout, Dusty already had a cigar in one hand and a beer in the other.

"What were you worried about, Skip?" said Dusty. "I had it all the way. And how about that homer? I guess that was a cheap one, too."

In two games at the Polo Grounds we used only three players who weren't in the starting lineup—Rhodes and Liddle and Grissom.

I was concerned about my hitting, though. In the two games I was 0 for 5. Although I didn't let it affect my fielding or my running, I was the cleanup hitter, batting fourth, and I knew I had to produce immediately. World Series don't last longer than seven games. In Game 3, we were facing the Big Bear, Mike Garcia, a 19-game winner and the American League leader in earned-run average and shutouts. In fact, the first three Cleveland pitchers we faced all led their league in something. Yet, we never were too concerned about being underdogs or facing a team with such a famous pitching staff. We knew the Indians better than anyone else in baseball, better than any of the American League teams that played them. For a couple of years we were the only teams that trained in Arizona, so we had to face each other a lot. We got to know them very well, and we seemed to be able to beat them often enough.

Luckily, I didn't have to wait long to get my first hit of the Series. With two down in the first and Mueller on second, I singled him home. That was the only run of the game when we got up in the third. This time, Leo did it again— Leo and Dusty, that is.

We loaded the bases, and Monte was due up. Now, Monte was one of the best clutch hitters I ever saw. He had led the league in RBI's when I was a rookie. But Leo made the move again. He brought up Rhodes. Sure enough, Dusty ripped Garcia's first pitch into right, Mueller scored from third, and I came in from second. That was it for Garcia. We went on to win the game 6–2. We all knew how good we were, and we knew we could keep handling the Indians.

Jeff Chandler, the white-haired actor, sang the national anthem before Game 4. Leo's pals, Danny Kaye and Toots Shor, sat in box seats provided by Durocher. The Municipal Stadium crowd of more than 78,000 fans cheered when they heard the pregame announcement that Rosen, despite a hobbling thigh injury, was returning to third base, replacing thirty-eight-year-old Hank Majeski, who had taken the slugger's place in Game 3.

I was glad for Monte in that final game. Sure, I was glad we won, too. We beat them, 7–4, and swept the team that was a 2–1 favorite to beat us. Monte had a big hand in this one. In the second inning, he doubled Hank Thompson to third. A couple of errors by the Indians, now jittery, led to a pair of Giants runs. Then, in the fifth, we had the bases loaded and a 4–0 lead. Hal Newhouser, a lefty, was pitching in relief of Lemon, and maybe Leo figured Monte would have a better shot against the southpaw than Dusty. But this was the type of situation where Leo had made a move in the earlier games. Monte even looked at Leo to see if he was going to bring in Dusty. Not this time. Leo just clapped his hands and yelled, "Let's go." Monte stayed in. He slammed a single to score two runs.

Leo started to hug me when the game was over, and he didn't stop for the next ten hours, through a nonstop party. You see, Leo had never managed a World Series champion before. This was a vindication for him. He had tears in his eyes as he thanked me for my contributions.

I understood. This victory made Leo something more than just a feisty baseball character who was known as a great manager "between the lines." He always had been hounded by the fact that his teams had never won that big final game, as if there was some character deficiency he had that prevented that ultimate triumph. Now, he was in the record books with McGraw and the rest of them. He tried to explain some of this to me afterward. But he really didn't have to.

Leo lived it up to the hilt. He became even more of a celebrity, if that's possible. So did Rhodes. That big character milked his success, and who can blame him? He became an instant television star, often teaming up with Leo. Dusty showed up for one appearance with Leo wearing a velvet jacket with rainbow colors.

"Where'd you get that thing?" Durocher asked. "It looks like a carpet."

"Yeah, it's a great coat, Skip. How about a C-note?"

10

WHEN IT WAS OVER, I felt like collapsing. I had a Most Valuable Player award, my Male Athlete of the Year award, my Professional Athlete of the Year award. My team had won a World Series, I had played 151 games, in a sense had played at two positions at the same time. Because of what Leo had wanted me to do—cover for Mueller in right—it seemed I was always thinking, always having to anticipate every pitch, every play. Even when I was on the base paths, Leo seemed to leave it up to me. I didn't know how much rest I'd be getting, even with the season over, though. In addition to the offers I had to speak and to go on television and to start business deals, I was even offered a nightclub act in Las Vegas.

Besides being tired, I was concerned about the rumors I kept hearing that Leo would not be back. We heard stories about how he didn't get along with Horace any more, and that after the Series, Leo would quit baseball and get into private business. With all his Hollywood friends, he might even go into show business. Leo told me he wasn't quitting, though, and that he would live up to his contract, which had another year on it.

Meanwhile, I never got a winter of rest. Herman Franks, our third-base coach, was managing winter ball with the Santurce team in Puerto Rico. He wanted me to play. He had some really good players—Roberto Clemente, Don Zimmer, Jack Sanford, Ruben Gomez, Sam Jones, and George Crowe. Herman felt he had a shot at the championship and the extra money. I told him I was tired. But he needed a favor, and so did Stoneham. The owner of the club in Puerto Rico was a good friend of Horace's. Since the Santurce club wasn't drawing too well, Stoneham asked me if I could go down there to help. So I made an unusual deal. I agreed to play until the team got a seven-game lead. Then I'd be able to come back to New York. I was surprised when he agreed.

"Fine," he said. "Only keep reading the newspapers, and if you see us start to fall back, you hop on a plane right away."

I didn't expect my arrival in Puerto Rico to become such a major event. Puerto Rican baseball had been around for a long time, and major-leaguers had gone there for many years. The Puerto Rican hero was Orlando Cepeda's father. He never made it to the big leagues. At that point, no one from Puerto Rico had made it big in the States. Roberto Clemente was about to change things, though. Nineteen fifty-five would be his rookie season in the big leagues. He was going to be Puerto Rico's first star, and they all knew it.

I guess I was the first MVP and batting leader they had ever seen down there. When my plane touched down in San Juan at six forty-five in the morning, a thousand fans were waiting for me.

Before my first game, one of the coaches told me that Clemente would be in leftfield and Bob Thurman in right, but that they knew to leave alone anything that I shouted for. My first day was tough. I struck out my first two times up, hitting against Arnold Portocarrero of the Athletics. I got two hits after that, though. I was experimenting with a new batting stance that I had started after the second game of the Series, when I had gone hitless again. Leo had told me to make some adjustments, that I had been going back to my old stance of standing erect and trying to pull everything. Anyway, after my first game in Puerto Rico, I went on television. The show was conducted by a man who spoke Spanish and English. I didn't realize that it was sponsored by a milk company—and I already was connected with a milk company back in the States. When I found out afterward, I was terribly embarrassed. It bothered me so much I wouldn't even pose for any pictures. I was afraid someone would sneak a commercial endorsement in. Perhaps to some people it seemed I had changed, that I wasn't as easy-going as I had been, not as willing to give my time.

The arrangement worked out great for me overall. I'd be able to stay in New York for a week or so at a time before jumping down to Puerto Rico for another week. I commuted the whole winter. It didn't take me long to learn about the playing fields. They weren't anything like the majors. They were bumpy and the grass was high. I once lost a grounder in the grass, but I decoyed the runner on third into thinking I had it. I faked picking the ball up with the glove. By then, Clemente had found it and thrown it home.

Despite the commuting, I had gotten a hit in the first five games I played. The first pitcher who stopped me was a left-hander from the Dodgers named Tom Lasorda. He told people he had figured out my weakness, that I went for the first pitch, so he was going to tease me with the first one, give me something that looked good but really wasn't.

Two weeks later I hit my first Puerto Rican home run. It was off Lasorda, and did he mumble. Our Giants-Dodgers rivalry went beyond the playing fields and the bars of New York. Now things were heating up in Puerto Rico. I hit homers the next two games, too, just when Stoneham came down to offer me a new contract. Actually, I think he flew in because the New York papers ran a story that Ruben Gomez and I had been fighting. It wasn't over much. We started to argue over whose turn it was in the cage for batting practice. Gomez jumped ahead of me in the batting cage, but the practice pitcher refused to throw to Gomez. But Gomez, remarkably, sat himself down at home plate and refused to budge, claiming it was his rightful turn at bat. I wouldn't leave, either. So I stood a few feet off to the side and told the pitcher, Milton Ralat, to start pitching. Instead, Ralat threw a high, fast one near my head. Can you believe that?! I started to scream at Ralat. The next pitch was a slow one, so slow that I caught it bare-handed and threw it back so hard it hit Ralat on the shoulder.

The pitcher started cursing me in Spanish and I started to walk menacingly toward the mound. Then Gomez, bat in hand, tried to stop the controversy. I thought Ruben was trying to defend his fellow Puerto Rican and I wrestled with him. I then knocked him down with a right-handed punch. Gomez got up and headed for me, but was stopped by Franks and George Crowe of the Braves, who was playing first base for Santurce. Gomez then picked up several bats and tossed them at me, and I threw them right back.

After all this, we made up in the locker room, but I was still furious. I started to pack my things.

"I'm leaving," I told Franks. Instead, the manager calmed me down and I stayed. The next day, fans found out about the skirmish. When I came to bat the next game against San Juan, I was booed, but I wasn't about to let that get to me.

On my first at bat, I smashed a tremendous triple, and ran all the way home when the outfielder bobbled the ball. Immediately the fans started to cheer again. With each following at bat, they continued to stand and applaud for me.

Two weeks later, I added the Puerto Rican Winter League batting title to my list of honors. I batted .395, and, although I did not play in every game, I still performed in 48 games and led in total bases, triples, and slugging percentage while slugging more than a dozen homers. And remember, I had actually played more than 200 games, counting spring training, in less than a year.

The contract Horace Stoneham brought to Puerto Rico was for $25,000, which was double what I had started for in 1954. But by the end of 1954 I was getting more. Horace tore up the original contract twice. Before signing for 1955 I told him I had to speak to my boss.

"What do you mean, 'boss'? I'm the boss," he said.

"No, I mean Mister Leo," I told him.

Horace smiled and called Leo at his home in California. After I spoke to Leo I hung up the phone. Horace wanted to know what Durocher had told me.

"He said you should give me five thousand more." And he did.

Things were different around the Giants camp that spring. We really had the feeling now that Leo would be leaving. He just wasn't himself, and we had heard stories that he wasn't getting along with Stoneham. We found out that Stoneham and Leo had been at a stag roast in Leo's honor, and that Danny Kaye had cut up Horace pretty good. Horace wasn't laughing at the jokes about his drinking, but Leo was, and Horace believed that Leo was behind the whole thing. I couldn't imagine what it would be like on the Giants without Leo. I knew that Leo was the first "outsider" the Giants had ever hired as coach. After John McGraw had left, Bill Terry and Mel Ott had managed them, and they were home-grown players. Leo was changing his managing style under the pressure, I think.

We didn't get off to a good start, and that didn't help things. In the middle of May, Leo pulled me aside. He seemed nervous.

"Willie," he said, "I want you to start going for more home runs."

I was really shocked. All of the last season he had been worried about me swinging for the fences. Now that's just what he wanted me to do. He explained to me that the club needed help.

"It's not as good as Stoneham thinks," he said. I told him sure, that I'd try it. I had the feeling that this wasn't only to help the team, though, it was to help Leo save his job. That was fine with me. I approached it as a challenge. It's something I've always done, and it could be that I've hurt myself by putting myself under too much pressure. But whenever Leo, or anybody I respect, asked for help, I would give as much as I could. By the middle of June I had hit 17 homers and had 42 RBI's, but my average was only about .270. That's the part Leo didn't like. He asked me to change again. Once again, he told me I was trying to pull everything to left and that the pitchers had picked it up. That's why they were getting the ball on the outside corner. He told me to go with the pitch. He also was annoyed that I hadn't been doing that, and I was in a slump, hitting only 3 for 26.

A week later we were playing in Milwaukee. I went hitless the first day. When I got to the ballpark the following day, my name wasn't in the lineup. I figured Leo was playing a joke on me. He had Dusty Rhodes in rightfield, put Bobby Thomson—who had come back to us—in center, and kept Irvin in left. I went over to Freddie Fitzsimmons, one of our coaches, and asked what was going on. Was I being benched for the first time?

"Go see Number Two," he said.

But there was no way I was going to see Leo. I knew he was hot that day, so it was wiser to keep away. There never was a longer game for me, sitting and watching. Leo kept me out the next day, too. When I finally asked him about it, when I could play, he growled at me and said, "Don't need ya. We won without ya." They won two in a row without me. And then he had a meeting with me in the clubhouse. I was down and I guess everyone could see it.

"Look," Leo said to me, "I've asked you but you haven't tried. If you go to rightfield you'll become one of the greatest hitters of all time. Maybe not percentagewise, but home-run-wise, powerwise. You can hit the ball out of any park. It'll be like an airport for you."

I looked at Leo and said, "Okay, Mista Leo, I'll go to rightfield."

"You better," he told me, "or I'm not gonna put you back in there. Think about what I've said."

Not put me back in? Well, luckily it never came down to that. I did exactly what he asked. The trouble was, Leo couldn't get everyone else to. What's more, injuries wrecked our club. We lost Dark for about 40 games, we lost Davey Williams for more than half the season. Antonelli had arm problems and couldn't repeat and we traded Maglie to the Indians. So there went our double-play combination and our two top pitchers. And Leo was next. When I found out, it was my saddest moment in baseball. We were finishing the season against the Phillies at the Polo Grounds in a doubleheader. Leo called me over to his end of the dugout halfway through the second game. We went down the tunnel between the dugout and the stands and squeezed into a small bathroom that was there for the players. Leo placed both his hands on my shoulders.

"I want to tell you something," he began. "You're the best ball player I ever saw. There are other great ones, sure. But to me you're the best ever. Having you on my team made everything worthwhile. I'm telling you this now because I won't be back next season."

I couldn't understand for a minute what he was saying. How could he leave? I finally asked him. We were just getting started. I was back from the Army for only two years. He told me it didn't matter, that Stoneham had already made the change and that Bill Rigney was going to be the new manager.

"I already talked to Rigney about how to treat you," Leo told me. "Besides, I'll always be looking out for you. All you have to do is call me."

I had tears in my eyes. I'll never forget that scene, me

standing on the dugout toilet because there wasn't enough room for the both of us in there.

I pleaded with him. "But Mista Leo, it's going to be different with you gone. You won't be here to help me."

Then he said something I'll never forget. "Willie Mays doesn't need help from anyone."

He leaned over and gave me a kiss on the cheek.

With a week to go in the regular season, we had no chance to catch the Dodgers, but I had a chance to set a Giants record for homers. Johnny Mize had once hammered 51. I had 50. I also had homers in six straight games to tie a major league record. Now we were playing a doubleheader against the Pirates in the Polo Grounds. I missed the record in the opener, although I got a single, double, and triple. But in the first inning of the second game, Dale Long hit a terrific fly to dead center. I ran back against the wall and jumped, the ball bounced off the wall, and so did I. The impact banged up my thigh and back. Now I wondered whether I could even tie Mize's record.

Luckily, the next day we were off. On Friday, we were playing the Phillies at the Polo Grounds in our final series of the year. Leo asked me if I could play, that the record was something I'd always be proud of. But against Saul Rogovin, I got nothing but four pop-ups in four at bats.

My old friend Robin Roberts started against us in the first game of a doubleheader on the last Sunday of the season. Robin always led the league in giving up homers because he always had the ball around the plate. He also usually led in innings pitched and victories. He gave very few walks. If you were going to beat him, you had to beat him yourself. He wouldn't mess himself up.

I faced him in the first inning—and I got one of his strikes and tore into it. Homer Number 51. We won the first game. Then we went into the ninth inning of Leo's last game trailing by two runs. We tried to give him a going-away present. Joe Amalfitano singled and Whitey Lockman walked.

Bobby Hofman, who had been a great clutch hitter for us along with Dusty, was at bat against Curt Simmons. He nailed a fastball on a line and it looked as if it would land in centerfield. Amalfitano and Lockman took off and they were in full stride. But Ted Kazanski ran over from short-stop and caught the ball on the line, then flipped it to second to double up Joey, and the throw to first nailed Whitey. Our last play for Leo, we hit into a triple play. Well, I had a record now, but I had lost Leo.

The Dodgers, meanwhile, went on to win the World Series. They had failed seven times previously, disastrous defeats that had helped coin the phrase—a cry, really—"Wait till next year!" Now, the day after they had toppled the Yankees, a beaming Walter O'Malley, the Dodgers' president, said the victory would add fresh impetus to plans for building a new Dodgers stadium at Atlantic and Flatbush avenues in Brooklyn.

"Right now the matter is pretty much out of our hands," he said. "But I don't see how anyone could want to see the Dodgers leaving Brooklyn. Certainly we don't ever want to go anywhere else, and I am now more confident than ever that something will turn up that will enable us to build a new home befiting world champions."

Despite the turmoil afflicting the Giants on the field and in the front office, I had a pretty damn good 1955 season. I became the seventh player in major league history to hit 50 home runs. I hit 51, actually, to equal Mize's Giants record. I led in triples with 13, slugging average with a .659—and also led outfielders in assists with 23. For the first time, I also was among the leaders in stolen bases. My 24 were topped only by the Braves' Bill Bruton.

Willie's 1955 Numbers

G	AB	H	2B	3B	HR	R	RBI	BB	SO	SB	BA	SA
152	580	185	18	13	51	123	127	79	60	24	.319	.659

11

AFTER LEO LEFT, a lot of people who had praised him and had thought he was the best manager in baseball suddenly said, "I told you so." Now that Leo was gone, all the things that he had done and that had worked were now being used against him—including the way he had handled me. Some people were saying that because he treated me differently, other players in the locker room objected. If they did, no one ever told me about it. All I know was that Leo lasted longer than any other manager in the National League while I played for him.

I know it wouldn't be the same, and how could it be?

There wouldn't be any more stickball games in Harlem, either. I also was getting married. Stickball would be behind me now, along with Leo and the carefree days in Harlem and the ballpark.

Just a week before I was to report for spring training in 1956, I got married. For about a year I had been discreetly dating Marghuerite Wendell, a beautiful woman. She was several years older than I was, and she had been married twice before. One of her ex-husbands was a singer in a very popular group, the Ink Spots. The fact that I wasn't even twenty-five seemed to strike many people as worrisome, and there were protests from the media about my marrying her. But I had made up my mind. We decided to get married so

quickly, we had to go to Elkton, Maryland, where you
didn't have to wait. I drove so fast on the way to Elkton
that I was stopped for doing seventy by a trooper on the
New Jersey Turnpike. That really wasn't so much over the
speed limit, but maybe my light-green Cadillac caught his
eye. We got married and moved to a nice block in Upper
Manhattan, not far from Columbia University, into a home
I had just bought.

When I got to spring training, I knew immediately it was
all going to be different. Rigney had been a utility infielder
with us when I came up. He was the quiet type even then.
Actually, he was a loner. I wondered whether he had
changed at all. Rigney had won the Little World Series managing Minneapolis in 1955, so he seemed to deserve the
promotion. Besides, he was an ex-Giant, and that was important to Stoneham. I knew Rigney didn't have Leo's bub-
bly personality, but I also wondered what else would be
different.

Rigney had come up the hard way. Like many players in
the late Depression years who had hoped to make it to the
big leagues, his career had been stalled by World War II. He
spent six seasons in the minors and another three in the
service before making it with the Giants as a twenty-eight-
year-old utility infielder in 1946. His big-league career
ended in 1953, and in '54 the Giants sent him to Minneapolis as a manager and part-time player.

I suppose the team he inherited from Leo had suddenly
gotten old and lost its identity. He probably could only
count on me, along with Lockman, a singles hitter. In the
midst of this collapse, the fans deserted us. Attendance had
shrunk by more than 330,000 fans in 1955 compared to
the championship season of 1954.

Rigney appreciated a struggle. We had nicknamed him
Old Bones when he played for us. We appreciated the way
he performed despite repeated bashings to his 165-pound

body, which often was the target of players trying to break up double plays.

He was a high-strung player, on edge much of the time. In fact, he used to tell Leo he could not play second games of doubleheaders because of what he described as a nervous stomach.

Within a week of taking Leo's place, he described it as "a new era." I never really thought there was anything wrong with the old one.

Leo always used to tell me I was born to play baseball. So I approached the 1956 season that way—I would have fun playing a game I love. Rigney didn't go out of his way to talk to me or listen to ideas I had, but that was just his way. He certainly wasn't playful like Leo, and at times I didn't know what Rigney was thinking. With Leo, you always knew what he was thinking and where you stood. Leo would either yell right there on the spot, or talk to you privately about it. I could see this wasn't Rigney's approach. Still, I approached spring training the way Leo said I should. I had a big spring. I hit 11 homers and batted .476.

Once the season started, though, we couldn't get it together. I woke up on my twenty-fifth birthday on May 6 and realized we were in sixth place and not getting any better. I couldn't remember when the club had been that low. I had never been with a second-division club before. We were playing the Cardinals and I decided I had to do something to get us going. I really felt it was on my shoulders, even though I was the youngest everyday starter on the club.

The Cards were starting a fastball-throwing left-hander named Wilmer (Vinegar Bend) Mizell. He was pitching carefully to me. In the first inning I walked. Then I stole second, which upset him, I know. As a southpaw, he had a natural move to first base. The next time up I singled and

stole second again. When I walked my third time up, I knew
that Mizell and the catcher, Bill Sarni, would be watching
me. It didn't matter. I just had to go. I got a good jump and
I had my third stolen base. I looked at Sarni and I could tell
he was getting frustrated and angry. So I stole third base,
too. Now I had four stolen bases in one game. My last at
bat I got another hit, and everyone knew I was looking to
steal again. Mizell pitched out twice, but I didn't move.
Then I knew I had him. The next pitch I took off for second.
I had five stolen bases. The next pitch, Mizell gave up a hit,
and I scored the winning run. We beat the Cards, 5–4.

But even performances like that didn't seem to be enough
to fire up the team. Looking around, I noticed I didn't even
know my teammates. There was no one around I was close
to. Not only was Leo gone, but Monte had been traded to
Chicago. Hank Thompson was suffering headaches from a
beaning earlier in the season. Mueller had a leg injury and
was having a bad year. Rigney had shaken the team up, and
we had a rookie, Bill White, playing first. He had a terrific
first year, though. Red Schoendienst came in a trade with
the Cards for Whitey Lockman and Dark. Red played second. Daryl Spencer was at short and Foster Castleman at
third. Sarni, who came over in the trade, wound up catching
for us. I shared the outfield with Mueller and Jackie Brandt.

These were some of the reasons I felt I had to do it myself.
Even getting on base wasn't enough. I felt I had to get all
the way around the bases on my own. I led the league in
stolen bases with 40. It was the first of four straight years I
finished first in stolen bases, and it was to be the most I ever
stole in one season. No one else was stealing that year, on
my club or anyplace else. Those 40 stolen bases were 19
more than anyone else in the majors stole. Meanwhile,
when I was up, I was trying for homers. The big trade didn't
help us. It probably hurt us. You don't lose players that are
part of a winning tradition, such as Dark and Lockman,

without feeling an emptiness. We sank toward last. Our pitching couldn't pull us out. Johnny Antonelli had come back with a strong year, but no one else could get any outs.

When you lose, everything takes a turn for the worse. Just after the All-Star break we were playing in St. Louis. I hit a high foul pop behind home plate and just stood there, waiting for Hal Smith to catch it in foul territory. Sure enough, the wind blew the ball back and he caught it fair. I walked back to the dugout, and I could tell right away that Rigney was upset. He looked at me and said, "I'm fining you a hundred dollars for not running." After the game I asked him why.

"You know why," he said.

It just seemed so unfair. I asked him when was the last time he had ever seen me not run after hitting a fair ball.

"That's just the way it's going to be," he said. "No exceptions, you or anybody else."

He was making an example of me, I realize, trying to show who was boss at a time the club was in trouble. But he shouldn't have fined me. It had the opposite effect from what he intended. It would have been enough for him to tell me not to do it again. I wondered then whether Rigney was annoyed that I never confided in him as I had with Leo. I always felt Rigney had his own ideas about managing, so I left him alone. Conversely, Leo never managed me. He just let me play. Rigney that first year managed me. By his second and third year, he let me play. He told me to go ahead and be myself, do what I had to do to win. That fine upset me so much I called Leo. He told me there wasn't anything to do but accept it, that this was Rigney's style. But I never again had the same respect for Rigney.

A few weeks after the fine, I was in a batting slump. The Giants were in Milwaukee, and I ran across an old friend of mine, a dentist named Maurice Saklad. Leo had introduced us during my first year in New York, and then the doc had

moved to Milwaukee. I had made a few hospital visits with
the doc to cheer up patients, but this time it was Maurice
who was trying to cheer me up.

"I think I know why you're in a slump," the doc suddenly
said to me. That shocked me. What in the hell did a dentist
know about hitting? He explained that he was going to see
Leo the next day, and he was going to mention some of his
theories to him when Leo arrived in Milwaukee. You see,
after Leo left the Giants he went to work for NBC, and he
was broadcasting their baseball game of the week.

I ran into Leo in the clubhouse before the game and
teased him about not saying anything about my slump on
the air. I was cutting up with the other players, and for a
moment it seemed like old times. Except, of course, that
Leo wasn't really part of it any more.

Anyway, Leo had heard what the doc said about my
hitting problems, and from what he knew about me—
which was more than any man who ever lived, at least in
terms of baseball—he said to me, "Willie, I think I can help
you with the batting slump. But first, I'd better check with
Rigney."

This was more than common courtesy. It was something
Leo would have wanted as manager himself. So Leo went
to see the man who had once been his infielder.

"Rig, do you mind if I talk to Willie about his hitting?"
he asked.

This is what Rigney replied. Leo said he'd never forget it:
"I don't care. Talk to the son of a bitch. You want to talk
to him, then go ahead and talk to him."

I'm still sorry that Rigney didn't care for me. But I kept
playing for him. I hit .296. I hit 36 home runs and I drove
in 84. My 40 stolen bases were the tops in the majors. And
we still finished in sixth place, 26 games behind the
Dodgers. In some ways, it was one of my most difficult
seasons. I played 152 games—14 more than anyone else on
the club. Only one other Giant stole more than three bases

—White. That was the first season where I put everything on my shoulders, and still I was worried that it wasn't enough.

Willie's 1956 Numbers

G	AB	H	2B	3B	HR	R	RBI	BB	SO	SB	BA	SA
152	578	171	27	8	36	101	84	68	65	40	.296	.557

12

LEAVE NEW YORK? The Giants? Un-unh. No way. The New York Giants were New York through and through as far as I was concerned. But I shouldn't have been surprised when I started hearing those rumors about our move before the 1957 season started. Other things—things no Giant fan could ever believe—were going on.

Before the winter even started the Giants made a trade for Jackie Robinson. Who would have thought that was ever possible? Jackie Robinson a Giant! No, I couldn't believe it, either. But I never would have believed that Sal Maglie would end up in Brooklyn, either, which is where he was in 1957. Jackie never signed with us, though. He decided to retire instead. I don't know whether he quit to prove a point—some people wrote that when he said he'd never leave the Dodgers it was just to get more money out of the Giants. Or maybe he believed, as he told me, that he couldn't help the Giants. He had played for ten years and was thirty-seven years old. He said the Giants had to rebuild. That's just what Leo had said the year before.

Then, before the 1957 season even started, we lost three good young players to the service—White, Brandt, and Willie Kirkland. In the outfield, I played between Mueller, who was never a fast man, and Hank Sauer, who was the oldest guy on the team. He was thirty-eight years old, a pick up after the Cardinals dropped him.

We were struggling. And then we heard the news. The Giants made it official. We were moving to San Francisco after the '57 season. The Dodgers were going to Los Angeles. That would keep our rivalry alive.

On top of our problems on the field, Leo started a controversy. He wrote a story for a magazine and criticized the Giants for messing up—all the way from the front office to the way Rigney was supposedly mishandling me. Leo was finally getting back at the club he had been forced to leave. I guess he had never forgiven Stoneham for firing him two years before. Leo said in the article that he treated me special because that was the best way to get the most out of me day after day. He said he gave Rigney that advice, but Rigney didn't listen.

When the story came out, I wound up in the middle, of course. Because Leo praised me and rapped the Giants, I suddenly became the bad guy out there. People wanted to know if I was feuding with Rigney. They wanted to know if I was causing dissension on the club. But I never spoke against Rigney to the other guys. I tried to explain to writers and broadcasters that when you talk about Leo and Rigney, you're talking about two different personalities, two ways of trying to win. But no matter who the manager was, I still had to go out and try to play baseball. That's what I was paid for.

I knew, of course, that Leo and I had a relationship that never could be equaled. His departure was a source of regret that stayed with me for the rest of my big-league career. He was there at the beginning at the most important point of my career. I have always felt that if I had come up to the majors with the start I had in 1951 under any other manager but Leo, I probably wouldn't have made it. Remember, I was so depressed after that start I wanted to quit. I needed somebody to lift my spirits, to give me the confidence I

needed at that low point. Leo was that person. He knew
what I needed. Any other manager would have sent down a
twenty-year-old kid. But Leo made me believe in myself. He
forced me to. Leo wasn't only my manager, he was my
friend. He didn't pamper me, not the way Rigney thought.
Leo encouraged me. Leo's way was different, though, and
that might have made others believe he was holding me up
higher than the other ball players. He was loud and showy
because he felt it was the most effective way.

People forget that Leo disciplined me, too, whenever I
made a mistake. He benched me when he felt I needed it.
He knew my insides were hurting when he benched me for
two games. After the article came out, as much as I disliked
it, I had to apologize for Leo.

Okay. I admit that first year there was a coolness between
me and Rigney. We didn't give each other a chance. He
came in and wanted to do things his way. That was his
option, as it should be. But a manager also has to understand the personality of his players. A manager can't come
in and assume everyone is the same and requires identical
treatment. But after a while, our relationship improved. He
told me to go out and play my game. Nothing more, nothing less. And I did.

The old order was leaving baseball in many ways in 1957.
The Brooklyn Dodgers got old all at once. Pee Wee Reese,
their captain, and Roy Campanella, their catcher, had de-
clining seasons, although Don Drysdale, a twenty-year-old
right-hander, won 17 games, and a twenty-one-year-old
southpaw named Sandy Koufax struck out batters at better
than one per inning—when he could get the ball over the
plate. Bob Feller, Phil Rizzuto and Al Rosen all retired. The
Braves, managed by Fred Haney, were coming on with their
young sluggers, Hank Aaron and Eddie Mathews, and a Big
Three pitching staff of Warren Spahn, Bob Buhl, and Lew
Burdette. The Yankees were the only familiar equation,
with Mantle leading a solid group by batting .365. The

Braves, though, were on their way to toppling the Yankees, taking the '57 World Series as Burdette won three games.

Before that happened, the Giants had to finish out their season—or, rather, their career, in New York. Now, looking back, I see that our leaving symbolized the start of the urban decay that was to infect the country's great cities.

We lost our New York finale to the last-place Pirates 9–1. Bob Friend yielded six hits, two to me.

Old-timers who were part of the rich Giants history—the team, after all, had captured fifteen pennants between 1904 and 1954—were on hand. There was Rube Marquard and Larry Doyle for the pregame ceremonies. And sitting close to the dugout was Mrs. John McGraw, widow of the Giants' famous manager. She carried a bouquet of flowers presented to her before the game.

Rigney had a lineup that was filled with as many starters as possible from the 1951 and 1954 pennant winners: Antonelli pitching; Westrum catching; Lockman on first; Thomson on third; and Mueller, Rhodes, and me in the outfield.

When we made our last out, the clock atop the ancient, weather-beaten clubhouse in centerfield read 4:35 P.M. On Sunday, September 29, 1957, New York's oldest baseball institution came to an end.

There was a near riot at the Polo Grounds. The Giants would never be coming back—at least, not as the home team. So hundreds, perhaps thousands, of fans charged onto the field when the final game was over and took anything that could be moved. It was a commingling of affection, nostalgia, anger, excitement. Fans ripped up the regular and warm-up home plates, the wooden base beneath the main plate, the pitcher's rubber, two of the bases, and the foam-rubber sheathing protecting outfielders who crashed into the centerfield walls. The fans who stayed until the bitter end also broke down and smashed the bullpen sun shelter, gouged out patches of outfield grass, and carried off telephones, signs, and even telephone books.

But I'm told that the fans' special reaction was reserved for me. Every time I came up they cheered wildly—even in my final at bat, when I made out. It was as if they were attempting to preserve that last link to the Giants' greatness. Now I was taking part of New York and Giant tradition out West with me. So when the game ended and fans ringed the clubhouse steps—the ones I'd nearly run up after the catch on Wertz—they started to chant for me. As the chanting grew louder, more and more fans made their way to the centerfield area, each of them joining the chorus. I never appeared, though. Rigney told everyone to stay in the safety of the clubhouse. But their cheers meant more to me than I can say.

Finally, the fans left. So did Mrs. Blanche S. McGraw, Muggsy's widow.

She was asked what she was going to remember most.

"Why," she said with a tear in her right eye, "Mr. McGraw winning pennants."

In my last season as a New York Giant, I became the first player in National League history to get at least 20 triples, doubles, and home runs. I batted .333, led the league with 38 stolen bases, scored 112 runs and drove in 97.

As the Giants said good-bye, New Yorkers were talking about the fact that integration was gaining in the city's schools. More than fifteen hundred black and Puerto Rican children were being transported up to two miles from home to achieve that end. And out in the suburbs, Levittown, Long Island, was celebrating its tenth anniversary—a community that symbolized many urbanites' search for a piece of grass and blue sky. Americans, meanwhile, were watching Little Rock, Arkansas, to see what Governor Orval E. Faubus would do to counter the use of federal troops to help integrate the state.

In Boston, with its eye on history, newsmen reaffirmed

their decision to keep women out of the press box. The Supreme Court also ruled that baseball was a sport specifically not covered by the antitrust laws. Over in Brooklyn, a schoolboy found a hollowed-out coin that contained microfilm hidden by a Russian spy, Colonel Rudolf Ivanovich Abel. The best-seller list was headed by John F. Kennedy's *Profiles in Courage,* with *The Organization Man* also making a strong showing. In fiction, *On the Beach* and *Peyton Place* were leaders.

At the movies, *The Pajama Game* was at the Music Hall, while *Search for Paradise* was the headliner at the Cinerama Theater. On Broadway, *West Side Story* and *Auntie Mame* pulled in the crowds. Boy, I was going to miss this town.

Willie's 1957 Numbers

G	AB	H	2B	3B	HR	R	RBI	BB	SO	SB	BA	SA
152	585	195	26	20	35	112	97	76	62	38	.333	.626

13

THE SAN FRANCISCO FANS didn't exactly take me into their arms right away. I couldn't understand it. It was as if I had done something wrong by doing well in New York. I have always thought that the fans' coolness toward me was because of something that Rigney said before we ever got out there, something he said to get the fans' interest. He tried to sound like Durocher, and it did more harm than good. Before I even took one swing in San Francisco, Rigney predicted I would hit 61 home runs there and break Babe Ruth's record. And he didn't stop there. He said that I would hit .380 and knock in 150 runs. The only person in San Francisco who had ever approached those numbers was Joe DiMaggio, the hometown hero, when he had played for the Seals 25 years before.

The first two years in San Francisco we were going to play in Seals Stadium until the city built a new ballpark along the bay. Seals Stadium immediately made the fans recall DiMaggio and the other great local hero, Lefty O'Doul. The way I figured it, the San Francisco fans, who had not seen DiMaggio in the majors, now were getting to see a centerfielder from New York—and it wasn't DiMaggio. Not only that, I was supposed to hit more home runs than the Babe!

When I went to buy my first house, I quickly discovered

that San Francisco was different from New York. The owner and the real estate broker got so much pressure from the other homeowners in the neighborhood that the offer was withdrawn. The owner explained that because he was a home builder himself, he might lose business. I couldn't believe it. When Mayor George Christopher read about the incident, he called to apologize—and offered to share his house with me and Marghuerite until we could get one of our own. I thanked him, but said no. Finally, in the middle of November, we moved into a house on Miraloma Drive—the house that was originally denied to us.

We had been in the house about a week when a brick came through the living-room window. Marghuerite was terribly upset. I don't think she got over it even when the season started. But as bad as the incident appeared—and it made national news—I don't think it was done by somebody from the neighborhood. Some neighbors actually called to ask if they could help. So I didn't feel concerned about racial tensions in my neighborhood once the season was about to start.

When I joined the Giants for spring training in Phoenix in the spring of 1958, I had a $75,000 contract. If Leo had been around, I'm sure he would have gotten me $5,000 more. Thinking about it, I'm sure Leo could have worked Stoneham for an additional $10,000. After I signed, Horace admitted to me that Frank Lane, the Cardinals' general manager, had offered a million dollars for me.

Still, I was looking forward to a new beginning in San Francisco. The last couple of years in New York had been filled with tension—there was a losing ball club, a manager we didn't all get along easily with, and the constant rumors of a move. Now, the move had finally taken place, and it seemed to take the pressure off us. I was one of the few Giants remaining from New York. Antonelli was still with us, and so were Gomez and Grissom, all pitchers. I wasn't yet twenty-seven years old, but I had suddenly become the team's elder statesman, even though Hank Sauer still was around. Just seven years before, I had been a rookie surrounded by a team of veterans. Now there was no Bobby Thomson, or Don Mueller, or Hank Thompson, or Dusty Rhodes, or Wes Westrum.

Everything was just the opposite of a veteran club. Even Rigney started to look like an old friend. The club was loaded with rookies, and I had plenty of outfield company. There were four good-looking youngsters for the outfield—Felipe Alou, Willie Kirkland, Jackie Brandt, and Leon Wagner. There were good newcomers in Jim Davenport at third, Bob Schmidt catching, and a pair of tremendous first basemen—Bill White, back from the Army, and Orlando Cepeda. I was impressed with the twenty-year-old Cepeda, and I told Rigney he could help us. Despite a good core of youngsters, we were picked no better than sixth in some polls, which should not have surprised me. I had a good feeling about this team, but the people who do the picking aren't able to project how well a youngster is going to do.

With all his rookies, Rigney was determined that I was going to hit those 61 home runs our first season in San Francisco. He decided not to play me much during the exhibition season. He believed that I started the season cold because I had gone stale from playing too much in the spring. My style was always to go all out, whether I played four innings or nine. That's how I played all my life, and I think that's the reason I would suddenly collapse from exhaustion or nervous energy or whatever it was called. Rigney, though, really had done his homework. He explained to me that in the last three seasons, I missed only six games out of 462—and to have a shot at Ruth's record, I would have to play in practically every game.

Governor Goodwin J. (Goody) Knight proclaimed the first week of the 1958 season "Major League Baseball Week" in California. And quite a week it was. It opened with the Giants playing host to the Dodgers in San Francisco for three games, then moving to Los Angeles for three more—a six-game West Coast series. When our charter landed in San Francisco two days before the opening, a few hundred fans turned out. They immediately recognized me and shouted "Hey, Willie," while a band played "California, Here I Come," and "Take me Out to the Ball Game."

When the teams finally met at Seals Stadium, it was, in truth, a National League game. I posed in my Giants uniform with Duke Snider wearing a Dodgers flannel. But I had "SF" across my cap and the Duke had "LA" across his.

I collected two hits in five at bats and drove in two runs as the Giants beat Don Drysdale, 8–0. Cepeda blasted a homer before 23,448 fans. Of course, Mrs. McGraw was at the game.

Back in New York, National League fans were left with a disarming thought—watch the Yankees play or give up baseball.

"We're trapped," one ex-Polo Grounds fan said. "The Giants are gone. Brooklyn's gone. So what are you left with? You're left with a winner. I guess I'll see a few Yankee games."

But one Brooklyn fan insisted, "I'll never go for the Yankees. Not even to see them lose. I'm a Brooklyn fan and a National League fan. Why did the Dodgers leave? I'll tell you. Because they were greedy. They made money here. But they wanted more."

Perhaps. But the anger also was tempered with resignation. As one Giants fan snapped, "It makes me sick when I think that now some phony Dodger will break Babe Ruth's home-run record by bunting homers in that new phony field of theirs in L.A."

Over at the Polo Grounds, the outfield grass where I had roamed was ankle-deep. On the scoreboard there were no inning-by-inning goose eggs, no numbers of pitchers in other games. Instead, there was a blank scoreboard. One of the few signs remaining said, "Warning—anyone wagering on any contest in the Polo Grounds will be ejected and denied any future admission."

I went at it too hard once the season began. I tried to please the San Francisco fans, while I had rookies on both sides of me and Rigney expecting me to take charge of a young team. Yet the first six weeks of the season were a dream. The team was near the top, sometimes in first place, sometimes out, and I was hitting more than .400 in early June. I couldn't have been happier. Nobody expected us to win, and my high average surprised a lot of people.

Suddenly, I stopped hitting. My average fell to about .380 after I got five hits in 26 at bats. Slumps didn't bother me. But something else did. For the first time I began to feel tired. When it continued, I started to worry, thinking that I had an illness of some sort. I told Rigney how I felt. When the team had a road trip to Philadelphia, I continued on to New York and checked into a hospital. After two days I was released. The doctors told me I was okay, but needed to rest. At least I found out there was nothing physically wrong. That was important to me. I was worrying as much about my health as I was about hitting.

But when I got back in the lineup, my slump continued. I thought about Leo. If he had been around, maybe he could have told me what was wrong, just as he did that time in Milwaukee. I was hitting at a .240 pace after falling below .400, and by August my average was around .320. Then, just as it disappeared, it came back again. It all came together after we dropped four straight to the Braves in Milwaukee. Don't ask me why. I still can't explain what turned it around for me. I hit a home run, my first in a month, against the Cubs in Chicago. We took off and had a bit of a run against the Braves, but our pitching was too weak. Still, we finished third, 12 games out of first. Even with my slump I finished strong, too. I even wound up battling the Phils' Richie Ashburn for the batting title. He beat me on the last day of the season, .350 to .347.

Rigney tried to get me the title. He had me batting lead-off, hoping that I would have enough at bats, and enough hits, to catch Ashburn. I went 3 for 5 that last day. I started the game with a double to deep left center. I hit a homer into the rightfield seats, my 29th, and I also beat out an infield grounder. But Ashburn went 3 for 4, all singles. Still, I was proud of my year: I got 208 hits, led in runs scored with 121, led again in stolen bases with 31, and drove in 96 runs.

Willie's 1958 Numbers

G	AB	H	2B	3B	HR	R	RBI	BB	SO	SB	BA	SA
152	600	208	33	11	29	121	96	78	56	31	.347	.583

But at the end of our first season, the *Chronicle* polled its readers and asked them to vote on the Giants' Most Valuable Player. Cepeda won the vote. He had had a good season and was Rookie of the Year, but I always felt the fans were disappointed that I hadn't hit 61 homers—and anyway, Orlando was theirs from scratch. They didn't inherit him.

14

THE FIRST TIME I ever got hurt seriously I was playing an exhibition game against the Red Sox the following spring—1959—in Phoenix. I tried to score from second on a high grounder to short. As I slid into home, my leg slammed into Sammy White's shin guards. I was stunned for a few seconds, but basically all right—but when I got up I saw the blood stain on my pants. Frank Bowman, our trainer, helped me back to the clubhouse. I didn't think the injury was too serious. At least, I didn't have any broken bones. But Bowman ordered me to the hospital. He told me I'd need stitches. When I arrived there, they were waiting for me in the emergency room with a wheelchair. Thirty-five stitches. I couldn't play for two weeks.

But I wound up enjoying that time off. After the 1958 season, Marghuerite and I adopted a five-day-old baby from a San Francisco hospital. We named him Michael. We became very close and I spent as much free time with him as I could. Both Marghuerite and Michael were with me at spring training. Michael never went to sleep unless I drove him around the block every night. I had a lot of fun doing it. I put his crib in the backseat and drove off. Just like clockwork, by the time I finished driving around the block, Michael was asleep. Since I had nothing much else to do while I recuperated, I also learned to change diapers.

When I got back on the field, I was impressed with another big rookie. Willie McCovey had power and could hit a long ball. But he was also a first baseman, and after the rookie year Cepeda had had, I didn't think there'd be room for McCovey on the club. It was one of those situations, though, that you knew if we got into a pennant race, he'd be called up to give us an extra bat.

Meanwhile, we'd be playing another year in Seals Stadium. There were lots of political problems over getting our new stadium built. Our attendance in 1958 at Seals had been fantastic—double what we had drawn at the Polo Grounds. We attracted almost 1.3 million fans to a stadium that didn't hold much more than 22,000 people. That was an average of about 16,000 a game. The Dodgers had flopped their first season in L.A. They wound up seventh. In San Francisco, the fans liked calling them the "Smodgers," because of the smog. We seemed to have gotten the West Coast jump on the Dodgers.

By early August in our second year, though, we were fighting the Dodgers and Braves for first. We were in first place by a game. I was playing against the Reds in Cincinnati when I slid back into first after a long single. I jammed the little finger of my right hand on the bag.

This one really hurt. I knew it was much more serious than the leg injury I had suffered in spring training. Rigney came over from third to look at it, along with our trainer. Bowman figured it was broken. Afterward, Rigney wanted to now how serious it was. I told him it wasn't that bad. But it was swelling up pretty quickly.

"I'll be able to play tomorrow," I told him. But I also told Rig not to say anything about my finger. I didn't want anybody to think I was using an alibi.

I knew the finger was broken. So did Bowman. I played the rest of the season with a broken finger, but kept it a secret. If the other teams had found out, they could have jammed me every time I got up to hit. In the next two games, I played only as a pinch runner. After that, I pressured Rigney to put me back into the lineup. I pointed out that I could still play the outfield, and even if my hitting would tail off, we now had McCovey back with the team to pick us up. Rigney saw it my way.

On September 17 we played our last game in Seals Stadium. We clobbered the Braves 13–6, while I went 4 for 4. That gave us a two-game lead over the Dodgers, with only eight left. I was hitting over .300 again and with five RBI's had knocked in an even 100. I started to feel good again, but that feeling didn't last. We went to Los Angeles and lost three straight to the Dodgers. Then we dropped two out of three to Chicago, and lost a doubleheader to the Cardinals on the final day of the season. Even so, Rig thanked us at the end for coming so close.

Willie's 1959 Numbers

G	AB	H	2B	3B	HR	R	RBI	BB	SO	SB	BA	SA
151	575	180	43	5	34	125	104	65	58	27	.313	.583

Rigney asked me about the finger and told me to get it examined again. I told him I'd do it when I got back to New York. Marghuerite and I were selling our San Francisco house and moving back East.

It was almost as if I had had to start all over again in San Francisco. The first two years I played in every game except five, just missed leading the league in batting the first year and hit 34 home runs the second one. Whatever I had accomplished before reaching San Francisco didn't seem to matter. In fact, it seemed as if it was being held against me. Some writers didn't help the situation much, either. They hadn't seen me play, and couldn't relate to the New York part of my career. Many of the fans felt the same way. I was a Giant who had traveled West, and whatever I had done back East would forever go unnoticed.

Instead the fans showed their feelings for the new Giants who joined the team when it started in San Francisco. Cepeda was a favorite and so was McCovey. Both were excellent players, and I could deal with the applause they received. It was deserved. But the boos for me were hard to understand. I never let on that they hurt me. One writer said of the situation, "San Francisco's the damndest city I ever saw in my life. They cheer Khrushchev and boo Mays."

When the 1960 season started, I was determined that I would be able to play for any manager and in front of any fan. Perhaps it would be different in our new stadium, Candlestick Park. I felt it was a new beginning, and here was a park presumably designed just for us. I had a good spring, and Stoneham made me the highest-paid player in baseball with an $85,000 contract. As usual, it was no big deal to come to terms. Those days, we didn't ask advisers or agents about it. We didn't have much choice. But I also felt the Giants were fair with me. Once Stoneham made me the offer, I said to him, jokingly, "You think I ought to have that much?"

"Yeah. I'm giving it to you because you're the best," he said.

"If you're giving it to me because I'm the best, then I'll take it."

"You deserve it."

We also felt we deserved the pennant. We had come close our first two years in Seals Stadium. We had strong hitting. Our only question was pitching.

You'd think that if you were starting from scratch, you'd build a park that was made for your type of club. Cepeda, me, Alou—right-handed power hitters. Give us something to shoot for in leftfield. But the first thought I had when I took my first turn in Candlestick Park was that if Seals

Stadium was too small, this place was too big. We had our first workout the day before the season opened, and it confounded me. I had never seen anything like it in all the games I had played and in all the places I'd been.

The wind started off blowing one way. Before the day was over, it shifted the other way. I thought to myself, "Willie, you're the centerfielder and you have to be sure out there." Seals Stadium had some wind, but this was really going to be a challenge. I had played a shallow centerfield my whole life, in every park, and I wasn't going to change now. Somehow, I had to figure out the wind.

That first day was windy, but it also was cold because of the strong winds blowing off San Francisco Bay. You could feel it at bat, too. My first practice swing remains with me. It wasn't because I smacked the ball into the wind. The ball split my bat in half. I worried about that, thinking that this might not be a good park for me to hit in. To top it off, one of the architects told me that I'd need all of my speed to run down some of the balls that would twist and turn in the wind. He got that right.

Sure, I was really intent on starting a new chapter. But I didn't want it to get to the point of having to learn to catch a baseball all over again. Usually the wind blew from left to right, another factor that favored a left-handed hitter. I ran like hell in that place—often, I would run far after a ball that started out toward me yet wound up in rightfield. Or I'd keep charging in for a ball that seemed to have been hit to center, and instead I'd end up shaking hands with the second baseman.

It took me some time to learn how to play the outfield at Candlestick. In all the years in all the ballparks I had played in, I usually had been concerned more with the shape of the park, or the condition of the field. Here I had a whole new situation: a wind I couldn't control. And control had always been one of my strong points. Physically, I could dominate a ballpark in the field. Today's ball players play back. They may make a lot of leaping catches against the fences, but they also let a lot of balls drop in front of them. If something dropped in front of me, I felt I'd let our pitcher down.

Yes, it took me time to learn how to play Candlestick. There were no enclosed parts behind the stadium, and at times the wind would blow the ball back as if it were a Ping-Pong ball. I remember one ball that I thought was going out of the park—only to land at my feet as it dropped for a single. These were the strangest weather conditions I'd ever played in, even on "normal" days. It was no wonder that no centerfielder in the league looked forward to playing in Candlestick.

But I discovered the secret of playing there. I used it my entire career in San Francisco, and never let anyone else know about it.

When a ball was hit, I didn't move. From the moment it was up in the air, I started counting to five: one, two, three, four, five. At "five" I began to run. I made the catch look easy. Believe me, it was a science as much as baseball skill. I don't think an airplane engineer could have solved the mystery of Candlestick. But somehow those five seconds gave me a chance to see whether the wind would take the ball, and if it did, where it would go. Every day I would measure the wind in my mind—how hard it was blowing and in what direction. There were days when it blew exactly the opposite of the way it had the day before, and I'd have to allow for that. Once the game started, I had to think along with the pitcher. The first three innings he'd be strong, then the next three he'd be a little weaker and I would have to compensate for how I played the batters. If I knew our pitcher had a good fastball, I figured that in the first inning the batter wouldn't be able to get around on it and I'd play him to hit the ball late. But as the game went along, I might play the hitter to pull the pitch. Before the game even started I'd go over the hitters in my mind, and I knew what they could do with a certain pitch. If a new ball player was in the lineup, I'd make it my business to check up on him.

The other outfielders would play off me. In that regard, the responsibility was totally on my shoulders. Every inning was different. In a way we played the game backward. If I was playing the outfield one way, the infield was playing the other way. A batter could pull a ground ball—but it would be harder for him to pull a fly ball. So in the late innings, we'd have the infielders play in the holes and leave the middle open. On every pitch, the other players would look at me. I positioned them by raising my hand. The player would move in that direction and stop when I dropped my hand to my side. I made it very clear to the other players. If you want to play, look at me. If you don't, then go home. When Hal Lanier was a young player with us in 1965, he didn't obey my signals. He was at shortstop one game and I raised my hand, signaling him to move. He ignored it. I called time. Herman Franks, who was managing then, came out of the dugout.

"What's wrong, Willie?" Franks asked.

"Nothing, Herman," I said. "You can go back to the dugout. I just have to talk to Hal."

I went over to Lanier and told him, "You didn't obey my signal. The next time it happens, you won't be playing."

I took my spot in the outfield and raised my hand again to set the defense. Lanier didn't bother to look. I knew what I had to do next. The next day I went to Herman and told him that Lanier wasn't playing the game. Herman accepted it. But when Lanier came out to the dugout before the game, and saw that his name wasn't in the lineup, he came over to see me.

"Why ain't I playing?" he asked.

"You know why."

"No, I don't know," he insisted.

"Well, let me tell you for the third time. You're not

watching my signals, which means you don't want to play with us. You want to play by yourself. When you're ready to play with the team and not by yourself, just let me know."

Lanier didn't play for a few games. We won each of the games, and my point looked stronger. When he came back in the lineup, he was wiser than before.

The Candlestick winds also affected my thinking as a hitter. You couldn't hit the ball into the bleachers even in batting practice. I had to change my batting stance at home and on the road. That also was something opposing pitchers never knew. At Candlestick, I went more to right center with the pitch. On the road, I went back to pulling the ball more. I didn't have any problem having two different styles. It went back to Leo. Back in 1954, he made me an inside-outside hitter, and that benefited me tremendously now.

Everyone in San Francisco quickly grew aware of Candlestick's wind problems. It was a local joke, a San Andreas Fault of stadium building. But the baseball public around the country grasped the magnitude of the wind in 1961, when the first of that season's two All-Star Games was staged at the park. In the ninth inning, Stu Miller—ironically, a Giants pitcher—came in as a relief hurler and promptly was blown off the mound, committing a balk. The wind also led to a throwing error by Ken Boyer in the 10th, which gave the American League the lead. The Nationals, though, won in the 10th, scoring twice as I stroked a key double.

Not only was it windy in the park, it was also cold. So they installed a heating system, but it was worthless.

Despite the playing conditions, we got off to a good start in 1960. But the Pirates were giving us the toughest time of all the clubs. In late June, we met the Pirates in a three-game series at Candlestick. We went into the series with a 33–22 record—better than .600. But the Pirates swept us. The fans booed us in the final game, but there was worse to come. I was sitting on my stool when someone came up to me and said that Rigney was fired.

I felt bad for Rig. We had our differences at the beginning, but over the past year we had gotten along without any problems. I thought the timing in firing him was very bad. The season wasn't even half over, and despite the three straight losses, we were still pretty close to the Pirates. Perhaps the booing got to Stoneham's ears. He was trying hard to please the fans and the press. On top of that, it was our first season in the new park, a place that was getting criticized because of the winds, and that displeased a lot of people because of its cost. Horace felt pressured into making a decision that he thought would make everyone else happy, when actually the only decision necessary was to keep going as we were.

Tom Sheehan replaced Rigney, which surprised me, but after I thought about it, I understood the move. There was a lot of local pressure on Stoneham to hire Lefty O'Doul. He had been our spring-training batting coach, and already had been a San Francisco favorite. Sheehan, though, had been with the Giants a long time, especially as a scout. Now it was clear to me. He would be only an interim manager for the rest of the year while Stoneham decided who would be our manager in 1961. It was obvious it wouldn't be O'Doul. If Horace had wanted him, he would have been hired on the spot.

Sheehan was a quiet type, up in years. He was in his midsixties and no one expected him to try to launch a managerial career now. He didn't have anything to prove and he didn't have to make points with Horace. Sheehan didn't make any dramatic changes. He was a good baseball man and was secure in the organization—so secure, he wouldn't do anything to jeopardize his position. I felt kind of sorry for him. We both knew that he was only a temporary fill-in, and that's a tough spot to get anything done. He was in uniform in body only. He didn't offer us any inspiration. The club played that way, too. We played under .500 ball for Tom and finished the season in fifth place, 16 games out. I was the only player who hit over .300. I also led the league with 190 hits.

Willie's 1960 Numbers

G	AB	H	2B	3B	HR	R	RBI	BB	SO	SB	BA	SA
153	595	190	29	12	29	107	103	61	70	25	.319	.555

Although we were finishing three years in San Francisco, there was still a sort of New York–West Coast split. Some New York writers still were covering us, and their presence annoyed some of the San Francisco area reporters. I had the feeling that I was on one side of the Golden Gate Bridge— the side closer to New York—and that the rest of the Giants, the new ones who had joined the team since the move in 1958—were on the other side, along with the local writers. That feeling became obvious in the spring of 1961.

15

THE NEW MANAGER was Alvin Dark. He was no stranger to me. Once again, Horace Stoneham went back for someone who had worn a Giants uniform. I think I knew, after I first met Alvin in 1951, that some day he'd be a manager. He was always thinking baseball, and he taught me some tricks. When I played with him, he used to put his hands behind his back at shortstop. He'd signal with one finger (fastball) or two fingers (curveball) to let me know what pitch the batter would be getting. That gave me an extra edge. If I knew a fastball was coming, it helped me figure where to play the hitter. If he couldn't hit the fastball and swung late, that would mean he probably would hit the ball to the opposite field.

Alvin hated to lose. We all did. But with Alvin, losing turned in his stomach and it would eat away at him until he took it out on something or someone. He also was ready to fight anyone. I remember once he took out Jackie Robinson on a rolling slide into second base, then immediately jumped up, ready for whatever Jackie might do. Leo used to call Alvin his "upside-down shortstop" because Alvin always seemed to end up on the ground from going after every ground ball hit between second and third. If it was 10 feet away from him, he still dived after it.

About a week after he was named manager, Dark wrote

me a letter. He told me that the greatest privilege any manager could have is knowing that I'd be playing for him. I had never gotten a letter from a manager before and it impressed me and made me want to really play for him.

That spring there was an airplane strike, and Dark was having problems getting all his players in camp. I made it a point to be there and I drove over from San Francisco to help an old friend—and also to show the rest of the team that I supported him. It seemed like old times when I got there. Three of his new coaches were my old teammates from 1951—Whitey Lockman, Wes Westrum, and Larry Jansen. All five of us had been in the lineup that day Bobby Thomson hit his home run against the Dodgers. We played that game over and over in camp.

To add to that New York feeling, more reporters from New York joined us, attracted by Dark, an old Giants hero. I didn't realize it then, but this created a terrible problem. Dark knew all the writers from his New York days, and I guess that, naturally, he tended to hang around with them and not the San Francisco reporters. The first four or five days of camp, it looked like New York Giants press conferences. The San Francisco media didn't get a chance to know Alvin.

Meanwhile, I could tell that Dark wasn't going to have anything to do with O'Doul. I don't know the reason, whether he objected to Lefty's presence or just that he hadn't hired him. For the past three years, since we had moved to California, Lefty had come every spring to act as our batting coach. But Dark didn't recognize him as that at all. One day, a writer called O'Doul the Giants' batting coach.

"A batting coach?" Alvin answered. "I really don't have one. If any of the players want to ask O'Doul for help, they better do it on their own time."

A week later, O'Doul went back to San Francisco. That did it. Lefty was a genuine San Francisco folk hero. Now the writers, who were hoping that Lefty would be the manager instead of Dark, had something more against Alvin.

Alvin's style further complicated the relationship. Dark didn't socialize with the San Francisco press people. He wasn't a drinker or a smoker and he made this clear from the beginning. The New York writers already knew this and they didn't feel put down when Alvin wouldn't join them for a drink after practice. But when he refused to go out with the San Francisco people after a game, that bothered some of them. He told them that if they wanted to talk to him, they'd have to do it during daylight hours, no late-evening interviews in motel bars. Every other manager around the league fraternized with the media over a bottle of beer, but not Alvin. In the old days, Leo had a table piled with liquor in his office in the Polo Grounds. Dark's desk was nice and neat. He didn't encourage drinking.

Alvin would go to bed early and wake up early. Once workouts began, he wouldn't hang around the dugout and chew the fat with the media. Instead, he'd go onto the field and remain there until the workouts were over. His work habits and communication with the players created a new atmosphere on the club. We felt we could win, that someone up there knew we could and had confidence in us. I could see that the players accepted his discipline. That meant they would play for him.

Dark earned a great deal of respect in just one exhibition game. It was a hot day and we were playing the Red Sox in Scottsdale, near Phoenix. We were tied in the bottom of the ninth and the Red Sox had the bases loaded with two out. Bob Bolin, a rookie, was pitching for us. He threw a pitch that looked like a strike. Usually, on a close pitch in that situation, the batter swings to protect the plate. If not, the umpire will usually give the pitcher the benefit of the doubt. But the hitter didn't swing and the umpire called the pitch Ball 4. The winning run was forced home.

We all left the field. But suddenly Dark ran out of the

dugout and started to really argue with the ump. Just the three of them were on the field—Alvin, the umpire, Bolin. It was only an exhibition game but we were all getting the message from our new manager: Dark knew that Bolin was fighting to make the team and Dark was out there fighting with him. That showed us, very early in the spring, that he was a manager who would fight for his players.

In getting ready for his first season as manager, Dark made only one major change, and I felt it was a good one. He talked to me about switching Cepeda from first base to the outfield and putting McCovey on first. Then Dark took me by surprise. He said he wanted to put Cepeda in right-field.

"But, Cap," I told him, "rightfield is tougher to learn than left."

"I know that, Willie, but I have a good reason for doing that, something I thought about a great deal."

And what was that?

"The fans," said Dark.

"What do they have to do with it?" I wondered.

"They'll realize that Cepeda is learning a new position and they'll have more patience. It'll be easier on Cepeda since he'll need the time to learn how to play the tough field."

Alvin was beginning to remind me of Leo. But then again, that wasn't so unusual, because Dark, along with Stanky, was one of Leo's boys. Leo couldn't pick between them. That's why he had made Dark and Stanky co-captains. They were both smart players, very tough players, and they both ended up as managers—just as Leo had predicted.

For a time, Dark even sounded like Leo. He compli-mented me a lot, not only directly to my face but when talking with the fans and the media as well. He said he couldn't understand their coolness to me. On one radio show he said, "Without Willie, the Giants are just an ordi-nary team." On a television show, he said, "Willie's the greatest ball player I've ever seen, greater than Ted Williams, Stan Musial, or Mickey Mantle."

As usual, when I tried too hard I didn't do well. When the season began I had it in the back of my mind that we needed a big start under our new manager. I was swinging too hard because the deepest part of dead center was only 410 feet away. And the winds, as usual, were a distraction. No one else could figure them out, though. But as I learned more about them, I had an advantage over the visiting players. In a game against Pittsburgh, Jose Pagan, our shortstop, was at bat. He hit a pop-up that their second baseman called for. A routine play. All of a sudden he started running back into rightfield and stopped. He kept looking for the ball but it never came down. Instead, the wind carried the ball all the way to the top of the fence in right—more than 330 feet away. All of us in the dugout were laughing like crazy. Then Hobie Landrith, one of our catchers, said something that made sense.

"Boys, I'm beginning to realize they hate it worse than we do." At that moment, I began to realize what an advantage we had knowing about Candlestick Park and its crazy winds.

I slumped early. We opened with a couple of victories in Los Angeles, where I managed a few hits. We moved on to Milwaukee, and who should greet us but Warren Spahn! Still pitching at the age of 40—and he no-hitted us. The next day we broke out with 15 hits, but I was the only Giant who didn't get one. I went 0 for 4. Combine that with my 0 for 3 against Spahn and now I was showing only 10 hits in my last 40 at bats. I wasn't helping Dark at all, and I certainly wasn't helping myself.

After the game, McCovey and I went for a walk. Willie was my roommate, and used to astound me with the way he could eat so late at night. We passed a take-out joint that specialized in ribs. Willie said we should take some back to our hotel room. He ate most of them. After watching television for an hour, we turned off the lights and went to sleep. But I got up earlier than I expected. I was sick.

About three A.M. I started to throw up. McCovey quickly called Doc Bowman and he came in with Jim Davenport. Doc told me I had an upset stomach and told me to get some sleep. He gave me a sleeping pill. I did get about five hours of sleep, but it wasn't enough. When I got to the park, I felt dead. I certainly didn't feel like playing, but I still got dressed.

I was standing at the batting cage watching Joey Amalfitano take his cuts. I wasn't out with the regulars, so Joey, an infielder, must have known I wouldn't be playing.

"You're not playing today?" he said.

"Doesn't look like it," I told him. "I ate some bad ribs last night and I don't feel too good."

"Too bad, Willie," he said.

"Maybe I could use a day off, the way I've been hitting," I said.

He looked at me and smiled. Then he said, "If you change your mind about playing, try this bat I've been using. It's heavier than yours."

We laughed about it. Joey was a singles hitter.

Just then, Dark came along. He wondered how I felt, and I told him not too great. Anyway, since I had a bat in my hands, I figured I might as well take my turn in the cage.

Was I surprised. Everything I hit went into the stands. I took fifteen swings and I must have sent a dozen into the seats. After that, there was no way I was going to sit on the bench.

"Cap, don't leave my name out of the lineup," I told Dark. "The balls are jumping off my bat."

Of course, I expected it would be tougher against Lew Burdette, the Braves' starter. He was a right-hander who had great control. He had a good fastball along with a curve and slider. He also had another pitch, a spitter.

My first time up, he threw me a slider—I socked it over

the left centerfield fence, 420 feet away. In the third inning
I hit one 400 feet. Hey, this really was getting to be as easy
as batting practice.

By the time I was up for my third at bat, Seth Morehead
was pitching for the Braves. The lefty threw me a sinker and
I got into it and smacked it over the fence in dead center.
Must have been 450 feet away. Now, for my fourth at bat,
Moe Drabowsky, another righty, was pitching. I got a hold
of this one, too, but I lined out to center, to Hank Aaron.

In the eighth inning, Don McMahon, a fastball right-
hander, was pitching. I got around on him and hit the ball
on a line over the centerfield fence. Another 400-foot homer
—my fourth of the game. What a thrill I had rounding the
bases. Here I was, not even expecting to play and now
becoming part of baseball history, the fifth player ever to
hit four home runs in a game. The fans were great, even
though it was Milwaukee. As I touched each base they
cheered.

I even had a chance to become the only player to hit five
in a game. In the ninth inning I was the on-deck batter when
Davenport got up with two out. The Braves' fans were
screaming for Davenport to get a hit so I could get up. But
he grounded out. Still, what a day. I was out of my slump
—4 for 5, all homers, and eight runs batted in.

"How 'bout some more ribs?" McCovey asked me when
I got back to the dugout.

Two months later I got another thrill. I had not been in
New York to play a game since we moved out in 1957, not
even a stickball game. But we had an exhibition game
against the Yankees in the Stadium. I didn't know what to
expect from the crowd since this was Yankee Stadium, not
the Polo Grounds, and the Yankee centerfielder was Mickey
Mantle. Before the game, they arranged a home-run hitting
contest—Mantle and Roger Maris against me and Cepeda.
It rained, so the homer-hitting contest was called off, along
with the usual pregame warm-up. It didn't appear that we

could play ball at all as fifty thousand people sat and waited.

The rain finally stopped and the game began an hour late. The public-address announcer started to call out the starting lineup. I was batting third. Before he could even finish saying "Willie," the crowd stood and the noise rocked the stadium. You couldn't hear a thing except their cheering. It lasted for about a minute and I was frozen. I had tears in my eyes. New York hadn't forgotten me.

The '61 Giants had a decent season, finishing third, eight games behind the first-place Reds. For the first time in my big-league career, I played in every game. Once again, I led the league in at least one category. This time it was with 129 runs scored.

Willie's 1961 Numbers

G	AB	H	2B	3B	HR	R	RBI	BB	SO	SB	BA	SA
154	572	176	32	3	40	129	123	81	77	18	.308	.584

Oh, yes. In addition to my four-homer game I hit three in one game eight weeks later. I also played in both All-Star Games, going 3 for 8. The year before I went 6 for 8 in both. With those 40 homers, I had cracked the 300 barrier for my career, and I was only thirty years old.

16

THEY SAY IN SPORTS that just when you think you've seen everything, stick around. You ain't seen nothin' yet. And that's what 1962 was all about. It was as topsy-turvy a year as any we've ever had, certainly as unusual for me as 1951.

I shouldn't have been surprised. It just had to be different. That's the year the Mets were created. Not only were they created, but their manager turned out to be Casey Stengel. He was returning at the age of seventy-one, a year after the Yankees had fired him for being too old.

The National League had expanded for the first time, and now it had ten teams. Along with the Mets, there were the Houston Colt .45's.

We were good, but the Dodgers were better—at least for most of the season. They were pumped up. After their years of struggling with Los Angeles officials, they finally were able to open their new stadium in Chavez Ravine. A strange thing happened when we'd play there. I'd know the fans were watching us. But they would also hold their hands to the sides of their heads. Why, they were listening on the radio to what they could see just yards in front of them. Strangest sight I ever saw in the stands.

Of course, for the most part they heard good things all season. That's why the Dodgers drew more fans than any other team in baseball history, almost 2.8 million. Maury Wills had become the greatest base stealer in the history of our game. He broke the one record they said would stand after Maris broke the Babe's single-season homer record of 60. No one figured anyone could steal more bases than the 96 Ty Cobb stole in 1915. It took forty-seven years, but Wills broke it—not only broke it, shattered it. He stole 104 times. Amazing. And Tommy Davis hit .346 for the Dodgers and drove in 153 runs. He was to earn the Most Valuable Player title. Don Drysdale was on his way to a 25-victory season and the Cy Young Award. In those days, they only gave one for all of baseball, not one for each league.

Despite all that power and pitching, the Dodgers' luck started to go bad on July 17. Koufax, at twenty-six, finally was having the sort of year the Dodgers had been waiting for since Brooklyn. But he was lost for the season with a circulation problem in his fingers. At that point Koufax was 14–7 and led the league in strikeouts and earned-run average.

With Koufax out, there was no question in my mind but that we could make a run at the Dodgers. Hey, we had some sensational players, too, especially on the pitching staff—Jack Sanford (who won 16 games in a row), Billy O'Dell, Juan Marichal, and Billy Pierce. Besides, I was hitting homers at a league-leading clip, and Orlando Cepeda and Felipe Alou were slugging right up there. It was getting hot in the pennant race. But none of us wanted to take a day off. I pushed myself as I always did. Then one day it got to me.

I was flat on my back on the floor of the dugout when I came to. It was hot and muggy in Cincinnati, even though it was September. We were in a pennant race.

It was our last road trip of the season, and we were only a half game behind the Dodgers. I was sitting on the bench when the inning began. I was hot and felt dizzy. The next thing I remembered was Doc Bowman looking down on me, a bottle of smelling salts in his hand.

"What's wrong with me?" I asked.

"It's all right, Buck. You just fainted. How do you feel now?"

"I just feel like I don't want to move. I can move, but I don't want to."

Bowman ordered a stretcher, and the next thing I was aware of was being in an ambulance on the way to a hospital. It reminded me of the other times I had passed out over the years. In New York, back in '54, it was on a night like this, hot and muggy. I knew I'd be okay, that I was just exhausted from playing hard in another pennant race. The doctors told me the same thing, except that they prescribed a few days of rest. I hadn't missed a game all season.

How could I take off time now, with first place so close? Dark didn't push me, despite the pressure of the pennant race. That meant a lot to me. He told everyone I'd be back in the lineup when I felt I was ready to play. He insisted that I continue to rest until I had completely recovered and felt strong again.

I missed three straight games—the only games I was to miss that year. Yet Dark had to explain constantly to the news media what was wrong. They were wondering why a thirty-one-year-old athlete could be so tired that he couldn't play a game of baseball—and in a pennant race, when it was so important. Alvin tried to explain that in any other business, if a person was overworked, he'd simply take the week off. But in baseball, you can't hide. After that, I wanted to play for Dark very badly. We were on a roll, with seven straight victories.

But starting with the first game I missed, we lost six straight. When I returned, I hit a homer, but we had lost our momentum. When we returned to San Francisco for the last days of the pennant race, we were four games behind with only seven to play. The odds were terrible.

Through all our problems, though, Dark never gave us a tongue-lashing. We had lost six straight games back in June and he didn't say anything then, either. The only time he really chewed us out came before a Dodgers series in Candlestick. We had lost eight of 11 games to them and he brought us together behind closed doors. There was some feeling that a couple of the players were giving up, that they felt there was no sense in trying to catch the Dodgers.

"Boys," he began, "they tell me some of you think school's out. If you think that, I know we'll all be glad if you sit down and think again. I don't care if you want to quit. I do care if you want to quit on me."

We swept the three-game series from the Dodgers.

Now we were meeting them again. It's uncanny, but virtually ever year it always seemed to come down to a crucial Giants-Dodgers series that would be the key to our season. Our rivalries extended from player to player, to team to team, and borough to borough when we were back in New York. Now it was extending across an entire state. This pennant race was getting bigger than just comparisons. The first one I remember was between Duke Snider and myself. We wound up kidding each other about the rivalry, which was greater in the newspapers than it was between us.

I recalled that first time in Brooklyn, when Campy told me that Newcombe was going to throw at me. I struck out on three pitches, but when I got back to the dugout I was sitting there and laughing. Leo came over and wanted to know just what in the hell was so funny that I could laugh after striking out. I told him we were just having fun.

"Don't talk to Campanella any more," Leo ordered.

Another night Sal Maglie was on the mound pitching for the Dodgers against us. He must have been thirty-eight years old by then, but he still had the reputation of throwing close to batters no matter who they were—sluggers, rinky-dinks, former teammates. He always liked to be in complete control of a game, and the way he did this, or thought he had to do it, was by pitching batters close. You always had to worry about a brushback pitch from him. You knew he would throw it, but you didn't know how close he would make it. Sal the Barber.

This was a hot, muggy night, and the first pitch Maglie threw brushed me back. Since it was hot, I gave him the benefit of the doubt. Maybe the pitch had slipped out of his hand. After the next pitch I knew differently. He knocked me down. If I hadn't gotten out of the way so quickly, he would have beaned me. I got up and stared at Maglie, really angry. But he turned his back to me and rubbed the ball as if it were slippery. I looked at the plate umpire, Tom Gorman, and said, "What about that?"

Gorman called time and went out to the mound to warn Maglie. As the ump returned to home, Maglie called him back and said something. When Gorman walked past me, I asked him what Maglie had said.

"Maglie said to tell you that he's sorry," said Gorman.

I dug in and waited for Maglie's next pitch, knowing I was going to take a good cut becuase he had to come in with it. I swung and caught all of it. I drove it into the leftfield stands. I could see Maglie was hot. As I reached second base, I yelled, "Sorry, Maglie," and kept running around the bases. That home run gave me a lot of satisfaction, not only because Maglie knew he couldn't intimidate me, but because it came against the Dodgers.

Now, in 1962, we had the Dodgers to contend with again. I think this presented an even greater challenge than the 1951 miracle finish. I realize we had come from farther back in '51, when we were 13½ games out in August. But we also had had more time to make up ground. In the final week of the 1951 season we were closer to the Dodgers than we were in 1962. We had to pick up four games with only seven remaining just to tie the Dodgers. I don't think any team in history had ever been able to finish like that before us.

Dark thought our chances were good. "Willie, the Dodgers could have taken charge and they haven't. I think something's wrong down there in L.A.," he told me.

The Dodgers were in a slump of their own. After losing Koufax they couldn't get rolling. They were on the way to losing 10 of their final 13 games, which would go down as one of the great collapses. We got to the final Saturday of the regular season and we were a game and a half behind them. On Friday we had been rained out against Houston —our only rain-out of the year in San Francisco, and our only one until 1964—while the Dodgers were losing to the Cardinals. So we had to play a doubleheader on Saturday while the Dodgers met the Cards again that night. If we won the doubleheader, we'd be only half a game behind and the pressure would be terrific on the Dodgers that night.

Before our doubleheader began I saw an old friend. Joey Amalfitano was now playing for Houston. He said something strange to me: "Can you guys score a run?" I couldn't figure out what Joey meant.

"If you can score, you got the pennant. They're never going to score another run," he said.

We beat Houston in the opener to cut the Dodgers' lead to only one game. Now a sweep would be sweet. It could mean we'd be tied going into Sunday. But we couldn't do it. We dropped the second game. I didn't get a hit in either game. But the Dodgers didn't do any better. The Cards shut them out, and now it was down to Sunday, the last game of the season. We needed to win, and we needed the Dodgers to lose.

Eleven years earlier, I had crouched in the on-deck circle

at the Polo Grounds praying, "Please, God, don't let it come down to me." Bobby Thomson had saved me from the unknown at that moment.

Now, on September 30, 1962, I came to bat in the eighth inning of the final day of the regular season. The Giants were tied with Houston at 1–all. We needed the victory and we needed the Dodgers to lose. The Dodgers, though, had been in first place continuously since July 8.

Dick Farrell, the Colts' strikeout pitcher, started for Houston. He was still on the mound when I arrived at the plate in the eighth. I knew I wouldn't see many fastballs because the last time we had met, in Houston, I had crunched him for a pair of homers. So today, Farrell was serving me curves. Hitless in my previous at bats that day, I saw a curve on my first pitch of the eighth. I fouled it into the rightfield seats.

Then I knew what was coming next.

I figured he just might try to slip the fastball by me. I was right. Only he didn't get it past me. I got all of it and drove it deep into the leftfield seats.

It landed fourteen rows back and it lifted the Giants to a 2–1 victory. But a strange thing happened at Candlestick after it was over. Many of the fans in the crowd of more than 41,000 people didn't leave. Instead, they stayed to hear what was going on in Chavez Ravine to the south, where the Dodgers faced the Cardinals. My teammates and I clustered around a radio in the clubhouse, and suddenly Dark let out a soft "Wahoo," when he heard that a Cardinal catcher named Gene Oliver had tagged Johnny Podres for a homer. It was to be the only run of the game as the Cards stopped the Dodgers—and forced a best-of-three game playoff.

"Well," said the Dodgers' Duke Snider philosophically, thinking back to 1951, "we owe the Giants something."

That homer against Houston was my forty-seventh, and it gave me back the home-run title. I had been hitting ho-

mers at a good clip all along, but I hadn't realized that I had
not led in homers since 1955, when I hit the 51. I knew I
couldn't stop now, though. The Dodgers' pitching was extremely tough, and you had to get big hits off them to put
them off balance.

This Giants' team dreamed, just the way the '51 club had.
After our last road trip to Pittsburgh, pitcher Billy Pierce
told us he had had a dream in which we ended up winning
the pennant. The guys laughed him off. They told him to
dream again and let them know the result.

"I had the same dream again," he said a few days later.

"I don't want to hear it," one of the players shouted.
"Every time you dream like that we lose."

Pierce was upset. "I have no control over what I dream,"
he said.

"Okay, try it one more time."

The next day he came into the clubhouse and shook his
head and said, "Same dream." Someone threw a towel at
him.

As if Pierce's dream wasn't bad enough—ball players
hate to be "jinxed"—Harvey Kuenn's mother also was
dreaming. She met Harvey when we got to St. Louis and
told him she had dreamed we won the pennant. This started
to become a running gag with us. Then Whitey Lockman
asked, "What do you suppose Leo Durocher is dreaming
right now?"

"Never mind Leo," said Larry Jansen. "Hey, Harvey, can
your mother stay with us a couple of more days?"

Leo was now coaching the Dodgers. It made me think
that either his dream or Pierce's dream wouldn't come true.

The opening playoff game would be at Candlestick, then
the next two at Chavez Ravine, where the Dodgers finally
were playing after spending their first four years at the Los
Angeles Coliseum. Pierce had a chance to make his dream
come true in the opener. He was pitching against Koufax,
who was trying to pitch again.

Alvin, though, wanted to make sure we weren't bothered by the Dodgers' singles hitters—their base stealers such as Maury Wills, who had set the record. Alvin was a smart baseball man, all right, so smart that his moves in this series would lead to his being nicknamed the Swamp Fox.

Before the opening game at Candlestick, Dark ordered the groundskeepers to water down the area at first base. That made a lot of sense. You make the first-base dirt heavy and it cuts down Wills's ability to take a big lead and to take off for second. Then Alvin also told the grounds crew to turn the hose on the path between first and second.

That tactic didn't escape Jocko Conlan, who was one of the most experienced umpires I ever met, and who was in charge of the umpiring crew that day. Jocko knew to come out before the game and inspect everything. He didn't like what he saw. He went right over to Dark.

"Now, Alvin, that's enough water. You have the field too wet as it is."

That really teed off Dark, who felt he could do what he wanted to with his field. After all, everyone knew the Dodgers played games with their field, fixing the baselines so that Wills's bunts would stay fair.

"Jocko, I don't know what you're talking about," Alvin told him. But Conlan insisted that Dark call the head groundskeeper and fix up the base-paths.

"What for?" said Dark. "You call him yourself."

That was all Jocko had to hear. He wasn't a future Hall of Famer for nothing. He liked to be in control. He yelled at Dark. That's just what we wanted to hear. Some of us who were on the field early for practice razzed Conlan: "That's right, Jocko. Give it to him. You don't have to take that."

But this was only one of Alvin's tactics. Nobody ever knew that he had been watering down the left side of the field long before Conlan ever discovered what was happening on the right side. We had slow fielders on the left side—

Pagan at short, Davenport at third. And the other teams pulled a lot of balls to the left side. By slowing the field, we slowed down their grounders. If Conlan had arrived on the field even earlier than he did, he would have seen how heavily the left side was being watered.

Just the day before, we had held a fan appreciation day, and we were giving away automobiles. The head groundskeeper warned the master of ceremonies not to park the cars on the left side of the infield.

"Why not?"

"Because the cars will sink to their hubcaps."

It was no wonder to me they called Dark the Swamp Fox. All the strategy didn't help when you were facing a Sandy Koufax, though. You had to beat him pure and simple, or not at all. Pure and simple meant making contact with that great fastball of his.

I came up against him in the first inning of the playoff opener. With two out, Felipe Alou hit a double just past Andy Carey at third. I worked Koufax to a 3–1 count. Then I tagged his fastball over the right centerfield fence. We led by 2–0 and, as it turned out, we didn't need anything else. Still, during my next at bat, Ed Roebuck threw a duster that knocked me down. I singled. When I came up in the sixth, I tagged Larry Sherry for another homer. That turned out to be my forty-ninth of the season, and gave me the major league title for the season, one more than Harmon Killebrew of the Twins. I was back in action—3 for 3, a walk, 3 runs scored, 3 batted in, a stolen base. We won, 8–0.

Interestingly, when it was over Dark felt he had to explain to all the assembled newsmen just what it was about me that made me important to the team.

"Now, you *really* know Mays," he said. For the questions before the playoffs, and even after the first game, had concerned my "collapse" late in the season. A strange thing was happening concerning my play. I was being measured by a different standard. Great things were expected. When

I did the ordinary, or simply didn't deliver, to some observers it became a failure of my personality, or will, or a diminishing of my talent. Here I was, thirty-one years old, a man who had never failed to score less than 100 runs since moving to San Francisco five years earlier, who had never whacked fewer than 29 homers, nor driven in less than 96 runs—and when I had a bad week it was subject to analysis. So here was Dark sounding as if he almost had to apologize for me, as if I had to win the first game single-handedly or else be considered a failure for the season. People who knew, though, understood.

"There are three leagues," said one observer. "Minor league, major league, and the Mays league."

We had to win one of two games in Los Angeles against a Dodgers team that suddenly had forgotten how to hit. With Pierce's shutout, they hadn't scored in 30 straight innings.

Leo was trying to help the Dodgers get back into action, so he pulled out his old superstitious tricks. He wore a T-shirt that he had had on the day Bobby Thomson hit the home run in 1951. I couldn't believe it, but Leo must have actually saved the things he wore that day, knowing that there'd come another time when he'd need the luck they brought. So after we beat the Dodgers at Candlestick, he had gone through his old things and found a cardboard box that contained clothing and equipment from that 1951 game. He also pulled out old socks and shorts. Leo believed they had enough power to work again.

We grabbed a 5–0 lead against them in Game 2. It lasted only until the sixth inning, though, when they came back with seven runs. Maybe Leo's underwear was working. We tied it, but they won it in the ninth. It was the longest nine-inning National League game in history, more than four hours. But what concerned me was that they might have some momentum.

Well, Leo had his good-luck charms. And everyone sud-

denly realized that Game 3 of this series was taking place
on October 3—exactly eleven years to the day after Thomson's homer. Someone asked Dark whether he had any
good-luck charms from '51, the way Durocher did.

"Only Willie Mays," Alvin said.

The Giants took a 2–0 lead in the third, but the Dodgers
pushed ahead, and when the final inning of the 1962 National League pennant race began, the Dodgers were leading
by 4–2. But we loaded the bases with one out, and I came
up against Ed Roebuck, a reliever with a 10–1 record.

I wanted to be up. This was something I had been waiting
for for . . . how long, eleven years? I wanted it to be on my
shoulders. No scared rookie now. I knew what had to be
done. I smashed a liner back at Roebuck. It was hit so hard
it knocked off his glove. He had no play, a run scored, the
bases were still loaded, and our comeback was underway. I
came around eventually as we scored four times.

Just three more outs to go. Dark didn't take any chances
in the bottom of the ninth. He brought in Pierce. Maury
Wills made out on a grounder. Jim Gilliam hit a fly to me.
Then Lee Walls was up as a pinch hitter. I said to myself
that if I caught the ball, I'd save it for Pierce. Walls hit a fly
and it came to me. But I had forgotten what I told myself. I
took the ball and started dancing. Then I flung it into the
rightfield seats. We had won the pennant by beating the
Dodgers in a playoff. Again.

Everyone was drinking champagne except Dark. The
Latin players were whooping it up in Spanish and English
—Cepeda, Marichal, Pagan, the Alou brothers. In the mid-
dle of all this, I started to laugh to myself. For some reason
I thought back to 1951, when Leo said after Thomson's
homer, "Hell, we just wanted to make it look close."

Willie's 1962 Numbers

G	AB	H	2B	3B	HR	R	RBI	BB	SO	SB	BA	SA
162	621	189	36	5	49	130	141	78	85	18	.304	.615

That night, fifty thousand people waited for us at the San Francisco airport. The next day we were going to start the World Series against the Yankees. Our plane had to circle for an hour and a half so they could clear the runway area. When we finally landed, we tried to sneak away and they unloaded us at a terminal about a mile from the main buildings. But it was no good. The fans found us. A couple of them climbed on top of our bus. Some of them even smashed the windows to get a look at us and shake our hands. Somehow, I was the only player to find a taxi and I escaped in it. The airport was closed down and planes were rerouted to Oakland across the bay. But now, people were shouting, "We want Mays. We want Mays." It had taken them only five years.

17

ONCE UPON A TIME it was called a subway series. Now it was strictly for the jet set: the Giants and Yankees in the World Series.

These two legendary ball clubs had met six times in Series play going back to 1921, when the Giants owned New York. They won that year and the next one, too. The Yankees got back at them in 1923, but not before Casey Stengel, playing for the Giants, hit a home run into rightfield at Yankee Stadium. Throughout the series Casey had been razzed by the Yankees, especially after he almost lost a shoe in running out an inside-the-park homer that decided the opening game. So when Casey hit one into the seats in the third game, he ran around the bases thumbing his nose in the direction of the Yankees' bench. That angered the bombers' owner, Jake Ruppert, who complained to Commissioner Kenesaw Mountain Landis:

"That man, Stengel, insulted me and my patrons."

The judge replied, "Well, Casey just can't help being Casey," but he fined Stengel fifty dollars.

Almost forty years later, Stengel was managing the Mets, a club created in the upheaval generated when the Giants and Dodgers left New York. That man had longevity, and brother, did he love the game.

The Yankees were favored, and that was only right. They

were rested and they could work their pitching rotation any way they wanted. That meant they might be able to get three starts out of Whitey Ford if they needed to.

The Yankees were going to wear us down any way they could. Before the first game even started, they asked Commissioner Ford Frick to make sure the field was examined. They knew what Dark and his groundskeepers had done to the Dodgers.

Whitey Ford was just fine with me. I'd always hit Whitey in the past, and I was looking forward to facing him three times if we had to. Whitey and I had always kidded each other in All-Star Games, and I knew he scuffed up the ball or used a spitter against me.

We were carrying the load for all of San Francisco. This was the first time any major league team from the city was playing for a world championship. Now we were heroes, as if all those other good years we had had really didn't count. This was for a title.

In the second inning, I led off with a single against Whitey, and I got to third on Davenport's hit. I tried to rattle Ford by taking a big lead off third. He threw over there once and nearly picked me off. But I got back. Then, Pagan laid down a nice bunt that Ford fielded, but I was able to get home on it. That wasn't enough for the game, though, as we lost, 6–2. We couldn't do much against Ford, even with my three hits. Around the fourth inning, he was having trouble with the wind. His curve wasn't breaking. I found out later that his catcher, Elston Howard, had told him to forget about the curve and throw only the slider or fastballs. Too bad we didn't know about it. We got nothing off him that mattered over the last six innings.

As usual, Dark had worked up some theories to try to change things around for us. Roger Maris had gotten two hits in the opener, driven in two runs, and scored once. Now Alvin tried something new for him, the Ted Williams shift (this was "invented" by Lou Boudreau of the Indians):

use three infielders on the right side of second base, since
Williams pulled everything. So Dark had our shortstop,
Pagan, on the right side of second base, with Chuck Hiller,
our second baseman, playing closer to first. Dark had gotten
the idea to use it against Maris when he was watching
Roger bat against right-handers in batting practice and saw
him pull everything to the right side. And since we were
starting a right-hander, Jack Sanford, this was the time to
do it.

It worked sensationally. Hiller took two hits away from
Maris on balls that normally would have been through between first and second. Meanwhile, on offense, Dark
benched Cepeda because a righty, Ralph Terry, was pitching for the Yankees. Instead, McCovey played first. Willie
hit a homer, and that made Dark look even smarter. We
won the game, 2–0, on Sanford's three-hitter.

The Yankees came back with good pitching again in the
first game in New York, even though Pierce had a shutout
until the seventh. But Bill Stafford stopped us on four hits.
We won the next game when Chuck Hiller hit a grand slam.
But we also lost Juan Marichal. He was holding the Yankees to only two hits when he came up in the fifth inning.
He tried to sacrifice on Strike 3 and smashed his finger.
Because the pitch hit him, Juan argued that he should have
been given first base. But you can't do that when you're
swinging. That finished Juan for the series. One of his relievers was Don Larsen, and it turned out to be the sixth
anniversary of his perfect game over the Dodgers. Don won
the game in relief and we were tied at two games apiece.

Then it rained. We had an extra day off, which bothered
Sanford. He had psyched himself to be ready that day, and
we waited around an extra hour before the game was called
off. When we got it in the next day, Tom Tresh, who was
only a rookie then, hit a three-run homer against Sanford.
We went back to San Francisco down by three games to
two. This didn't bother us. The Giants' tradition had been

to bounce back, and we not only remembered what we had
done just a few days ago against the Dodgers, but we all
knew what we had done eleven years ago. Guys like me and
Alvin didn't let the younger players forget that, either.

Alvin decided to put Cepeda back in the lineup against
Whitey Ford in the sixth game. Orlando had had a bad run
in big games. He had been 0 for 29 in All-Star Games and
the Series, a number that kept haunting him. Sometimes you
break out of big slumps with little hits. When he faced
Whitey in the second inning, he had been 0 for 12 in this
Series. Then he got a little grounder than kept bouncing up
the middle and took a hop over Tony Kubek's head for a
single. Who knows, but maybe the fact that the sixth game
had been rained out three straight days helped Orlando. He
told me he felt stronger, and was using a 35-ounce bat
instead of his usual 33 ounces. Orlando also got two other
hits, one of them a double, and he drove in two runs as we
beat Ford 5–2, with Pierce coming through again for us on
the mound. We were taking the Yankees to a seventh game.

Sanford came back for us, while the Yankees used Terry.
There was only one run in the game and it wasn't scored by
us. Bill Skowron came home on a double-play ball hit by
Tony Kubek in the fifth.

I didn't have a hit all game against Terry. Then I came
through in the ninth, but I look back at things that might
have been. In the seventh, I pulled the ball down the leftfield line. Tresh took after it and made a backhanded catch
on the run. The tip of the ball stuck out of the webbing. We
call it an ice-cream cone. Then McCovey really rocked a
pitch and hit it 400 feet, but the wind stopped it. He had to
take a triple and was left on third—although I thought he
should have kept going, since the ball was hit so deep that
Mantle had to rush his relay, and it sailed over Kubek,
bouncing around the infield. In a close game like that,
maybe you try to score when you have a chance. Instead,

McCovey stayed on third. But that's what happens when you lose. You think of what didn't happen.

In the ninth we had one other shot. Until then Terry was pitching a two-hitter. Matty Alou beat out a bunt. We were alive in the bottom of the ninth with none out. But Terry was tough. Felipe Alou and Chuck Hiller both struck out after trying to bunt Matty to second. Then I was up. I didn't figure Terry would give me anything to pull. I was looking outside, and that's just where he pitched me. I lined it over Skowron's head down the first-base line. It was hit hard enough to go for a triple and past Maris in the outfield. But the field was still very slow from those three days of rain, and it slowed up the ball enough so that Maris could cut it off before it hit the fence. Whitey Lockman, our third-base coach, held up Alou at third. If it had been me, I would have tried to score.

Some people don't like to take chances, to be criticized for being thrown out in the last inning. It wouldn't have bothered me at all. I'm trying to score if I can, especially here, where we hadn't been able to do anything all game against a tough pitcher. On a play like that, the pressure is on the guy throwing the ball, even a good outfielder like Maris. He has to make a good throw to the cutoff man, then there has to be another perfect throw to home plate. If the ball arrives at the plate the same time as I do, the catcher knows he's going to get hit. But that's me. I never had a third-base coach. I did whatever I wanted to do. I know I would have tried to score the tying run and I wouldn't care who criticized me if I didn't make it. How can you criticize someone trying to win a ball game?

So there I was on second and Matty Alou on third. I felt certain that with two out and first base open, the Yankees would walk McCovey and pitch to Cepeda—a right-hander against a righty—especially after the ball I had hit off him in the seventh. McCovey on first didn't mean anything.

Houk came out to talk to Terry. I was the winning run on second. I was surprised, though, when Houk let Terry pitch to McCovey. On the first pitch, McCovey drove the ball deep to right, but foul. Two pitches later he hit a line drive toward right. Everyone started yelling. I took off. But Bobby Richardson grabbed it, a sinking liner at second base. He didn't have to move a step. A couple of feet either way, who knows? Maybe we would have won the Series.

Later, Willie told me that he too had expected the Yankees to walk him, and he wasn't bearing down. When they didn't walk him, he at least figured Terry wouldn't give him anything good to hit, so he wasn't as aggressive at the plate. I thought about that, and about my double that had been held up in the soggy grass.

I didn't care if I never saw rain again.

18

I DECIDED TO check into Mount Zion Hospital in San Francisco a couple of weeks after the World Series. If nothing else, I wanted to ease my mind—and, I suppose, everyone else's—that there was nothing wrong with me physically. Sure, I had collapsed a few times. But I always assumed that it was because I pushed my body to play it to the limit day after day, and nobody except me really knew what that took. It wasn't only that I played so often and was in the middle of so much. I also went out as if every game was a World Series. That was how I used to play back in Alabama and I never stopped.

Somehow, people thought that because I was able to do a lot of things I just had a natural talent—as if I had never worked hard to get where I did. When I'd hit a cutoff man in the right place, people would talk about my "natural" vision—instead of maybe realizing that I had planned before the ball was hit where I'd throw to. All that studying I had done of the Candlestick winds paid off. All the analyzing I had done of other hitters helped me in the field, and my studies of pitchers' habits helped me at bat and on base. The thing is, if everything I did had been just "natural," I probably never would have suffered from exhaustion. But a lot of thinking also went into how I played and what I did—and that, combined with the

189

day-in, day-out physical stresses, helped knock me off my feet.

In the quiet of my hospital room I had time to think. Where was I going? How long could I play? I had now played the equivalent of ten full seasons. And yet, I thought I could play another ten. Stan Musial was ten years older and still playing for the Cards. Ted Williams had retired at forty-one only a couple of years earlier. It occurred to me that if I lasted, I could be up there with them.

I was thirty-one years old. Except for the dizzy spells, my body had never betrayed me. I didn't drink or smoke. I always made certain I got the proper amount of rest. My idea of relaxing was to sit around in my pajamas and watch television. Because I knew how well I took care of myself, I strongly believed I could play for ten more years. I thought to myself, hey, I'm even stronger than Musial. I wondered whether I could handle centerfield for that long, though. It's tough on the legs.

Suddenly, I had become the old man of the Giants, the oldest everyday player. It seemed like only yesterday I was a teenager, with the great Joe DiMaggio as my idol. Instead, kids were now looking up to me. One of them was O. J. Simpson, whom I had met the year before, when he was a fourteen-year-old. I found out I was his idol under unusual circumstances.

I got a phone call at home from Lefty Gordon. He was a youth counselor at the Booker T. Washington Center. He asked me if I could straighten out a sensational athlete, a kid of fourteen who was about to end up in a lot of trouble with the law. The boy's name was O.J., and he was a member of a youth gang that had robbed a liquor store.

The police were waiting for O.J. when he came home after a dance. They already had his buddies and O.J. joined them in San Francisco's Juvenile Hall for the weekend. He was living with his mother because his parents were separated. She picked him up on Monday and brought him home. He thought his father would come over and give him a whipping, and he went right up to his room and fell asleep.

That's when I got there. I spoke to his mother downstairs in the living room and asked her if it would be all right for the boy to go out with me for a couple of hours. I didn't have a lecture in mind. I just thought that by showing him I cared about him, I might be able to help him. Maybe it sounds goody-goody, but I believe that kids are affected by their sports heroes and that someone in my position could make a difference.

When O.J. came down the stairs he didn't look excited. He didn't even seem surprised. I think he was nervous about what was coming. He didn't know what to expect. I asked him if he wanted to spend the afternoon with me. He nodded "Okay." He probably was expecting a lecture. Instead, we hopped into my car and I just did what I had planned to do that afternoon. I stopped at the cleaner's and then at an appliance store. I went over to a friend's house. And then I took O.J. home. No lecture. We just talked about a lot of different things—cars, baseball, football. He already was thinking about going to college in Utah to play football. I advised him not to. I told him to go to Los Angeles. He'd be closer to home and he'd be in an area with a big television market. If he was as great an athlete as I had heard, that would help him get his name around. The two hours we spent together were my way of showing O.J. what to do by giving him an example. I didn't want to set myself up as a god, just as someone who tried to do the right thing.

That included following doctor's orders. I had three days of tests at Mount Zion. I did a lot of reminiscing, lying there in bed. For some reason, when things weren't going well with me, or I was nervous, I used to think back to my early days in New York. Leo. Monte. The good old Polo Grounds. Before the 1962 season, it had been five years since I'd set foot inside the park that still contained some of my fondest memories. That first time, of course, I was in the visiting team's clubhouse.

The Mets were New York's team in the Polo Grounds now, their first year of existence. Casey was their manager. As the visiting team, we took batting practice last. I stayed behind on purpose until everyone else had gone on the field to hit. I never knew you could get such chills in an old ballpark. The nervousness and excitement increased as I walked alone down the steps to the field.

It surprised me that the playing field was in good condition, although no baseball had been played since we had gone. One thing was different and it bothered me. The Chesterfield's cigarettes sign—the "h" would light up for a hit and the first "e" would light up for an error—high on the stands in left center was throwing off a glare. That glare had never been there before when I played for the Giants. I figured that meant they had either raised or lowered the sign for the Mets' first year. It was something to think about and remember.

That first day of June in 1962, New York was a different city.

To try to eradicate urban decay in Brooklyn and revitalize the city, a huge tract of land was going to be developed near a landfill, with schools and low-income housing. There was going to be more pay for teachers at the City University. And of course there now was a baseball team cavorting in the Giants' old place. They were the Mets, and they were going to lose a record 120 games.

This is what some people were talking about that day when we invaded New York. The Number 1 best-seller was *Calories Don't Count,* while the fiction leader was *Ship of Fools.* People also were reading Richard M. Nixon's *Six Crises,* and *Franny and Zooey* by J. D. Salinger. On Broadway, *My Fair Lady* was in its final weeks, but *A Funny Thing Happened on the Way to the Forum* was going strong, along with *The Sound of Music.* In the movie houses, *El Cid* was big box office, while Joan Collins and Bob Hope were on-screen in *The Road to Cairo*. At night, television viewers were playing along with *To Tell the Truth*, a panel show with Bud Collyer as host, or *The Price is Right*, with Bill Cullen. A blurb said that Ben Casey was jeopardizing his career to perform a brain operation on a boy. The *Huntley-Brinkley Report* news show went on at 6:45 P.M.

Baseball was no longer the same, either. As I've already mentioned, there were two more clubs in the National League: the Mets and the Houston Colt .45's. The leading batters in baseball were Dick Groat of the Pirates and Manny Jiminez of Kansas City. Al Kaline was leading the American League in RBI's, while Tommy Davis was pacing the Nationals. And I was leading the majors in homers.

More than 43,000 fans showed up for our first game back. Most of them were on hand for batting practice, calling for me to come up and blast a few into the stands. First, I went into the infield and took a few turns at each position. Then I got my bat and saw my old teammate, Johnny Antonelli, tossing batting practice. Antonelli was retired now, but had come in for the game.

The crowd hushed when I stepped into the cage. I was swinging for the fences, to be sure, but my first five hits were line drives.

"Shucks, I can't hit you, Johnny," I shouted out to the mound.

Antonelli smiled and grooved me one.

I knocked it into the upper deck. Then I belted one over the roof, and then connected with a drive that sailed 450 feet away into the left center stands near the bleachers. The crowd went crazy. Boy, it was great to be back.

The crowd went nuts in the game, too, when I belted my league-leading seventeenth homer in the third inning. We sent the poor Mets to their twelfth straight loss. That was okay. When their Mets were up, no matter what the score, the crowd would go crazy. Little rallies, such as Ball 3 on a batter, would stir them. Somehow, it seemed all right, though, if I was the one getting hits against them.

The next day I hit another homer as we swept a doubleheader.

Considering my return, I remember saying to an old friend, "It's wonderful to be back. The saddest part about going away was that I was just approaching my peak when I had to leave."

Was I being wistful? Was I leaving something there unsaid—that maybe it would have all been nicer in New York?

I admitted some things, things that have always been hard for me to say. I explained to my buddy, "For a while they seemed to expect me to hit a home run every time I got to bat. After a while they got to realize others are being paid to get me out, and everyone treats me swell now."

So did the Mets' fans. I hit Number 19 as the Giants, with Marichal pitching, swept the four-game series.

My appearance caused Arthur Daley of the *New York Times* to remark, "The center-field turf at the Polo Grounds looks normal this weekend for the first time in almost five years. Willie Mays has come home."

I hit pretty well on all my visits to the Polo Grounds. I even got a couple of home runs off Roger Craig. I started hitting against the Mets when they came to Candlestick. Early in the season I got two homers in one game and we beat them in the bottom of the 10th. My second homer came with a man on and got them, 7–6. But I did have trouble with the Mets one day at Candlestick. I was on second base and Cepeda was up. I took a big lead off the base but kept an eye on Elio Chacon, their second baseman, for a pickoff play. I knew that Chacon would just love to put the tag on me. The year before, when he was with Cincinnati, I had spiked him on a hard slide into second, and he had needed a bunch of stitches. Now, Craig tried to catch me leaning toward third base, but I slid head first back to second. Chacon started throwing punches, and Craig came over to help him. Before he got there, Cepeda rushed out and Craig stopped dead. It was the first fight I got into in the major leagues. The funny thing was, Chacon claimed he had started swinging because I tried to spike him. How could I spike him with a head-first slide?

Chacon hadn't forgotten that I'd spiked him, and I guess Craig hadn't forgotten that I hit a couple of homers off him. For that matter, Cepeda hadn't forgotten that I had come to his aid in 1958 when he was a rookie, and now he was returning the favor. We were playing the Pirates in Pittsburgh when pitchers Ruben Gomez and Bob Friend got into a beanball war. Batters were dropping like flies. Everybody was heckling from the bench. Danny Murtaugh, the Pirates' manager, led the Pirates, and Rigney screamed back at him. Now I again had a feeling something bad was going to happen soon.

When Gomez came to bat, Friend sailed one over his head. It was a payback pitch. Earlier, when Friend was up, Gomez had knocked him down. But this was all Cepeda had to see. In situations like this the Latin ball players stuck together. They really looked out for each other. I spotted Cepeda going to the rack and grabbing a bat. That was not the thing to do. I jumped off the bench and tackled Orlando from behind and pinned him to the ground. Orlando was one of the biggest guys I ever played with, six two and 210 pounds, and he was struggling to get up. I needed Hank Sauer, another big man, to help me keep Orlando down. The next thing I knew, three cops surrounded us. I have always felt that anything that goes wrong "between the lines"—on the field—should be settled by the players and umps themselves. As wrong as it was for Cepeda to grab a bat, it was just as wrong for cops to be on the field when players were brawling. Somehow, we've always managed to settle these things among ourselves. Players can deal with other players, but not necessarily with the police at the same time.

So there I was trying to keep Cepeda locked in place, when I looked up and saw a cop with a nightstick in his hand. Now I knew there could be big trouble. Sauer, with one knee on Cepeda, looked up at the cop and said, "If you hit him, then you got to take on both of us." The policeman backed off. The worst was over. Order was restored and the game continued with no other incidents. Orlando came up to me when it was over.

"I could have done something really bad, Willie," he said. "You kept me from doing it. Thanks very much."

Those first five years we were together, I always heard stories that we didn't like each other and that we were feuding. That wasn't the case. We had no battles. Chico had great talent and I pointed that out to management in our first spring training together in 1958. I even took time to help him. I knew he was someone who could help our club.

In a spring-training game against the Indians he was playing first base. There was a runner on first when a sinking line drive came straight out to me. Those are the most difficult ones to catch because you have no angle on the ball to tell whether it will sink or sail. Instinct is the key. As soon as I saw the ball coming I charged in. I caught it with a shoestring catch at full speed. I didn't hesitate once I caught the ball. I threw it to first to try to double up the runner. But the throw caught Cepeda by surprise. It hit him on the shoulder. "What happened?" I asked him later.

"I was watching you with my mouth open," he said. "After you made the catch I never figured you could throw it, too."

That hospital stay gave me the chance to reflect some more on our '62 season, too. Some people thought that we had not so much won the pennant as that the Dodgers had lost it. We had backed in, some believed. But to me, backing in is winning something while you're losing. We had to win at the end and we did—seven of our last 10 games. It was great that the Dodgers were losing, sure. But if we had been losing, too, then we never would have made it. Then we beat them in the playoffs—and on their own field. You remember those big games, but lots of things happened during the season between the two great rivals.

I'll never forget one time early in the year when Sanford was pitching for us, Ed Bailey was catching, and the ump behind the plate was Chris Pelekoudas. The Dodgers had a runner on third. The ball was hit in that direction. Davenport grabbed it and started to throw the ball home. Then he stopped because he spotted Bailey running toward first base to back up a throw there. So Davenport held the ball while the runner on third charged home.

Sanford was going crazy on the mound.

"Throw it!" he yelled.

"To who? Pelekoudas?" screamed back Davenport.

I know Sanford never forgot that. Pitchers don't forget any bad things that happen to them.

In 1954 the Cards' pitcher Harvey Haddix was having a good year. But at the Polo Grounds I caught one of his change-ups and I hit it so hard I've always thought it might have been the longest ball I ever hit. It sailed into the upper deck in left center, at least 460 feet away. Because it was a change-up, all the power from the shot came from me. Haddix never forgot and I didn't see one of his change-ups again for years.

Five years went by and Haddix was pitching for Pittsburgh. It was in Forbes Field and we were losing by a run but had a man on when I got up. Haddix was stubborn. He decided after all those years to try another change-up. I still remembered the other one, though. I jumped on him and sent it over the fence and we won the game. Then, a month later, he was pitching against us again and the game was tied in the bottom of the ninth. I came up with two outs.

Haddix called time and told his catcher to come to the mound. Haddix told him he wanted to walk me intentionally. I could see the catcher, Smokey Burgess, was arguing with Haddix. Then Murtaugh, their manager, got into the discussion. With two out and nobody on, you don't walk the winning run to first base. At least, that's what they were telling him. Then the umpire, Larry Goetz, got into the discussion to see what the delay was all about. The catcher told him that Haddix intended to walk me.

"Look at him," said Haddix, pointing to me. "He knows he's going to hit me and I know he's going to hit me, so I'm going to walk him."

But Murtaugh wasn't buying that.

"What happens if Mays steals second?" said Murtaugh. "Then we're in trouble, real trouble."

Haddix insisted on walking me, and I got to first base. Cepeda was up. On the second pitch, I stole second. Cepeda swung at the next pitch, hit a single, and I ran home with the winning run. I scored a lot of runs and drove in a lot in 1962. I had the best year of my career in both departments —141 RBI's, 130 scored. Best of all, we won the pennant.

One thing still haunted me about the Series. I could still see myself running to third on a triple as the tying run scored, instead of being stuck at second base because the watered-down outfield grass held my hit to a double.

I didn't know what 1963 would bring as I waited for the doctors' reports. It was good news. The doctors wrote: "Willie is in superior physical condition. It was a difficult season, very trying, and he is aware of his responsibility. Mays had a comprehensive physical examination that included all the routine tests. All yielded normal findings and his condition is perfectly healthy."

Indeed. I had just played 162 games, a number matched by only four other players in the National League. For the ninth straight year, I had played in more than 150 games. I led all outfielders in putouts with 429. With the majors-leading 49 home runs I had slugged, I already had 368 for my career—more than halfway toward the "unreachable" total of 714 slugged by Babe Ruth.

19

RESTING DURING THE OFF-SEASON after my discharge from Mount Zion, I realized I had wasted a lot in the course of my career. I don't mean talent. I mean I had given away time—maybe by not always being with people I should have been with. And I had also given away too much money. Everything had come quick and easy for me. I had spent money foolishly. I had lent it to people I thought were friends. I'd spent too much money on trivial things and never thought about the future.

With the coming of the 1963 season, I thought a lot about these things and I resolved to try to pass on some of my acquired wisdom to the younger players. Remember, hard to believe as it may be, I had already been playing twice as long as the average major-leaguer. That's a fact of life it's hard to get across to kids—that there actually is life *after* baseball, and that if you are not careful, whatever you do after your baseball career probably won't pay you as well and you probably won't have as much fun.

I was lonely, too, during those dreary winter months. I had left my wife, and my son, Michael, was now living in New York with his mother. I could see him only a few times a year. I wanted to have someone with me all the time. I had the sense that I was peaking as a player, and now it was

time to look for something more out of life. This was the
thought always lurking in the back of my mind—the back,
but hardly ever in the front. Maybe all this came up because
of my failed marriage. It turned out to be a mistake. Maybe
I should have listened to friends who told me not to marry
an older woman. The truth was, I was infatuated with a
beautiful older woman who had been married twice before.
One of her husbands had been a doctor, the other, as I've
said, a singer with the Ink Spots, one of the biggest singing
groups in those days.

Going through a divorce put an awful strain on me. The
court hearings were going on during the '63 season. I would
appear at court in the morning and then rush out to Candlestick to play a game. Because of the winds, our games
would start early and I'd have to leave the court before
noon. Still, I'd get to Candlestick barely in time to put on a
uniform and play without warming up. One day I was late,
and it cost us a game against the Dodgers. They hit a ball
over the centerfielder's head and it rolled to the fence for a
hit and knocked in a run. Durocher was coaching for the
Dodgers and he said later that I would have caught it if I
was playing.

A couple of days later, we were on a road trip in Chicago.
I was alone in my hotel room and I started to cry. I couldn't
sleep. I got out of bed and called Dark. He wondered what
was wrong.

"I have the shakes," I told him. He ordered me to get up
to his room.

When I got there, Doc Bowman had arrived, too. He gave
me a couple of sleeping pills.

"Sleep here tonight in that other bed, Willie," Dark told
me. We talked for a little while, and then I fell asleep.

My son, Michael, was three years old. I was upset at the
thought of losing him. But how could I raise him with my
life being what it was—ball playing? That was the only
reason I allowed him to stay with Marghuerite. I guess I

should have put up a fight. Still, I thought a young boy should be with his mother. When he got older, though, he began to spend more time with me.

No wonder my financial state was a mess at the time of my divorce. I had awful income-tax problems and very nearly filed for bankruptcy. I was talked out of it by a San Francisco banker named Jake Shemano, who helped get me organized again. I couldn't even begin to imagine how I had gotten into the predicament, me, a guy making $90,000 a year and now almost broke. What had done it was bad investments, such as real estate I had no business getting into, or restaurants, the quick way to find your way to the soup kitchen. It wasn't that bad, but couple these awful deals with my spending too much money. I had never checked with my wife on things she bought. Over the years I had borrowed against my salary from the Giants, and now my team wanted the money back. My actual income out of my $90,000 salary came to $35,000.

For the 1963 season, Stoneham was paying me $105,000. He wanted me to be the highest-paid ball player. Mantle had signed for $100,000, and Horace wanted to top that. As far as I know, it was also the highest salary anyone in baseball had ever earned. Maybe that was the reason Cepeda held out that spring. He was getting half as much, maybe. He had had a good year in 1962 and figured he was worth more than that. But his strategy didn't sit too well with Dark. In fact, Alvin got really miffed.

It wasn't so long ago, but in those days managers felt that no one should hold out, and if anyone did, the manager took it personally. So Alvin held a press conference one day. It was very unusual for Alvin to put Orlando down. In a sense, he actually said that Orlando wasn't worth the money he was holding out for.

Dark isn't diplomatic. He never was. The way he says things can offend you. His big announcement at this press conference was that he had been keeping a chart on what he called his key production system. You could call it clutch hits. He had been rating us on a point system. According to Dark's points, I graded out on top along with Davenport—but Cepeda was way down on the list in coming through with a key hit. Chico must have screamed when he heard about that. I didn't blame him. All he had done for us was hit around .300 and knock in around 100 runs every year. Alvin was wrong in pointing a finger. It seemed obvious to me what he was trying to do—act for management, show Cepeda he really wasn't worth all the money he was trying to get, and force him to come to camp.

Soon afterward I had my own troubles. I got off to the worst start of my career. I didn't know what .300, or even .280, looked like. But a few days before my thirty-second birthday, they honored me on Willie Mays Night at the Polo Grounds. My eyes were watery all night, from the time I stepped into the old place until I saw more than forty-nine thousand people cheering for me. I really wanted to do something special, but the most I could manage was a double as the Mets beat us.

That night I met a couple of old friends. Before I had left New York, I had developed a special relationship with two members of the Giants' board of directors. One was Mrs. Charles Shipman Payson, the other was Donald Grant. She was the greatest baseball fan I ever met. When we left New York she was very sad, and she always vowed that one day she'd bring a team back to New York. She could do it, too. She was a Whitney and her brother had been our ambassador to England. Donald Grant was also a wonderful fan. He used to advise her on business matters, and the two of them helped bring baseball back to New York. Now she was the owner of the team and he was the chairman of the board of the Mets.

Before the game, Grant and Bill Shea spoke to the crowd about me. Shea was the lawyer who had helped push the new stadium through as well as bring in a National League team, and New York was going to name the stadium for him. He gave me a gold key to the city.

Then Shea said something that thrilled and embarrassed me, but got the fans off their seats: "We want to know, Mr. Stoneham, Horace Stoneham, president of the Giants, when are you going to give us back our Willie Mays?"

Then Grant spoke. He said to me: "They could only love you more if you were a New York Met. If that is tampering, they can sue me."

My slow start continued into a slow season. Still, they voted me onto the All-Star team for the tenth straight year. I was in an All-Star groove even if I wasn't doing so hot in the regular season. I went 1 for 3, scored two runs and drove home two. I also became the first player in All-Star history to steal two bases in a game. My All-Star Game average for the ten years was .417. I had played 14 games because from 1959 to 1962 there were two games a year. I scored 15 runs, got 20 hits in 48 at bats, and drove in eight while hitting two homers.

But I wasn't hitting when they needed production from me. In the second game of the year we lost a good-looking rookie named Jim Ray Hart. He got hit by a pitch in the shoulder. It seemed that most of the teams in the league were throwing at us—something that seemed to be happening as a result of our having won the pennant the year before. Dark's view of this didn't help him with our fans. He felt our pitchers shouldn't retaliate against the other teams' hitters—only against their pitchers.

With things going badly, Dark tried a number of tactics, including clubhouse talks. A lot of them left us shaking our heads. He brought in stuff that just didn't belong in the clubhouse. Who cared if he supported Barry Goldwater?

He used to bring religion in, too. One time he said that Jesus was the only man in the history of the world who was perfect. Maybe Dark was searching, reaching out to us. But he didn't convert anyone to his politics or his religion, and, actually, no one took him seriously when he started that kind of talk.

On the field, he used to get steamed up if he thought you weren't trying. He didn't want a reason. One game, he benched Cepeda, which ate at Orlando, who sat on the bench really angry at everyone. Late in the game Dark called on Orlando as a pinch hitter. Chico had been waiting all game to do something and really wanted to show Dark. Instead, he hit the ball right back to the pitcher. He was so disgusted at failing that he didn't bother to run to first. That set off Alvin. In the clubhouse after the game, he screamed at Cepeda in front of everybody. I was watching Orlando. I knew that with his temper he might just explode and haul off at Dark. But Orlando kept it to himself. I wondered, though, if Dark was losing his ability to communicate with his players.

Soon we had our first blowup. We were playing the Cubs in Chicago. It was the bottom of the eighth and we had a six-run lead. A ball was hit toward me, going over my head. Who knows, if the game had been closer I might have chased it back against the wall, taken a chance. Maybe in the back of my mind I thought about the big lead we had and said to myself, "Take it easy. Don't get hurt on a ball that can't hurt your team." And maybe I just didn't hustle after it the way I should have. Anyway, the ball hit the wall and went for a double. That hit started a rally. They tied the game, and then they won it in extra innings. Dark snapped at me later in the clubhouse. I snapped back. I knew I should have gone after the ball as I always do. But when he raised his voice, I just thought it was unfair. I mean, I never dogged it, and here he started to make an issue out of one hit in front of everybody. We didn't talk for a few days. Then the issue just went away and things were back to normal.

The All-Star Game must have revived me. I started getting around on the ball in July. I got a couple of homers against the Mets, then had another big game when I scored the winning run against them—I walked, got to second on a groundout, stole third, tagged up on a short fly and slid home safely. Then the next game I made a shoestring catch and saved us two runs. I continued hitting into August, and finally got my average up to .300. One day late in August, I also got a big hit off the Cardinals and Curt Simmons—my 400th home run.

The pressure to get a streak going, to try to get us back in the race, got to me again. By September I was feeling tired. And then it happened again, just like the year before in Cincinnati: I collapsed during a game. We were playing the Cubs in Candlestick and I came to bat with the bases loaded in the fourth inning. I swung at the first pitch and fouled it off. I must have put everything into that swing. I never swung again that game. I dropped to one knee with that dizzy feeling. I couldn't believe it was happening again. Doc Bowman was out there with the smelling salts. I got up, groggy, and walked back slowly to the clubhouse. Once again I went to the hospital. Once again they told me it was fatigue.

A few days later I came back to finish the season. I wound up with my highest batting average in three years, .314. I hit 38 homers and drove in 103 runs and scored 115. To me, leading the league in any one category was never as important or significant as finishing in the top 10 in a lot of categories. It was the first time since my first full season in 1954 that I wasn't leading the league in some category. But once again, I was among the leaders in just about everything. Only McCovey and Hank Aaron finished ahead in homers. Hank also beat me out for runs scored. I played in more games, 157, than anyone else on the team.

Willie's 1963 Numbers

G	AB	H	2B	3B	HR	R	RBI	BB	SO	SB	BA	SA
157	596	187	32	7	38	115	103	66	83	8	.314	.582

We finished third, 11 games behind the Dodgers. Only a year ago we'd been the champs. We should have done better. Knowing that bothered me most of all.

20

I GOT A GOOD WORKING OVER from the umpires.

For the first time in my life, I brought the lineup card to home plate. Toward the end of May, Dark had named me captain of the 1964 Giants. We hadn't had a captain in eight years—not since Alvin himself had been captain.

It took a lot of guts on Dark's part to name me. I admired his courage for doing it. I was the first black captain in the history of baseball.

We were in Candlestick, and I handed the plate umpire, Ed Sudol, the lineup card. My first act as captain.

"Okay, twenty-four, let's go over the ground rules," said Sudol, enjoying this. "If the ball hits the scoreboard and sticks in one of the slots, what do we give the batter?"

I laughed. "Give him the scoreboard," I said.

"Any of your pitchers spit on the ball, captain?" Sudol asked me.

Of course, I told him the truth: "No, sir. We have a team rule that nobody breaks. None of the pitchers ever spit on the ball."

"Now, you're sure of that?" said Sudol.

"Oh, sure," I told him. "The pitcher spits in the glove and then puts the ball there."

Things weren't quite so funny around the clubhouse, though. A few days before he approached me with the offer

of the captaincy, Dark was in the middle of a racial controversy over some things he had been quoted as saying in a
book written by Jackie Robinson. Dark's most damaging
comments were these:

> There are a lot of people in the south who feel that
> everyone's a human being but that right now the social
> question is being handled a bit too fast. The majority of
> people in the south, especially the Christian people I have
> associated with, have really and truly liked the colored
> people. As for socializing with them on different levels,
> there is a line drawn in the south, and I think it's going
> to be a number of years before this is corrected, or it may
> never be corrected. . . .
> Being a Christian, I feel this will be solved one day in
> the south. But they're rushing it a little too quick right
> now. As for opening up the thoughts of older people
> down there, I don't think it would help at all because the
> older people in the south have taken care of the Negroes.
> They feel they have a responsibility to take care of them.
> That's my opinion of how things are.

I knew what Dark was saying. I was from the South, and
so was he. I understood what he was talking about. But it
seemed that nobody else did—or wanted to. The press, the
community, Stoneham—everybody was furious at Dark the
day he called me into his office.

"Willie, I'm making you captain of the Giants."

I was filled with admiration for Dark just then. Sure, it
crossed my mind that the timing was strange, that it looked
as if he was naming me just to get off the hook for the
things he'd said. But I sincerely felt he was naming me the
captain because he thought I deserved it. After all, I was off
to the best start of my career. The club was in first place.
He wasn't making a desperate move.

There was something else going on, and I thought I could
help if I was captain. He was losing communication with

the players. Why shouldn't I help him? He had helped me
the first year I joined the Giants. Dark, Stanky, Lockman—
three white guys from the South. They all had made it easier
for me in 1951.

I didn't know what changes my being captain would
bring. All I knew was that I was on a hot streak and so was
the club. I had always been a streak hitter, but this one
topped them all. In the first 17 games I banged 11 home
runs and was hitting .481. My slugging average was over
1.000. I had more total bases than times at bat. I was batting a thousand in slugging.

Because both Cepeda and McCovey also had had a good
spring, I felt we had a good chance to get back the pennant.
Chico switched to a 40-ounce bat, one of the heaviest I ever
saw. He claimed it helped his swing. The way he was hitting
in spring training, I wasn't going to tell him he was wrong.
He had changed a lot over the years, becoming more of a
team player, losing his temper less. One time he was at bat
and we needed someone to get on base to get a rally going.
He got himself hit with a pitch and that helped us win the
game. When it was over, I told him it was something he
wouldn't have done earlier in his career. He would simply
have gotten out of the way.

"It's something I learned, Willie," he said. "And if they
had let me alone, it's something I would have learned two
years earlier."

He had had a lot to learn, especially the outfield. He'd
come up as a first baseman. But after McCovey came up the
following year, someone had to move to the outfield. That's
when Dark decided to put Cepeda in rightfield, a tough spot
to learn. When that didn't work out, Chico was switched to
left. He wasn't that good an outfielder, and he knew it. It
bothered his concentration, and then you could see it carry
over to his hitting. It affected his personality, too, and he
became moody. He and Dark argued a few times.

Cepeda needed constant talking to. One time early in

1964, he heard boos when he came up to bat in Candlestick. He had been slumping, although I knew he had a bad knee, which was constantly swollen. That affected his swing, and then his timing went bad. Only yesterday he'd been hearing the cheers. But I know it's not easy to grow up. A person needs somebody to help him. I had always wanted to. I had a feeling that one day, when I retired, Chico would be the big guy on the team.

But first, he had a few things to learn. I talked to him from time to time. He had to learn to control his temper and he had to learn how to set an example. I had had to learn these same things, on and off the field. If you have the right attitude, the younger players follow your lead. It's not easy to get to this point. It takes a long time, I found out, but it's not really how old you are, it's the kind of ball player and person you are. It was all a matter of growing up, and that's what Chico had to do.

Because of my big start, I was getting most of the attention. Could I finish at .400? No. No one could hit .400 anymore. Ted Williams had done it in 1941, when night baseball still was practically unknown. I was playing a 162-game schedule, along with traveling cross-country. When Ted played, he had had only a one-hour time difference on his longest trips. He was in Boston and he'd go to New York, Washington, Philadelphia, Cleveland, Detroit, Chicago, St. Louis. By 1964 baseball life had come to mean checking into a hotel at three in the morning. Even when we played at home, the schedule was strange. We played night games on Tuesday and Friday, with day games the rest of the time, wind or no wind.

I knew I wasn't going to stay over .400 the whole season. The average started to drop in Houston. We had a standing joke in the clubhouse there. The Astrodome was still a year from being finished and Colts Stadium, where we played, had awful lighting. The gag was that it would be great to play a night game there when they finally turned on the lights. It was the worst stadium in the league. We took only one of four games there, and my hitting streak stopped after 20 games. I did manage to hit two out of the park in one game, a game Marichal was pitching.

Before it started he told me, "Willie, you owe me two home runs—one for tonight, and one because you didn't hit one for me the last game I pitched."

When this one was over and I had hit my two, I told him, okay, I hit for him, now he owes me a streak.

"Nah," he said, "I think you got a spy in centerfield. He was waving the signals to you."

That Houston series was part of a long slump we all went through. With rain-outs in other cities we were forced to play doubleheaders. Now we were losing, and we were tired. Dark was getting tough to live with. He was always snapping at everybody.

It was just before a game with the Phillies at Candlestick that he called the clubhouse meeting in which he told everyone he was making me captain. I went out and hit two homers. I got another one the next night. But after we lost three straight to the Pirates, Dark started to hear the charges of racism again. People ridiculed his choosing me as captain. Some journalists wrote that he had named me to cover his backside. Someone even suggested that the captaincy was too much pressure for me—especially since I had been rested for two games against the Mets. Of course, when else would you want to rest me than against the worst team in baseball?

Dark met with me and again asked me whether I believed the things that people were saying—that I was a captain in name only and that it was just a public relations move? I knew it wasn't true. The year before, Dark had set up a players' committee on the team and he made me chairman. He felt that there are times players would prefer to discuss some things without bringing him in. I told Dark I was still with him.

Overall, he still seemed to be making the right moves. One that I thought would help bring us the pennant was bringing in Duke Snider. The year before Duke had been with the Mets. Now he was getting up in years, but he could still drive the ball, and he was a left-handed batter. If this was going to be a close race, I thought, I wanted a guy like Duke around.

By the middle of June we had gotten back into first place with a big road trip. Snider started it by hitting the winning homer in St. Louis. Then I hit one in the eighth inning the next day off Curt Simmons. Johnny Mize used to say, "It's better to win a close game than a blowout." That way, you're not too high for the next game and you're concentrating. But I was concerned that we weren't hitting enough.

On the trip, we returned to New York. It was different now. It was as if the Mets fans no longer needed a connection to the old days. They had their own stadium this time, Shea Stadium, and the crowd acted differently. I could feel it when I went out. No more friendly Polo Grounds, no more fans yelling for us to do great. Now, they were pulling for their own team. I still got a big cheer when my name was announced, but I had the feeling they weren't as anxious for me to do well. If I did, it meant I was hurting their team.

Al Jackson saw me before the game and asked how I was hitting.

"Bad," I told him. "Throw me a curveball and help me out."

"Sure," he said. "But it won't help you any. I'll throw it behind you."

The Mets beat us the first two games, and then we had a doubleheader on Sunday. It was the longest doubleheader anyone had ever seen. We won the opener, but the second game . . . well, it lasted 23 innings and took more than seven hours.

At first, it was sort of fun—the 11th inning, the 13th, the

14th. Then parents started to get worried. They had sent
their kids off to a baseball game, and now it was about nine
o'clock at night and they hadn't come home yet. The New
York City Transit Authority started to get flooded with
calls. Missing persons bureaus at the police department
were asked whether they'd found a boy wearing a Mets cap.
The Shea Stadium food concessionaire, Harry M. Stevens,
started to run out of food by the ninth inning of the second
game. It was dark outside and the lights were on. Thousands of people hadn't eaten since lunchtime. Little by little
they started to leave. Those who did missed a Giants triple
play in extra innings that stopped a Mets rally. When it
finally ended, another part of lovable, losing Mets history
was safe.

I wound up playing shortstop for three innings, and I also
ended up so tired I could hardly swing the bat as the game
wore on. I began it with a 35-ounce bat and used a 31-
ounce bat on my last time up in the 23rd inning. Ed Sudol
was working home plate and he looked at it and said,
"What is that, a Little League bat?"

I couldn't move out of bed the next morning. Finally I
got up at noon. I wasn't going anywhere, though. I called
for room service.

"There's going to be a delay, sir. The Giants are here and
everyone seems to be eating in their rooms."

We didn't have many enjoyable days after that. In late
July, when we were getting into a groove and getting ready
for a pennant run, Dark's name hit the papers again. This
time it seemed even more serious.

Stan Isaacs, a talented writer for Long Island's *Newsday*,
one of the country's largest suburban papers, had gotten a
long interview with Dark. The conversation got around to
players and styles and, ultimately, managing black and His-
panic players. Dark said some extraordinary things. Isaacs,
a dogged as well as sensitive writer, felt that what Dark had
to say, and believed, was so important that it had to be

recorded. So Isaacs wrote two columns, in which Dark was quoted as saying:

> We have trouble because we have so many Spanish-speaking and Negro players on the team. They are just not able to perform up to the white ballplayer when it comes to mental alertness. You can't make most Negro and Spanish players have the pride in their team that you can get from white players. And they just aren't as sharp mentally. They aren't able to adjust to situations because they don't have that mental alertness.
>
> One of the biggest things is that you can't make them subordinate themselves to the best interest of the team. You don't find pride in them that you get in the white player. You don't know how hard we've tried to make a team player, a hustling ballplayer, out of Orlando. But nothing has worked for long . . . he doesn't sacrifice himself. I'd have to say he's giving out only 70 percent.
>
> Stoneham won't trade Cepeda or Willie McCovey. They know it and they know they'll get paid well if their averages are good.

After the two columns ran, I had to put down an uprising. Practically every one of the black and Latin players came to my hotel room for a meeting. I could see the anger in their eyes. But I knew I had to keep everyone calm. Not only that, I had to get them back into a groove. We had a pennant to win. Instead, this team was ready to fall apart. I knew that we'd now have to respond to the news media.

I told the players that I thought, and they knew, that Dark had treated them fairly. Forget what he said in the story, what was he like when it mattered? Then I tried to make them understand we could win the pennant with Dark as manager. Finally, I told them what I thought was most important: Don't ask for Dark's scalp now. When you change managers during the season, like we did in 1960, nobody wins. And anyway, I told them, Dark wouldn't be back the next year.

We wound up missing the pennant by only three games. It came down to a terrific fight—the Cards won, the Reds and Phils tied a game back, we came in fourth, and the Braves finished fifth, only five games out of first.

I had won the home-run title again with 47. Although I had that big start, my average fell under .300 for the first time since 1956. But I led the league in slugging average and once again I played in more games than anyone else on the team.

Willie's 1964 Numbers

G	AB	H	2B	3B	HR	R	RBI	BB	SO	SB	BA	SA
157	578	171	21	9	47	121	111	82	72	19	.296	.607

As everyone expected, at the end of the season Dark was gone. Before he left, he said, "Willie Mays is the Giants."

21

NOBODY EVER KNEW that I couldn't throw during the 1965 season. Yet, I had 13 assists, my highest since 1958. But early in '65 I slipped in a game at Atlanta and tore muscles in my shoulder and leg. I could tape the leg and run and you couldn't tell that there was anything wrong with me, but if my shoulder was wrapped, I couldn't throw.

The first thing we decided to do was keep it quiet. Before each game, the trainer would rub some hot stuff into my shoulder. That seemed to loosen it a little and relieve the pain, at least temporarily, which allowed me to throw a little. During pregame practice I would cut loose with two or three throws, to third and home plate. The throws were strong and accurate, and I did this the entire year without any other team knowing that I couldn't make those throws once the game began.

Yet I continued to cut down runners on the bases. A big reason for that had to be because I outsmarted some of them. There'd be two runners on, and the guy pulling into second with a double never thought I'd throw there. Or I might throw behind a runner when he didn't expect it and catch him taking it easy.

In 1965 I had my biggest home-run year—52, a Giants record. We also made a big run at the pennant under our new manager, Herman Franks.

Before Herman was hired, Stoneham asked me about him. I had known Franks for a long time, as long as I'd known anyone in major league baseball. I not only knew him as a Giants coach, but also had played for him in the Caribbean League. He could speak Spanish and he had a good relationship with the Latin ball players. I told Horace that Herman would relieve the tension that had cropped up on the club among the Latins, blacks and white ball players. Stoneham agreed. Then he asked me to go beyond being a ball player. He said I could fill a role as a sort of assistant manager. He wanted me to give advice to the younger players and watch over the older ones. As a captain under Dark I had had the title but not the job. Now I had it all the way.

Herman Franks was a completely different sort of manager. Alvin was not easy to talk to or even approach. With Herman, you felt the guy would make time for you. Everyone appreciated this very quickly. As for me, every day he'd say something to me. Not only about strategy—we discussed our personal lives as well. I began an investment deal with Herman that would help me during my retirement. Herman also encouraged the players, especially the younger ones, to talk to me. That knocked down barriers that might have existed because of the difference in our ages, experience, and salary. The big difference for me between 1964 and 1965 was that Herman consulted with me, which meant that I did more than hand the lineup card to the umpires.

The way we finished was a tribute to Herman. The players wanted to play for him. He got a good deal of mileage out of the club under very tough conditions. Cepeda had a problem with his knee, but it didn't come around after he had an operation on it. He was hardly able to play for us. Our pitching became inconsistent, and Herman made a deal for Warren Spahn, who was forty-four years old, to try to help us. On top of this, Herman had problems with Jim Ray

Hart. Hart broke curfew, and Franks not only fined Jim, he suspended him. I tried to talk to him. Jim needed confidence and someone who wouldn't scold him. Some of the players were disappointed in him, and Jim felt it. But they were concerned that he might be becoming an alcoholic and was hurting the team. I remembered that Dusty Rhodes had been a hard drinker, but he hadn't been a problem. I took the same approach with Jim Ray that Leo had taken with Dusty.

Hart was from a very small town in North Carolina where just about everybody did a lot of drinking. He probably never thought about it, and without knowing it, he just picked up the habit of drinking. Jim was the best guy you could ever want in the clubhouse and I was convinced that I could help him with the problem. I wanted him to admit that he had a problem. So I tried to get him to talk about it.

"I just got to have a little every now and then," he told me. I didn't know it was that bad.

"If I don't drink some, then I get all tight and nervous," he said.

I thought for a while about how to handle this, and then I came up with something. I told him, "If you play for me for six days, I'll give you one day." I meant that every Monday morning, if he stopped by my locker, I'd give him a bottle. We shook hands on the deal.

At first, Herman thought the arrangement was strange. But as far as I was concerned, it was going to work out, that we just had to play this little game with Hart. I reminded Herman that Leo used to give Rhodes some spending money, and it wasn't for the movies. So Herman went along with my idea.

Old Crow would do the trick, I figured. I bought a case and kept it in my locker. Next Monday, Jim came by and I gave him a bottle. He came by every Monday. He never lied to me all season. He was ready to play every day. No one played in more games for the Giants. He was in 160 and had a good season with 96 RBI's, 23 homers, and a .299 batting average.

When the season was over I took five hundred-dollar bills out of my pocket and handed them to him. I told him, "It's for telling me the truth and playing every day."

That money came out of my pocket, but I thought it was well worth it. Hart hit 33 homers the next season—because, I'm convinced, I showed him I believed in him.

The situation was typical of my relations with Herman. He let me do things my way. He allowed me to play the game at my own pace. I knew, for example, that late in the season I'd probably get tired. So I worked out a plan according to which I'd come out of a game in the late innings if we were far enough ahead—or too far behind. I'd save myself three innings here and there and they added up. Actually, I would have preferred staying in bed on a day off instead of coming to the ballpark. When I'm at the park, I never get any real rest because I'm always working myself up about the game. If I stay home, I turn on the stereo or television or maybe just doze off. At the park, you'd think I was in the game, the way I play from the bench.

Earlier in the season I'd appointed Hal Lanier the infield captain. That may not seem to be much of a job, but I had a reason. If I felt a pitcher needed a breather between pitches, I'd signal Lanier, our second baseman, to call time and walk to the mound and make some small talk. Even though he was only twenty-two years old, nobody resented his actions. They knew it was coming from me.

By the middle of August we were fighting—who else?— the Dodgers for first place. Sandy Koufax was in the middle of his five-year Hall of Fame stretch, and he was the most spectacular pitcher in baseball, along with our own Juan Marichal and the Cards' Bob Gibson. The Dodgers arrived in San Francisco for a big four-game weekend series. We were only half a game behind them. They won the first game on Thursday. In the second game, Tom Haller got ticked off when the home-plate umpire called him for tipping the batter's bat with his glove. The hitter got on base automatically. In the dugout Haller claimed that the Dodgers had been moving their bats back when the umpire wasn't looking. The next time Matty Alou got up, he held his bat farther back than he normally did and touched Johnny Roseboro, the Dodgers' catcher. Roseboro warned Alou.

This was getting to be a problem. You could just feel it. The next day, it was getting even uglier, with lots of talking back and forth from both teams. Roseboro had nicked some of the batters' bats with his arm while throwing the ball back to the pitcher. I was hoping that it wasn't going to get worse. This was a big series for both teams. There was lots of tension. The crowds were big and the fans screamed and every play seemed like a do-or-die World Series moment.

The Giants needed to win on Sunday to split the series. I had homered in each of the first three games, but we'd managed only one victory. The finale had a wonderful pitching matchup—Koufax against Marichal. This is how good they were in 1965: Koufax led everybody in victories with 26; and his 26–8 won–lost percentage of .765 was the best, along with his 2.04 earned-run average, his 382 strikeouts, and his 27 complete games. He took the mound against us that day with a 21–4 record. Meanwhile, Marichal led everyone with 10 shutouts, had a 22–13 record and a 2.14 ERA. That year, they were baseball's best.

Maury Wills started the Dodgers off with a bunt, a stolen base, and a run. When Wills came up in the next inning, Marichal tossed one right at his head. Out in center, I was beginning to get nervous. Ron Fairly, the next batter, also went down from a close pitch, although it may not have been as tight as Fairly claimed it was.

I was the first Giants batter up in the second inning. I figured I was going to get thrown at even by Koufax—who was to establish a record for cleanliness the following year by pitching 323 innings and not hitting a single batter. Now, though, I expected a "courtesy" pitch from the clean-throwing Koufax—and I got it. A real sailer, which is different from a headhunter. This one sailed a foot over my head. Nothing dangerous. The message was easy to read: Don't throw at my teammates.

Marichal came up for the first time in the third inning. Koufax did not throw close to him. The first two pitches were hardly dusters and the count ran to 1–1. But after the second pitch, Roseboro rifled the ball back to Koufax, and the ball whistled past Marichal's ear in the batter's box. I got tense in the dugout. I knew something was about to happen.

Marichal turned to Roseboro and screamed, "Why did you do that?" Roseboro confronted Marichal, and I knew it was time to get off the bench. Marichal had the bat in his hands and was facing the pitcher's mound when Roseboro brushed him. Maybe it was a swing.

Whatever it was, that did it. Just as I rushed out onto the field to prevent more trouble, Marichal took his bat and hit Roseboro over the head with it.

I couldn't believe it. It was the worst thing I had ever seen on a ball field. I grabbed Roseboro around the waist. He was trying to get at Marichal and I wanted to prevent a riot. Blood was dripping down his face, and I could hear the other players shouting and yelling. By now they were doing the same out on the field, fifty players tugging and screaming. I had to act fast and get Roseboro off the field.

"Your eye is cut, man," I said to him, trying to get him to relax and get it taken care of. "You're hurt bad. Let's get off the field." Actually, blood was dripping into his eye from the wound on his head, but I didn't know that.

We walked over to the Dodger dugout and I took a towel and pressed it against the bleeding. The trainer looked at it and said it wasn't as bad as it seemed. Just a nick on the

side of his head. But Roseboro started to curse me for holding him back. He started to go out again and I grabbed him
and calmed him down. Just then, Lou Johnson, one of the
Dodgers' outfielders, cursed umpire Shag Crawford. Johnson headed for Crawford, so I left Roseboro and cut off
Johnson. I had to tackle him. As I grabbed him around the
knees, he kicked me in the head and nearly knocked me out.
Some of the other players had to help me.

By the time everything had been straightened out, Koufax
was suffering from the delay. He got the first two batters
out, but then he walked Davenport and McCovey. I came
up knowing that I'd get a pitch to hit and that Sandy
wouldn't throw at me—especially after what had gone before and the warnings the umpires had given. Everyone was
on edge now, and if you looked over into both dugouts you
could see policemen there.

I was right about Sandy. I could set up for a pitch over
the middle or outside. He wasn't going to take a chance on
an inside pitch that might tail at me. One of his best pitches
was a jammer, inside. That would set you up, getting you
to lean back, and then he'd break a curve over the plate and
you'd be standing there just watching it. This time he would
not keep me off balance. He had to challenge me. So I was
thinking fastball, and it came. As soon as I hit it, I knew it
was gone. It landed over the centerfield fence for a three-
run homer. That gave us a 4–3 victory and a split in a big
series. I never finished the game, though. After my hit I felt
dizzy, probably from Johnson's knee. I asked Herman to
take me out.

Marichal's actions might have cost us the pennant. He
was suspended for nine days, which made him miss two
starts. That was a problem for us. Juan completed 24 of our
42 complete games. Our pitchers couldn't last the nine innings and that worked our relievers over. Herman had decided on a nine-man pitching staff early in the season, and
now they were all overworked.

We made it a heck of a season, though. We put together a 14-game winning streak. Meanwhile, I was headed for some records. I entered the season with 452 homers. The next big hurdle was Lou Gehrig's 493, and then 500. That was still a magic number in those days. In the pennant race in August, I got hot. As luck would have it, I was in New York when I broke Gehrig's mark with a pair of homers. That put me into fifth place among the all-time home-run hitters. My two shots not only got me past Gehrig, but the second was my 17th of the month. That broke a record that Ralph Kiner had set when he was with the Pirates. Now Ralph was a Mets broadcaster. He also had a show, *Kiner's Korner,* in which he interviewed the star of the game. Guess who was on his show after I broke his record?

Kidding him, I said, "Are you sore?"

"Sure, I'm sore," he said.

You're not supposed to think about personal records, but after I nailed those two, I thought about my next goal: Jimmie Foxx's 534 home runs. That was the most ever hit by a right-handed batter in all of baseball history. That was something to shoot for. Babe Ruth's 714? I didn't think it could be done—well, not unless I stayed healthy for the next six years or so.

The way I was hitting, and with Marichal back, we were doing great. By Labor Day we got into first place for the first time all season. We even opened a four-game lead over the Dodgers. But the Dodgers just didn't lose at the end. While we were going for the pennant, I was hitting more homers, and near the end of September I cracked Number 499. Then every news organization in America seemed to send someone out to watch me hit the 500th. We had to concentrate on a pennant race and I had to cooperate with the writers and broadcasters doing a job I knew they had to do. Maybe I lost my concentration, maybe it was just a simple small slump. And anyway, you can't hit a home run just because fifty writers traveled cross-country to see you

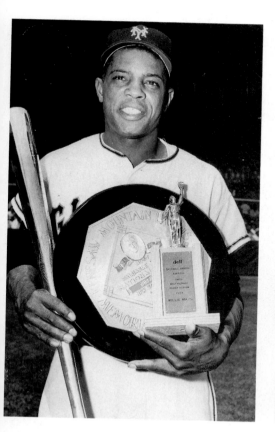

Being a Most Valuable Player has its rewards.

For a change of pace I always love to play a few games of pool.

19

Me and my boss, Horace Stoneham, accepting more awards after the 1954 season.

20

It felt strange walking down to the field from the visiting clubhouse during my first return to the Polo Grounds in 1962.

Me and my dad and Manager Al Dark at Shea Stadium in 1964.

Some candid shots of me and my son Michael.

23

24

Me hitting one of my
four home runs in a game
against the Braves.

25

My old roommate Monte Irvin
(right) meant a lot to me when he
played for the Giants.

Four of a kind (home runs) aren't
easy to come by in the game.

27

Me and the Mick.

Fans want autographs all the time.

29

Me being helped off the field against the Dodgers in 1963.

Me and Stan the Man, another all-time great.

30

It wasn't much fun getting brushed back by a Sandy Koufax fastball.

I've always enjoyed making special appearances for youngsters.

"I'm feeling fine," I said as this picture was snapped. But the night before I'd collapsed in the dugout and remained unconscious for fifteen minutes.

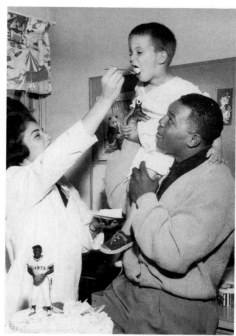

32

33

The New York cabbies didn't forget me when I returned to the Big Apple to play the Mets. And I didn't forget to tip them either.

34

35

I had a lot of respect for
the umps, but every once in
a while you had to make a
stand. I guess you can
imagine who won this
argument!

36

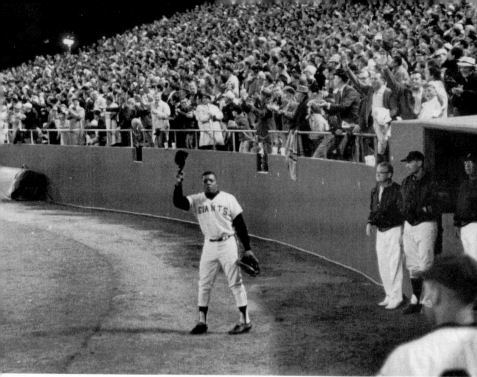

Acknowledging the standing ovation after hitting home run number 512.

A lot of home runs flew off these three bats.

Hamming it up with a fellow from the Police Athletic League.

Connecting for my 600th home run in a pinch-hit appearance against the Padres in 1969. At the time only the Babe had hit more.

39

CONGRATULATIONS WILLIE

41

Back home in New York again, this time with the Mets.

A TIP OF THE DODGER CAP

TO WILLIE MAYS...

INDUCTED INTO THE

HALL OF FAME SUNDAY

Even my old rivals the Dodgers took time out to congratulate me on my induction into the Hall of Fame.

(opposite) One of the biggest moments of my life.

Me with my beautiful wife, Mae, who is a Hall of Famer herself.

44

My boyhood idol, Joe DiMaggio, and myself in the Hall.

I'm proud to wear the Bally's insignia on my sportscoat.

46

I have a nine handicap out on the links.

47

No mistaking who drives this car.

48

49

It sure felt great to be back with the Giants for spring training in March 1986.

do it. Finally, a week after I hit my last one, I cracked Number 500.

It was September 13 in the Houston Astrodome. The Astros were playing out a moribund season in which they would finish out of first place by 32 games. Only the Mets were worse. But almost twenty thousand people showed up to wait and watch. Jim Wynn of the Astros smacked a homer off Marichal in the first inning, and the crowd, of course, applauded.

I led off the fourth with a 450-foot line drive into the centerfield runway off Don Nottebart. The crowd stood and chanted, "Willie! Willie!" as I jogged around the bases to join Babe Ruth, Jimmie Foxx, Ted Williams, and Mel Ott in the 500 club. The fans didn't seem to care that I had just touched off a rally that would send their team to defeat.

Warren Spahn, now a Giant, greeted me on the steps of the dugout.

"I threw you the first one and now I've seen the five-hundredth. Was it the same feeling?" asked Spahn.

"Same feeling. Same pitch," I replied.

Everyone was still talking about Number 500 when I came up with another blast the following night. It was one of the most dramatic, even though history records it merely as Number 501.

Going into the ninth inning, Bob Bruce of the Astros was holding a 5–2 lead. With one out he walked Bob Burda. So the Astros' manager, Luman Harris, called for Claude Raymond, a smallish right-hander with a blazing fastball. Raymond retired Schofield on a grounder for the second out. But Jesus Alou singled to right, making it 5–3—and I was coming to bat.

This was one of those remarkable situations in which everyone—even the popcorn sellers—knew that I would be swinging for the big one. I took two mighty cuts that brought me to my knees. Misses. Then I got the count to 3–2. I fouled off three pitches. Raymond threw again, and this time I clouted the pitch into the leftfield seats to tie the score. The Giants won it in the 10th.

That drive convinced us nobody could stop our team. We won 14 of our last 22 games, 22 of the last 30—the Giants' best finish since coming to San Francisco. But the Dodgers were even better. They beat us out for the pennant by two games.

A lot of people started asking me whether I'd like to manage some day. All I could think of was playing. During our last trip to New York, I'd seen Mrs. Payson, the Mets' owner. She was always telling me that one day she'd get me back to play in New York. I told her she'd better hurry and get me fast. "I don't have much time left," I said.

Perhaps, but in 1965 I still managed to be voted the league's Most Valuable Player—eleven years after I'd gained the honor the first time. My 52 homers not only led baseball, so did my .645 slugging average. In my last two years I had hit 99 home runs, scored 239 runs and driven in 223. My average of .317 was my best since 1960. I would not hit .300 again, although I still had more than 150 homers left in me.

Willie's 1965 Numbers

G	AB	H	2B	3B	HR	R	RBI	BB	SO	SB	BA	SA
157	558	177	21	3	52	118	112	76	61	9	.317	.645

22

THAT 52-HOMER SEASON had a major effect on my life. It seemed I now had been elevated to a somewhat mythic status. I was, perhaps, the last hero of the 1950's still able to play effectively. Over on the Yankees, Mantle's skills were eroded not only by time, but by those extra-long evenings he's written about in his own autobiography.

Ironically, both Spahn and Snider ended their careers as my teammates on the San Francisco Giants—Snider in '64, Spahn in '65. And yet I was still playing.

I now was called on as an elder statesman even though I had not yet turned thirty-five. I was asked to talk to youngsters in the Job Corps, which I did willingly. In addition, I discovered that people would pay tremendous amounts of money just to play a round of golf with me. And, what the heck, I loved golf. I played virtually every day in the off-season, getting my scores into the low 80's. At night, I lined up fifteen or twenty balls on my living-room carpet and knocked them into a "golf hole" designed for indoor putting. I was besieged for requests and was the honored guest at baseball writers' annual dinners in New York, Baltimore, Washington, and St. Louis.

I seemed to have entered a new phase: legend in residence. With that hallowed status goes an insistence by some people that I also be able to solve the world's problems, or at least those troubling America. This, I refused to do. I had a narrow framework of operations I was comfortable with and that I enjoyed doing. My work with the Job Corps had started shortly after the season ended. I was invited to Washington and met with Sargent Shriver, who headed the program, and Vice President Hubert Humphrey. They asked me to help with the program.

"Willie," said Humphrey, "the kids will listen to you. All you have to do is talk to them. They look up to you."

Not long after that meeting in Washington I was preparing to go onstage at a movie theater in Salt Lake City and talk about the Job Corps. I had been feeling good that winter and never had a warning of what was about to happen. Before I realized what was going on, I got a dizzy feeling again, dropped to one knee, and passed out. When I came to, I was sitting in a chair backstage. My collapse was different this time. First, it happened in December. The season wasn't even on. What's more, I had passed out for five or ten minutes—it had never lasted as long before.

I didn't go to a hospital. Instead, I rode a police car to Herman Franks's house. After I was examined by a private doctor, I felt better. The place and the time might have been different, but I heard the same old story from many different physicians: I was tired and exhausted.

My appearance in Salt Lake City was only one stop on a nationwide tour for the Job Corps. I guess I blacked out from the heat and from the excitement of being around the kids. I had been on the move every day, not only for the Job Corps, but for personal appearances which kept pouring in —especially after I got the MVP award. Franks insisted I end my commitment with the Job Corps. I was reluctant, but he insisted I spend a few days at his house and rest.

That incident settled it for Herman. He was determined I would get more rest this year. He didn't plan to sit me out of games, but to take me out in the late innings, especially if the game no longer was on the line. So he traded for Don Landrum of the Chicago Cubs to back me up.

By now I was intensely aware of where I stood on the all-time homer list. I needed 30 to move into second place behind the Babe. Foxx had 534, Williams 521, Ott 511, and I was at 505. The thing about Ott's homers was that they made him the biggest home-run hitter in the history of the National League. I might not catch Ruth, but I certainly intended to become Number 1 in my league.

Over the years I came to think "home run" in certain situations. There are times you just have to be looking to drive the ball—it's two out, the hitter behind you isn't having any luck against the pitcher, you've got a chance to win the game. But until now, I don't believe I was ever thinking *number* of home runs, how many I'd hit. I started to analyze where I hit my homers. Nothing would ever top the nine I hit in 11 games in Ebbets Field one season back in New York. And I knew that as long as we were based at Candle-stick, I'd always have to be content to hit more homers away from my own home park. Of the 52 I hit in 1965, 24 were at Candlestick and 28 were on the road. As I examined other home-run hitters, it was clear to me that if you have a park designed for your strengths as a batter—not intentionally, of course, but just play in a park that happens to be compatible with your style—you are at a tremendous advantage. Of all the top all-time home-run leaders, my park worked for me less well than any of the others' did for them. Aaron's ball took off in Milwaukee, and Ruth had the short rightfield porch in Yankee Stadium. I played 44 games in Ebbets Field—and I hit 26 homers there. That's the field where Gil Hodges became the top right-handed home-run hitter in National League history.

It's a great game to play, "what if?" What if I had played at Ebbets Field during my time in New York? I would have averaged 40 homers a season *at home*. What if Ted Williams had played at Yankee Stadium with that short porch in right, and Joe DiMaggio had played at Fenway Park with that short green monster fence in left?

The spring of '66 was good for me. I hit the ball great in spring training, and then, when the season started, I was still hitting. I got a quick four home runs in the first few weeks to give me 509. I was two behind Ott when we returned once more to the Astrodome.

The Giants were shut out in the first game of the series. The only homers were hit by Astros, blasts greeted by the whizbang message board's snorting bulls, fireworks, and shooting cowboys. Robin Roberts, now thirty-nine years old, was with the Astros. He had 281 career victories and was hanging on trying for 300. Roberts had it that night, though. Through six innings he held the Giants to one run. But I came up in the seventh and smashed the ball five rows behind the 406-foot sign in leftfield.

I didn't take batting practice the next day; we had a day game following a night game. I didn't take fielding practice either.

John Gregory Dunne, the writer, was in the locker room with me before the game and watched as my left hand, which was pretty banged up then, was treated with an ice pack. Dunne recorded the conversation between me and Eddie Logan, the longtime equipment manager. Logan was reminiscing about Ott.

"Ottie would have been glad it's staying with the Giants," said Logan, speaking of the home-run record.

"Haven't broken it yet," I replied.

"It's only a matter of time, Buck," Logan insisted. "You ever see him play?"

"Only in the newsreels," I replied, somewhat wistfully. "He was only a little guy. Don't know how he ever hit kicking out his foot like that."

The Giants had another tough game against the Astros. Houston was winning by a run when we got up in the top of the eighth. Jim Owens was the new relief pitcher. He threw two balls, and I figured he wouldn't be coming in with a curve just then. He didn't. I hit the belt-high fastball into the stands in left center, took two steps, then watched the ball land in the stands.

"Say, Judge Hofheinz," someone asked the Astros' owner, "maybe you could light up the scoreboard for that one." It had never been done for a visiting player.

"Well," growled the judge, "maybe . . . if he breaks the record here."

It took me ten days to get it. It felt as if San Francisco was holding its breath. I was, too. After the Astros series we had a 10-game home stand. They had everything waiting for me—a cake, a hundred bucks for the fan who caught the ball. But the thing was, I started to think home run every time I got up. My average dropped to under .300. I was hitting 3 for 23. In the series against the Reds, I got a cold and my stomach was upset. Herman took me out of one game and sent me home. I got back the next day, but Herman saw me getting dressed in the locker room and told me to take off my things and to go home and get some rest. Against the Cards, I fell over first base as I was running out an infield grounder.

Finally, we were playing the Dodgers. Their pitcher was Claude Osteen and he was having a big season. He struck me out the first two times up. When I got up against him in the fifth inning, he had pitched 92 straight innings without giving up a homer. I could see what he was trying to do— move the ball around on me, inside-outside. He threw me a high outside change-up. I set myself, waited, and then jumped on it and sent it over the fence in rightfield. Number 512. Twenty years earlier, Ott had hit his last home run. Now, as I ran happily around the bases, I thought to myself, heck, I've got a lot more of these in me. You always think that way after a homer. As I rounded each base, the excitement within me grew.

When I got into the dugout, I heard the fans shouting "We want Willie! We want Willie!" I had to come out and tip my cap to them. It was one of my great moments.

Later, when everyone had left the park, Herman sat down next to me. I told him I was worried that the same thing would happen when I got close to Ted Williams and Jimmie Foxx.

"Nah, you've got nothing to worry about until Babe Ruth," he said.

"Babe Ruth? I'd have to hit forty a year for five years," I told Herman. "Let me alone."

As usual, we were fighting the Dodgers that season. As usual, we didn't catch them. This time we missed by a game and a half. For the second straight year we finished second. In fact, we finished second five straight seasons. Herman was right about the other homers. I got Number 521 in June in Chicago to tie Williams. The funny thing about that day was that the crowd gave me a bigger cheer when I reached into the vines along the centerfield wall to take a base hit from Ernie Banks. In August I tied Foxx with a home run against Al Jackson of the Cards. That gave me 534. The next day I got in front of everyone—everyone except Ruth, with his 714. I hit No. 535 on a 3–2 pitch off Ray Washburn. I was second, yet I still trailed the mighty Bambino by 179 homers. Imagine, 179—you'd have to hit 18 homers a year for ten years to break that mark. Until I actually got that "close" at 535, I don't think I gauged how monumental his record was.

Near the end of the season, San Francisco was hit by some bad racial riots. The police took over Candlestick Park as a staging area. We were playing the Braves in Atlanta. The governor and mayor imposed a curfew in the critical Hunter's Point and Fillmore District areas of San Francisco. No one could be on the streets after eight P.M. To keep people home, Mayor Shelley asked the Giants to telecast their game with the Braves. A special feature of the broadcast was a tape-recorded message I read for the fans in which I didn't mention a problem. I didn't tell the youngsters to stay home. But I was credited with helping to calm the volatile situation. I simply said, "Root for your team." And I added, "I know I'll be out there in centerfield trying my best."

The Giants won that night, keeping us in third place, moving to within three games of the Dodgers and 1½ behind the Pirates. But we had to win our final four games—against the Pirates—while the Dodgers would have to lose at least three of their remaining four. We did sweep the Pirates, with one game rained out, but the Dodgers split their remaining games and so the Giants finished 1½ games out of first.

For the first time in 12 straight seasons I failed to score 100 runs—I got 99. But for the eighth straight season I had driven in more than 100. My 37 home runs were more than anyone except Aaron and Dick Allen struck in the National League. I also performed in 152 games.

By the end of the 1966 season I had established or tied these records:

- Most consecutive years of 150 or more games—13 (major league)
- Most consecutive years of 300 or more total bases—13 (major league)
- Most consecutive years of 100 or more runs batted in—8 (National League)

In addition, the record showed that I was the first player to hit 50 or more home runs and steal 20 or more bases in a season, which I accomplished in 1955, and was the first National League player to hit 30 homers and steal 30 bases in the same season—which I did in 1956 *and* 1957. I was one of five players to hit 20 or more doubles, triples, and home runs in one season, 1957.

Willie's 1966 Numbers

G	AB	H	2B	3B	HR	R	RBI	BB	SO	SB	BA	SA
152	552	159	29	4	37	99	103	70	81	5	.288	.556

23

IN A SENSE, the 1966 season capped my career—or so it seemed. I batted .288, a figure I had not fallen to in any of the years since my return from the Army in 1954. I would not clout 30 homers again or reach triple figures in runs scored or RBI's. On the other hand, I didn't play as often. Not only did my number of starts diminish, but so did my playing time. Yes, there wouldn't be single-season records anymore. But there would be remarkable career marks added to, records that put me up among the leaders in a special array of categories, from fielding to hitting to running. And there still were pennant races to be fought.

I felt relieved with the coming of the 1967 season. The pressure of hitting Number 512, and those that followed, was gone. But even though I had a good spring, I was beginning to wonder about the reliability of my skills when the regular season began. In a game against Cincinnati, Gary Nolan struck me out four times. Okay, the kid was good. But he was only nineteen. And I had never struck out four times in a game before. Everyone else was also struggling. For only the second time since we had moved out to the Coast, we had a losing April. Soon, I got into one of my streaks. Strange, wasn't it, that I could not go all out day in and day out, but when I got hot, it didn't matter that I was thirty-six years old? I even got my average to over .300.

Before half the season was over I already had 12 home runs, and had driven in 38 runs. But that good two-month stretch was the best I could do.

One cold night in July in Candlestick, before the game started, I began to shake. I had a fever. I told Franks that I was better off in bed. He agreed—but he asked me to stay in uniform long enough to hand in the lineup card, then hang around for a few innings, and slip out. I understood what he was doing. He wanted it to appear that I was ready to play in case he needed to make a move.

Ty Cline started in my place. In the first inning he pulled a muscle running to first base and had to leave. The only other outfielder around, besides me, was Jesus Alou, and he had a leg injury. I unbuttoned my jacket, grabbed a glove, and headed for centerfield. My legs felt heavy and the bat seemed to weigh five pounds. I finally took myself out of the game and went home. The next day I checked into a hospital and spent five days there.

After I got back into the lineup, I never felt strong again for the rest of the season. We were going through a .500 season in August when I got revived one day. I was ready to tear down the stadium. We were leading the Braves, 1–0, in the third inning. We had runners on second and third. Hart was at bat when Billy Hitchcock, the Braves' manager, signaled to walk Hart intentionally. They were loading the bases to pitch to me! That had never happened to me before. I was furious and embarrassed, but raring to go. Then again, I had never struck out four times in a game before this season. Maybe I couldn't blame Hitchcock. But I also couldn't wait to get up to bat with the bases loaded. Did I concentrate! Make me look bad, huh? I smacked a single past first base and the runs were enough for a victory.

We put on a big September drive, 20–7, but we couldn't do any better than another second. This time it was the Cards who finished first, beating us by 10½ games. My own numbers were the lowest of any full season I had had. My

batting average fell to .263, my runs dropped to 83, my
homers to 22, and I drove in 70 runners.

Now people really were getting after me about retiring.
Yet most players with those statistics would call it a decent
year. I admit I didn't think so. My standards were higher
than the numbers I put up. But I wasn't going to retire, even
if I had another bad year, and I didn't intend to have another one like that.

Willie's 1967 Numbers

G	AB	H	2B	3B	HR	R	RBI	BB	SO	SB	BA	SA
141	486	128	22	2	22	83	70	51	92	6	.263	.453

Maybe if I played a little first base in 1968 I could keep
from getting tired. I knew that a good start was important,
a confidence builder. I was going to be thirty-seven. People
simply didn't play centerfield at that age. They usually were
converted to being first basemen, or played third base. By
that age, my idol, Joe DiMaggio, had retired, and so had
Mickey Mantle. But I got the quick start I was looking for
—eight hits in my first 17 at bats.

I got to Houston on my thirty-seventh birthday. This time
Judge Hofheinz decided to let the scoreboard play some
tricks in my honor. He also wheeled out a big cake that
weighed 569 pounds—one pound for every home run I had
hit.

From the beginning I had driven it into myself that I
wouldn't have a bad year, and I didn't. I got into 148 games
and had almost 500 at bats, and I brought my average up
to .289. I had no trouble playing first, but I still preferred
the open space and freedom of center, where I could run
and throw. What was troubling me now was that we once
again finished second, although this time we won only 88
games. It was the poorest record Franks had during his
tenure with the club, and sure enough, he was gone.

Willie's 1968 Numbers

G	AB	H	2B	3B	HR	R	RBI	BB	SO	SB	BA	SA
148	498	144	20	5	23	84	79	67	81	12	.289	.488

Roger Kahn, the chronicler who wrote *The Boys of Summer*, whom I had first met back in the New York days, visited me during the spring-training season of 1969. The talk got around to my image and whether or not I was getting involved enough in civil rights causes.

"They want me to go on some campus?" I said to Kahn. "Why should I lie? I don't know a thing about campuses. I never went to college. I wanted to play ball."

But what about the black movement?

"I help. I help in my own way," I said. "I think I show some people some things. I do it my way."

Do you ever speak aloud on issues such as schools and jobs?

"I don't think I should. I don't know the full value of these things. I'm not the guy to get on the soapbox. I'm a ball player."

Look back over the record from the time the Giants moved to San Francisco in 1958, through 1968, and you'll see the same spot in the opening-day lineup—Willie Mays batting third. The exception was 1964, when I batted cleanup.

But in spring training of '69, Clyde King, our new manager, had it figured differently.

It was obvious what was expected of King—a pennant. When he arrived he was greeted with a letter that read, "Welcome to San Francisco, Mr. King. It's nice to have you. But we're tired of finishing second."

To the world, King and I put up a united front. I accepted the lead-off role without any complaint. Why? I had to do it for the team. I said so publicly. King had come up with figures to show how badly the Giants needed a top lead-off batter: In 130 games in 1968 the Giants failed to score in the first inning.

But Willie Mays batting lead-off? Lead-off is the position for Eddie Stanky or Pee Wee Reese or Richie Ashburn. Willie Mays batting lead-off is Wilt Chamberlain playing guard, it's O. J. Simpson blocking for the fullback.

Yet it was I, who needed 13 homers to reach 600 and who with one more stolen base would become the first player in history to achieve both 300 stolen bases and 300 homers, who became the lead-off batter. I hit .320 in spring training. I was becoming a lead-off man for the first time since the last day of the 1958 season, when Rigney had put me on top so that I could get the at bats I needed to try to catch Richie Ashburn. Actually, I also led off the 1968 All-Star Game. In the first inning I beat out a single, went to second when Luis Tiant tried to pick me off, took third on Tiant's wild pitch—and scored the game's only run on a double-play ball. I was named the game's Most Valuable Player.

From the beginning, though, I never got along with Clyde King.

"Why would you want me to lead off? I'm no kid, you know," I said to King.

"I know that. But you're not hitting home runs like you used to," he told me.

"I can still hit twenty or more. That ought to be enough," I told him. I explained that it couldn't be better for the team for me to lead off, that before the season was halfway over, I'd be too tired.

Actually, I started to slump in May. I had a knee injury and that didn't help. We were going to play three games in the Astrodome in June, and that had always been one of my favorite places.

But King said he was going to rest me in the series. I was taking my cuts for the second game, figuring I wasn't play-

ing, when Gaylord Perry told me, "Willie, you're playing."
I told him he was wrong.

"But your name is listed in the lineup," he said.

The lineup is usually posted on a wall in the corner of the
dugout. I went to the corner. My name was on the card all
right, leading off. I went into the clubhouse to take off my
sweat jacket and pants and put on my uniform. When I got
back to the dugout again, my name had been scratched off.

I exploded.

"What the hell is going on?" I shouted. "You took me
out of the lineup."

He told me he didn't think I wanted to play.

That really stirred me up. First he doesn't even tell me
I'm playing, and then he scratches me. I began shouting at
him in front of the other players. Perry and McCovey and
Larry Jansen must have thought I was going to go after him
because they surrounded me and pulled me back.

The funny thing was, in the second inning, Jim Ray Hart
hurt his shoulder and now King was asking me if I wanted
to play.

"You're the manager," I said.

After the game King told me, "You're fined."

"If I'm fined," I replied, "I quit."

King immediately telephoned Stoneham, who wouldn't
permit him to fine me. But when I got back to my hotel
room I got a call from Chub Feeney, who had been our
general manager all the years I had been there. Chub also
was Horace's nephew, but a respected baseball man in his
own right. He went on to become president of the National
League.

Chub asked me to apologize. I refused, but he explained
that it was for the good of the club, so the next day I told
King I was sorry. But I lost any respect I ever had for King.
I thought of him as a back stabber, and we didn't talk for
the rest of the year. If he had been allowed to fine me, I'm
sure I would have packed my bags and left. But Stoneham

protected me after all those years of playing for him, of putting people in the seats.

With my knees bothering me, the homers were slow coming. It took three weeks to get from Number 598 to Number 599. I really wanted to hit the 600th during a three-game series against the Dodgers in Candlestick. But I never came close. The next night we opened a series in San Diego and King decided to rest me. It was seven days since I had hit my last one. The Adirondack bat company had sent Frank Torre traveling with me. Torre used to be the Braves' first baseman. Now he was working for Adirondack, waiting for me to hit the 600th with an Adirondack bat. The poor guy never got a chance to go home.

The score was tied at 2–all in the seventh inning against the Padres when King asked me to pinch-hit. Ron Hunt was on second, so I was looking for a base hit to score him.

I stepped in against Mike Corkins, a rookie I didn't know anything about. Heck, he had been five years old when I broke in with the Giants. I wasn't thinking home run because I figured he'd keep the ball away from me. He made a mistake. He threw a fastball about belt-high and I got around on it. I pulled it into the seats near the leftfield line for Number 600. Adirondack awarded me not only a sports car, but a share of their stock for every foot the ball traveled. It went 390 feet.

Afterward, I said what I always said, and what I always believed—that winning the game was more important to me than any individual achievements. I also told Frank Torre to go home.

Meanwhile, we remained a mystery team—close again. Another second-place finish, this time to Atlanta as the league was split into East and West Divisions. For the time period since we had moved out to San Francisco 12 seasons before, we had the best record of any team in the National League—and only one first-place finish to show for it.

For the first time, my home-run total dropped below 20,

as I hit 13. There was some feeling of joy after the season, though, when I was picked on a team called Baseball's Greatest Living Players. I was finally in the outfield with DiMaggio.

Willie's 1969 Numbers

G	AB	H	2B	3B	HR	R	RBI	BB	SO	SB	BA	SA
117	403	114	17	3	13	64	58	49	71	6	.283	.437

Now I was starting to outlast my managers. The game was changing rapidly. Even Horace, who kept his managers on out of loyalty, was juggling them under pressure from the fans and the media. I had come up in the postwar era when Leo Durocher was supreme, and the Dodgers and Giants ran the league. Then in San Francisco I played while the Dodgers created a new dynasty, followed by the Cardinals' brief run at the top, then the Braves', and now the Reds'. Different teams were now kingpins, but I was still around. I was spanning generations of baseball.

By 1970, nineteen years after I had broken in, the Mets had already been created—and had captured a World Series. Pete Rose didn't arrive until twelve years after my first season. Cepeda was long gone, traded to the Cardinals. Ernie Banks was thirty-nine years old and slowing down, with only one year left.

Clyde King was gone in 1970 after 42 games, a 19–23 record that marked the Giants' worst start since moving West. Charlie Fox replaced him.

No, I wasn't thinking of taking over for King. I wasn't thinking of retiring yet, although I was taking it one year at a time. Coming into the season I needed 74 hits to reach 3,000. Only eight people had ever had that many. At the top, there was Ty Cobb with 4,192. I was about to get there, although Hank Aaron would be there first. After me, Roberto Clemente would get his 3,000th—the last hit of his life. Rose, I figured, would get to that number quicker

than any of us had. He was knocking out 200 hits every
year.

On a Saturday afternoon in July, at Candlestick, I was
hitting against the Expos' Mike Wegener. There were two
outs in the second inning. I took a strike, then fouled off a
pitch. At 0–2 you think contact on anything close to being
a strike. The next pitch was good enough to hit, and I got
it between third and short for a single. Hank had done it a
few weeks before. I was the ninth player to get 3,000 hits.

They stopped the game and someone gave me the ball at
first base. My old roomie, Monte Irvin, was there, and so
was Stan Musial, who at that time had more hits than any
National Leaguer had ever had. Carl Hubbell, the old
Giants screwball pitcher, was there, too. The Giants made
a big day of it for everyone—all the fans were given a free
ticket to another game during the season. The nicest touch
of all was the four-year college scholarship the Giants said
they would give to my son, Michael. I left the game after
getting another hit in the sixth inning. Another standing
ovation.

Overall, I was feeling pretty good. The week before I
played in the All-Star Game. I had 19 home runs and drove
in 47 runs, along with a .272 batting average. That really
pumped me up. My own ability helped keep me going in a
season that found us finishing third, although we did play
better than .500 ball for Fox. My 28 homers were the most
I had hit since 1966, and my .291 average was my best since
'65. I would have a 1971 season, all right, at the age of 40.

Willie's 1970 Numbers

G	AB	H	2B	3B	HR	R	RBI	BB	SO	SB	BA	SA
139	478	139	15	2	28	94	83	79	90	5	.291	.506

24

I HAD DONE a lot of thinking before spring training of the 1971 season. I wasn't concerned about being forty. Well, in a way I was. I had always been a Giant—I was now in my twentieth year with the team. Horace and his son, Peter, had always been proud of the fact that I was the highest-paid player in baseball. They realized my value to the team and the fact that I drew fans. For years, the Giants were the top drawing attraction on the road.

That spring I proposed to Horace that he give me a ten-year contract worth $750,000. I knew I wouldn't be playing that long. But I did think I had three years left. After that, I would want to remain with the Giants for at least the rest of the contract. I figured I could be a coach handling younger players, or get a job in the front office. I was now being paid $160,000 a year, so I felt the package I was asking for was fair to everyone. It was now time for me to plan seriously for a job other than as a baseball player.

It didn't work out. It was the first time in all my years with the club that I couldn't agree with Stoneham on a contract. Horace claimed that the board of directors would only authorize him to offer a five-year contract at $75,000 a year. Board of directors? I never heard that one before. When we had sat down in all the other years it was just him and me. Now I wanted security for all the years I had put

in, and I didn't get it. I was disappointed and hurt. I turned
down the offer and negotiated a two-year deal worth
$360,000.

There were no pressures to hit, and I had fun. I hit a
homer in each of the first four games of the season. In the
fifth, I got a triple and double. In the next game I was 1–2
and batting .417. Charlie Fox started to tell people that the
way I was playing, I could make a run at Ruth's record. To
pass him I'd need three seasons of at least 30 homers. I had
to tell Charlie to stop talking that way.

By now, many of the players were looking to me for
leadership as much as they were to Charlie. That was fine
with me. I always enjoyed passing on information, and I'd
sit with the kids in the dugout, watching pitchers, explain-
ing how a pitcher sets you up for his next pitch. In the field,
I still tried to run things, but Charlie had his ideas. So I
worked out a system to do things without Fox's even knowing.

We had two young players in the infield, Chris Speier at
short and Tito Fuentes at second. Fox didn't want me telling
them how to play. When I was out there, though, I would
position the players, the same as I had done for years. Fox
figured it was his place to do that. I told the kids that we
had to play two games with Fox—his and mine. I would
position them first, then let them do what Fox wanted. If he
told you to take two steps back, then take three steps forward and back up one. This way they'd be in the same spot
they started at. We did that all season. Fox never found out.

Turning forty was kind of fun. I was hitting .406 on my
birthday and the Giants were in first place. The team happened to have a day off and the baseball writers threw a
birthday party for me in San Francisco. Joe DiMaggio was
one of the speakers. Over the years, DiMaggio had always
praised me, and this night he synthesized his feelings.

"Too much emphasis is placed on home-run hitting,"
said DiMaggio. "He is a hitter all right, and one of the best

that ever lived. But this man does it all. He fields, he runs, he studies, he hardly ever makes mistakes. He is a very special person."

But at forty, I could not continue that pace, even though by the All-Star break I had, amazingly, 15 home runs. Then McCovey got hurt, and I had to play first. After that, whenever I got up, it seemed no one would pitch to me. They didn't have to worry about facing the next batter with McCovey out of the lineup. A strange thing was happening.

I walked 112 times—more than anyone else in the National League. It was the first time in my career I had ever led in walks, the first time I ever got more than 82 in a season, the first time I had more walks than runs or RBI's. Pitchers were still afraid of me, after all those years, which made me feel good, even though I would have felt better getting pitches to drive. Another thing: I stole 23 bases—my highest total since 1960.

I hit only three more homers the rest of the year. Now things were getting tough. The season had been such a lark. At one time we led by 10½ games, a lead we first took on April 12 and never relinquished. But boy, did we swoon.

We lost 19 of 26 games in September, and we entered the final day of the season with a one-game lead over the Dodgers—after we had enjoyed an eight-game lead on September 1. But we were ragged, and forced to play our final nine games on the road—winding up that last game playing the Padres at San Diego while the Dodgers were home against the Astros.

Marichal started for us, even though he had bruised his hip a few days earlier, and Dave Robin Roberts hurled for the Padres. It was scoreless when we came to bat in the top of the fourth. Tito Fuentes opened with a single. Then I rammed a double off the centerfield wall. We led, 1–0. Dave Kingman blasted a two-run homer and we led by 3–0. But by the time I got up in the fifth I wanted to finish them off. I walked with two out, then I took off for second with McCovey at bat. As I was heading for second I realized that the Padres' infield was overshifted toward the right side because of Willie's strength. The third baseman actually handled the throw to second as I slid in safely. So what the heck—I got up and took off for third. I didn't even have to slide. Two stolen bases on one play.

With Juan pitching strongly, we won. And a good thing it was, too. So did the Dodgers. So, tired but happy, we had won the Western Division championship by a fat one game.

Needless to say, I had yearned for one more World Series. But now, there was a new format in baseball: division play-offs. We faced the Pirates in a best-of-five affair. The winner would meet either the Oakland A's or the Orioles. Wouldn't it be something if San Francisco could have played Oakland? They were ready to call it the Freeway Series. We tried hard to get there. The Giants won the opener with Fuentes and McCovey hitting two-run homers. I contributed a walk just before McCovey's shot. I say "contributed" because I'm sure it helped get Willie into the right frame of mind. They walked me on four pitches, almost an intentional walk to get to McCovey, and no hitter worth his salt wants to see that.

Our pitching failed us in the second game, although we were able once again to collar Willie Stargell. The Pirates' slugger went 0 for 9 the first two games, stranding nine runners, after hitting 48 homers and batting in 125 runs during the season. But they had a surprise waiting for us, a fellow named Bob Robertson. He hit three homers. By the time I came to bat in the ninth we were trailing by 9–2. I smacked a two-run homer, but that's all we got.

We didn't do much better the rest of the series, which slipped away from us. Even though Juan pitched a strong game for us, we lost the next game at Pittsburgh by 2–1 as Robertson hit another out of the park. We were outslugged, 9–5, in the fourth game as Roberto Clemente came up with a couple of big hits.

I didn't know it at the time, but the home run I hit in the second game of the playoffs would be my last one as a Giant. Strange, it was on exactly that same date twenty years before that I had knelt in the on-deck circle in the Polo Grounds and watched Bobby Thomson bat. Why had all those years gone by so fast?

Willie's 1971 Numbers

G	AB	H	2B	3B	HR	R	RBI	BB	SO	SB	BA	SA
136	417	113	24	5	18	82	61	112	123	23	.271	.482

That November I decided to get married. I had known Mae Louise Allen since 1961, as she so often reminded me. The funny thing is, I had known her mother since 1951, when I gave her an autograph. She told me she had a daughter who was a baseball fan, so I looked around in my pocket and found a picture of me wearing a suit and I autographed it to this little girl in pigtails.

Ten years later, I met her. I was in Small's Paradise, a Harlem nightspot owned at the time by Wilt Chamberlain. That was the day I hit the four home runs in one game against the Braves in Milwaukee. Ed Sullivan immediately flew me in to be on his show that night. The next day I had to be in Pittsburgh, where we were opening a series. I had the evening to kill so I went over to see Wilt. I asked him if he knew any girls in Pittsburgh.

The next morning, I arrived in Pittsburgh. Before going to the game I called the phone number Wilt had given me. The conversation went something like this:

"Can I speak to Mae Louise?"

"Speaking."

"You don't know me, but I'm Willie Mays."

"And I'm Martha Washington," she said.

I guess she finally believed me—she knew the Giants were in town—and we had a date for lunch the next day. I enjoyed being with her. She was a graduate student at Howard

University, and she knew sports and had lots of interests. We saw each other that year, and the next year we spoke about marriage for the first time. But I had recently gotten divorced and I was scared of getting married again. I walked away from Mae. But she moved to San Francisco, doing social work, and we stayed close. After some years we started to date again, but when the subject of marriage came up, I felt I had to break it off again.

Finally, one day, I decided it was time for me to grow up a little. I decided to ask her to marry me. I got her over to my house by pretending I needed her to write a letter for me. Then I told her to open the safe. Her engagement ring was in it.

The wedding date was over the Thanksgiving weekend in Mexico City. As we waited in the airport lounge for our flight, I ran into my old golfing partner, Bob Hope.

"Where you going?" he asked.

"Mexico—to get married," I told him. He laughed and laughed. I guess it did sound kind of corny.

It seemed strange to me that the Giants never congratulated me on my marriage—no calls, gifts, nothing. And when the 1972 season began, there was another difference. I had a box at the park right next to Pete Stoneham's. During the 1971 season, Pete's wife had often talked to Mae. Now there was nothing—no conversation, no greetings. Something was going on, but I couldn't figure out what.

A week after my forty-first birthday I started to hear rumors that I was going to be traded. I didn't believe the story for a second. We were in Montreal when I got a call early in the morning from Mae. She had been up all night, unable to sleep. She told me she heard on television that I was going to be traded. I asked Fox about it. He told me it was just a rumor.

After we left Montreal and got to Philadelphia, I got a phone call from Red Foley of the New York *Daily News*.

He told me I had been traded to the New York Mets. I asked him the first question everyone who has been traded always asks:

"Who for?"

"Charlie Williams. He's a pitcher. And some cash."

25

WHAT A BLOW.

After all those years, I found out from someone outside the organization that I had been traded. My first reaction was anger at Stoneham. What happened to that family atmosphere he had always spoken of? I couldn't accept the fact that he hadn't called me when he was working out the details. Later, he explained to me he was losing money and would sell the club soon, but before he did, he wanted to make sure my future was secure. Whatever feelings I had felt for him over the years, at that moment I felt betrayed.

Then I thought about coming back to New York, coming home. I didn't think the Mets had traded for me as window dressing. They had a good ball club that was fighting for a pennant. They had drawn over two million fans in '72, so they weren't looking for me to sell tickets. I guess they got me because they wanted me. Mrs. Payson had been my biggest fan over the years, and she had always wanted me back. She told me not to worry about anything—just go out and play ball.

Virtually 21 years to the day after I joined a New York ball club for the first time, I returned. It was May 11, 1972. America had changed as much as New York—but the city's National League baseball team had Willie Mays again, Number 24.

People were reading about the Russians, who were angered over President Nixon's blockade of North Vietnam; the secretary of the interior opposed the building of the Alaska pipeline; the new F.B.I. director, L. Patrick Gray III, promised to liberalize the Bureau.

Play It Again, Sam, was at Radio City Music Hall. Other films around town included *The Concert for Bangladesh* and *Cabaret.*

On television, Dick Cavett's guest stars were John Lennon and Yoko Ono; the *Flip Wilson Show* was pulling in ratings. A new concept in news broadcasting on WABC-TV was called *Eyewitness News,* with Geraldo Rivera, Bill Beutel, Roger Grimsby, Tex Antoine, Melba Tolliver, and Frank Gifford.

In *The New York Times* of May 12, 1972, the story of my trade began this way:

> Willie Mays, a $165,000-a-year folk hero at the age of 41, was traded yesterday to the New York Mets by the San Francisco Giants after one of the most complex series of negotiations in baseball history. . . . When it finally was completed it returned Mays to the New York baseball scene where he had started his career 21 years and 646 home runs ago.

I brought with me the following statistics: I had played in 2,857 games, batted 10,477 times, produced 3,187 hits, and batted in 1,859 runs. I twice was voted the Most Valuable Player in the National League, appeared in the World Series three times, and played in 21 All-Star Games.

Beyond that, I seemed to be bringing nostalgia back with me. For many, it was a return to the 1957 baseball season and beyond, when there had been Giants and Dodgers in New York.

"We need him," a New York cabbie said outside the Mayfair House, where the deal was completed. "New York sports fans need charisma. They want to wave flags and yell, 'Let's see it, Willie. Do it.' They want to let it all hang out."

In the lobby, a fashionably dressed matron asked, "Is he here yet? I've got to get his autograph for my grandson."

I flashed a smile when the upside of the deal became clear to me and said, "When you come back to New York, it's like coming back to paradise."

In my new Mets uniform the first team I faced was my old club, the Giants. It was another of those moments you never forget. The crowd of more than forty thousand fans at Shea was cheering so wildly for me I got goose bumps. At first it seemed strange—maybe awful is a better word—for me to put on a uniform with "24" on it that wasn't a Giants uniform. My teammates now were Tom Seaver, Tug McGraw, Jerry Koosman, Cleon Jones, and Bud Harrelson. They made it easier for me. Yogi Berra was my manager now, another reminder of my first years in New York.

In my first at bat as a Met I walked against the Giants. It seemed to break the tension I felt. When I got up to the plate the second time, the score was tied at 4–all. This time I thought "home run." That's just what I did. It sailed out and I could feel the crowd on its feet and jumping up and down like we had just won the pennant. That hit also lifted my spirits. Since the trade I had been down. Mae wanted to fly to New York to be with me. But I told her I'd rather be alone until I got myself together. I spent time with old friends.

We didn't play in San Francisco until the end of July. I was hurting. A lot of players were injured and Yogi had to play me more than he planned. He promised me for the series in San Francisco that he'd use me only in the last game, on Sunday.

The team's arrival at the airport early Friday morning said a lot about how baseball had changed. Instead of making life easier, flying had taken its toll. It allowed teams to make schedules, all right, but it forced them into cities at odd hours. Now, with a game later in the day, the Mets arrived at the San Francisco airport following a night game in another town. Walking through the airport, distracted by thoughts of playing there again, I walked right into a pillar and nearly knocked myself out.

Berra announced that I would not be starting that night, and the crowd was kept to about eighteen thousand.

I went to Yogi before that game. He didn't want me to play, but I told him, "Yogi, I think I have to play. I think a lot of people are going to pay their money to come out, especially to see me play. If you pay four fifty to see a person play and he doesn't, I think you're going to be pretty mad."

That was some funny feeling in my stomach when I went into the visitors' clubhouse for the first time. The fans were actually rooting for me to get a hit when I came up in the first inning, batting second. I grounded out then and in my second at bat as well. In the fifth inning, Terry Martinez led off with a single and Jerry Grote doubled. Jerry Koosman flied out, but Bud Harrelson got us on the scoreboard when he drove in a run by grounding out.

That brought me up against Jim Barr. I hit his first pitch over the left centerfield fence, a high shot. I enjoyed hearing the San Francisco crowd rooting for me as I took off around the bases. It was the 650th of my career. I didn't know it, of course, but I had only 10 more left in my bat.

Despite the poorest figures of my career, I had the Mets' second-highest batting and slugging averages.

It was time to take a serious look at the 1973 season. I was going to be forty-two years old. So I asked Herman Franks to come down to spring training and tell me honestly whether he thought I could play another year. I didn't want to hang on. I had too much pride for that. Herman watched me for a few days and was convinced I could play another year.

Willie's 1972 Numbers

SAN FRANCISCO

G	AB	H	2B	3B	HR	R	RBI	BB	SO	SB	BA	SA
19	49	9	2	0	0	8	3	17	5	3	.184	.224

NEW YORK

G	AB	H	2B	3B	HR	R	RBI	BB	SO	SB	BA	SA
69	195	52	9	1	8	27	19	43	43	1	.267	.446

TOTAL

G	AB	H	2B	3B	HR	R	RBI	BB	SO	SB	BA	SA
88	244	61	11	1	8	35	22	60	48	4	.250	.402

"You can still hit, and if you don't get hurt, you'll make it through another season," he said. That was the thing—if I didn't get hurt.

I had problems with Yogi as well. One Thursday afternoon I left St. Petersburg to fly back to our house in Atherton, California, to be with Mae. She was pretty sick. I didn't tell Berra that I was leaving. I thought that since Friday was an off day, I could get back in time for Saturday morning's practice. But one flight was canceled and another was delayed. I got back Saturday afternoon. Berra fined me five hundred dollars and made his point. He was right and I was wrong.

I was having trouble in the workouts. My legs would get tired very quickly, and I would tape both of them. I also was troubled because I didn't know what position I would be at. Yogi didn't make up his mind on a centerfielder. To me, after all those years of calling the shots, it was unsettling. Then, when the season finally started, I hurt my knee and wasn't much good for the outfield. I had to move to first base.

In July I made up my mind. I was going to retire. I told the Mets they could announce it in September. Yet when August came around, I started to have second thoughts. I felt the best I had all year. But I knew I shouldn't go back on it. Franks told me to stick with the decision I had made.

Meanwhile, I found myself in a pennant race. The Mets got
hot and we won 18 of 23 games. So everything was pretty
exciting the night of September 25—all the more so because
it was Willie Mays Night. We were going to play the Expos,
a club we were fighting for first place, along with the Cards
and Pirates and Cubs.

That night topped all the others. There were more than
54,000 people on hand. This would be the hardest speech I
had ever had to make. But I didn't write it out. I never have
written a speech ahead of time. I just said what was in my
heart: "In my heart, I'm a sad man. Just to hear you cheer
like this for me and not be able to do anything about it
makes me a very sad man. This is my farewell. You don't
know what's going on inside of me tonight. Now that I
have all I need, I can teach other kids to be as great an
athlete as I am. If I see someone that has this talent, I will
help them. I want to say hello to all my friends, and Willie,
say good-bye to America."

As soon as I said the last words, I cried. Baseball was
my life, the only one I had ever known. I don't remember
walking away from the microphone until Mae and
Michael hugged me. There seemed to be nothing left. What
I had to do now was pack up my bags and go back to
Atherton. I was a retired player. Everyone knew that. But
Mrs. Payson wouldn't let me leave like that. She called
me at my apartment in Riverdale, a lovely section of The
Bronx.

"You can't go home now, Willie," she said.

So I stayed with the guys, not wanting to force myself on
Yogi. She promised to make it easy for me. We had a crazy
finish, winning the East. Then we beat the Reds for the
championship series. In my last shot at it, I was going to my
fourth World Series. This one was going to be practically in
the same two cities I had played my others—New York and
Oakland.

I got into the second game at Oakland. The funny thing is that Yogi put me into center for defense in the ninth inning while we were holding a 6–4 lead. I lost a line drive by Deron Johnson in the sun. That helped the A's rally and they tied the game. But in the 12th I got up with Harrelson on third and McGraw at first. I was facing Rollie Fingers, one of the best relief pitchers in baseball. I was worried about him, Maybe I could use a little experience to help me along.

As I stepped into the batter's box I called time. I said to the catcher, Ray Fosse, "Gee, you know, Ray, it's tough to see the ball with that background. I hope he doesn't throw me any fastballs. I don't want to get hurt."

Then I waited for Fingers's fastball.

It came, and I nailed it. I hit a hard bouncer over his head into center for the game-winning hit. I just felt I couldn't let the kids down. They hadn't seen me when I was young but they expected me to set an example. That's why I felt so good when I could come up with a clutch hit. I always was very emotional, but if you were watching me play, you wouldn't know it.

The Series went seven games, but I didn't play much after that. I got up seven times and I got two hits. I was very disappointed that Yogi didn't play me in the last game. It was in Oakland, and to me it would have been a storybook ending in front of fans in the Bay Area. But I didn't think of asking him. Still, after twenty-two years to end it in a Series game, maybe even getting the winning hit—that would have been nice. We took a 3–2 lead in games out with us to Oakland, but we couldn't win it. Those A's of Catfish Hunter and Reggie Jackson stormed back to win the Series. I wound up my career playing three thousand miles from New York. It symbolized how far baseball, and I, had traveled in those twenty-three seasons.

Willie's 1973 Numbers

G	AB	H	2B	3B	HR	R	RBI	BB	SO	SB	BA	SA
66	209	44	10	0	6	24	25	27	47	1	.211	.344

When I retired, only one player remained in Major
League baseball who had also played in the Negro Leagues
—Hank Aaron.

26

NO ONE KNOWS how much he will miss playing baseball until he stops. During spring training that next year, I was on a ball field for the first time knowing I wasn't going to play anymore. It was difficult for me to stand around the batting cage or even to sit on the bench. Once the season began, it became even harder. I had an unusual contract with the Mets. Mrs. Payson practically gave me an open ticket. It was a ten-year deal that came out to $500,000, but none of my duties were written out.

Over the years I had gotten very close with Sy Berger of the Topps bubble gum company—the one that sells baseball cards. Sy looked over my contract and said it could cause me some trouble. He told me I had better write down exactly what my Mets duties would be. We worked it out that I'd be at all the Mets' home games, work with the players, and then leave when the game started.

The first two years were very hard on me emotionally. I would get up at nine in the morning ready to play ball. Or I'd wake up in the middle of the night worrying about a situation in the game the next day and what I could do about it. Except there was nothing I could do about it. That was why I couldn't stay in uniform once the game started. I had to get out of there. It was as if I was in a bad dream trying to walk and something was holding me back. That's how I felt if I sat in the dugout and couldn't contribute. I would go home and watch the game on television.

There was another aspect of my new life. I was learning about a career outside of baseball. That was one of the hardest changes I've ever been forced to make.

Take a guy like me, who from the time I had been a teenager had almost no decisions to make about where I'd be working. The club told you when spring training started, when to get on the bus, when to come to play. Not only that, the club took you there. They paid your way to get to a game, took care of your meals, told you what time to get to bed and arranged for your wake-up calls.

What would I be doing when the playing ended? Ball players like to say they think about it. We don't. For me, that other world was brought into focus in my last year with the Mets. I was enjoying myself at an off-season golf tournament run by American Airlines in Puerto Rico. There are a dozen events like that every year, in beautiful settings where you get the best food and suites. I was playing with a businessman named Vern Alden, and he asked me this question:

"Willie, what are you going to do when you get out of baseball?"

I didn't know. I had played baseball from the time I was fourteen, and now I was beginning to wind down my career as a ball player. So I went upstairs and I thought about it for a while. Then I called Vern and I said, "Mr. Alden, you better explain what you mean." We talked for a while and we narrowed it down to public relations. He gave me the names of five companies, including Ogden and Colgate and a textile company down south. I wound up working with Colgate for twelve years, along with Ogden and the textile firm.

Now here I was forty-three years old, and I still was expecting people to make decisions for me.

After Mrs. Payson died, Donald Grant, the chairman of

the Mets, told me he wanted me to stay for the games, and also go on some road trips. But I had also gotten involved with those other companies, and they wanted me at dinners and golf outings.

At the time I didn't know it, but Grant ordered the Mets' general manager, Joe McDonald, to keep a diary on me—when I showed up at Shea Stadium, how long I remained. Grant collected the notes and called me into his office one day and said he was suspending me for not showing up at the park. We compromised. I would work with the kids, be at the games for four innings, visit some of the farm teams, and appear at booster-club dinners. We also agreed that McDonald would stop taking notes.

When I reported to spring training in 1975, there was another change. The Mets didn't seem to know what to do with me. They brought in Phil Cavaretta, the Cubs' former first baseman, to work with the hitters. Now, I really felt like a spare part. It's really too bad that my last years in a New York uniform were filled with politics and that I never had a chance to do what I enjoyed most—working with youngsters.

Still, one of my dreams came true while I was with the Mets—getting into the Hall of Fame. You aren't eligible for the Baseball Hall of Fame until five years have passed since your last game. The reason is that the committee wants to make sure you have lived an honorable life, and also that you haven't decided to return to play. It would be embarrassing to see a Hall of Fame player performing, especially if he no longer could play well. It's hard to get into the Hall in your first crack at eligibility. Duke Snider didn't.

I'm proud to say I got in—in fact, I was the only player elected for 1979. I became only the ninth player in history to get in on my first try. My total of 94.6 percent of the votes was the highest since the first year of voting, when Ty Cobb got 98.2 percent and Babe Ruth and Honus Wagner 95.1 percent.

Such players as Snider, Enos Slaughter, Gil Hodges and Don Drysdale didn't get the required three quarters of the votes of the senior baseball writers in '79. Indeed, the fact that I was omitted on 23 of the 432 ballots led Jack Anderson, the investigative columnist, to launch a search to find out why my name was off those ballots. That made me proud all over again.

We made the induction ceremonies a festival. I had two busloads of friends come up. This is the short speech I made:

"What can I say? This country is made up of a great many things. You can grow up to be what you want. I chose baseball, and I loved every minute of it. I give you one word —love. It means dedication. You have to sacrifice many things to play baseball. I sacrificed a bad marriage and I sacrificed a good marriage. But I'm here today because baseball is my number one love."

I hadn't been in the Hall of Fame long enough for my plaque to gather dust when I was kicked out of baseball.

My friend Sy Berger had been talking to me about Joe Louis, and how he had worked as a greeter for Caesars Palace in Las Vegas. Sy felt that this was something I could look into for extra income. There was a new hotel opening in Atlantic City called Bally's. Why not try them? I made a deal with Bally's to greet people, play a little golf with them. I wasn't even going to be where the gambling was. And I would be paid $100,000 a year, with a ten-year deal. I didn't realize what an earthquake that would cause.

How could I know that? The closest I came to gambling was on the golf course. I had been doing this for years, playing golf with the high rollers. One of the "perks" they gave the big gamblers, along with a private room to play in, was to set up golf games with sports celebrities. Heck, every big name in American sports—football, baseball, basketball, hockey—had been coming to Las Vegas or Atlantic

City for years for just such events. The casino would put you on the links with four people, just the high rollers. But nothing involving gambling. They'd fly us out, give us the room, the meals. Now the only difference was that the casino wanted me on a long-term basis and would pay me.

When Bowie Kuhn, the commissioner of baseball, found out about it, he told me I couldn't take the job and stay in baseball. This struck me as crazy. I was doing public relations for the place, not teaching people how to gamble. As an employee of a casino, by state law I wasn't even allowed to gamble within a hundred miles of Bally's. Besides, casinos were legal in New Jersey. I wasn't accepting a job with some shady operator. I knew that some baseball owners, such as George Steinbrenner of the Yankees, owned race horses. He was around gambling all the time. The Galbreaths of the Pirates were among the most famous racing owners in America. My contract even was drawn up with the help of Al Rosen, who had been the Yankees' president and knew the Bally's people. Al was one of the most highly regarded people in baseball. How much more respectability did you need?

I told the commissioner, "Look, I'm only going to Bally's to be doing the same thing I've been doing at The Dunes in Vegas for years."

Kuhn didn't want to hear any of it. He didn't care that for years he had never said anything about all those golf tournaments in Las Vegas. What was the difference between doing that, and getting paid then, and now doing this? It took me an hour, but I realized Kuhn would not change his mind.

He told everyone that I could not take money from two places. Well, that meant I could take it from only one. I left the Mets, left baseball, for Bally's Park Place Hotel. I felt as if I was practically being banned. Later, he did the same thing to Mickey Mantle. So Willie and Mickey were in the same boat again, only this time banned from the game we both loved so much. How's that for irony? Maybe Kuhn should have kicked out the Duke, too.

Going to Bally's was one of the hardest things I ever had to do. I didn't understand what the business world was all about. I wasn't aware of time. Oh, I understood, roughly, about keeping appointments. But in business, when they say eleven o'clock, they mean eleven o'clock, not 11:05. I had a problem with Charlie Tannenbaum and Bill Weinberger when I went there. Charlie is the senior vice president of Bally's Park Place and Bill is the president. Charlie sat me down and explained to me what was required. But, the first few years, I had a job to do and I didn't understand the job. They explained to me what the word "visible" meant. I had to be there and be seen.

That was the beginning of my growing up in the business world. I think in the years I've been there I missed only one appointment.

When you're the star of a ball club, when you get to the park you do nothing. You're just there to play. Everything is done for you. But in the business world it's different. You have to do things yourself, and I wasn't aware of that. But my new bosses at Bally's explained to me that they had to answer to other people, and I had to answer to them. It took me three or four years, but I grew up in learning what the business world was all about. I think I'm as comfortable now in the business world as I once was in baseball.

As it worked out, despite Kuhn's connecting me to gambling, I spent more time for Bally's at schools talking to kids than I did at the casino. Still do. I explained to Bowie that Mr. Weinberger had assured me I was going to be involved in the casinos only to play golf with the high rollers. Same as I'd been doing anyway when no one had found it objectionable. It had nothing to do with gambling. They didn't need me for that. That's what I tried to tell him. I never said anything publicly about Bowie or what he did to me. I thought about it, and I even discussed it with my friend Morty Rothschild. But he told me never to knock a man when he knocks you. Instead, praise him. The praise kills him more than the knock.

The morning I made the announcement that I would go to Atlantic City, I met one last time with Bowie. "Tell me what to do," I said, almost pleading. "How can I work it so that I can continue to make a living in baseball but not throw away another job?" He wouldn't bend. He said if I went to Atlantic City I couldn't be in baseball. It was that simple. I still don't know why.

The funny thing is, about a year after that I received an invitation to a benefit dinner for Bowie. A lot of people didn't think I'd go. But I went. And the first face I saw when I got there was Bowie's. His eyes made contact with mine. He came over and hugged me. I think he wanted to do something about his decision then, but he had made his stand. And you know how it is—you can't back down when you've committed yourself in front of the whole country. I never said anything. My attitude was: Whatever you say is all right with me. And I think that might have helped me get back in baseball again.

It's never come out before, but that wasn't the first job Bowie cost me. At the height of my career in San Francisco, I had an offer to go to Japan. But Bowie told me that he couldn't permit a major star to leave American baseball. It would be just as if Babe Ruth deserted the States to play in another country. What would that say about baseball in America? That the ball players didn't want to stay here? It could disrupt our game and start a flow of players to Japan, and lower the quality of our own game. Because the major leagues and the Japanese baseball establishment had a close working relationship, Bowie was able to use his influence to kill the Japanese offer.

He certainly shouldn't have worried whether I would hurt baseball's image by working in Atlantic City. In fact, it was almost as if gambling took a back seat to social work where I was involved. With all the problems it caused me, I guess it worked out okay because going to Atlantic City also spurred something I'm very proud of, the Say Hey Foundation.

Say Hey, my nickname. A lot of people say I got it when I became a Giant because I didn't know people's names. Instead of calling someone by his name, I'd go, "Say, hey!" But Barney Kremenko, an older writer friend who used to be with the *New York Journal-American*, insists he gave me that name. Barney says that I used to have a habit, when I didn't understand something, of answering, "Say what?" or "Say that again!" So Barney started calling me "Say hey." Whatever, I became the Say Hey Kid.

Because I was visible, because people knew the name Willie Mays, because I was now associated with a fabulously successful business, people had started to ask me to help out various charities. The average man connected me with casinos and thought I was very rich with an unlimited flow of money. I quickly realized I needed to have a reason to give people money, that just because something sounded worthwhile, I couldn't start making contributions. I was not rich.

I have always wanted to leave something for the world. Does that sound like a big ambition? Sure, but why shouldn't you have dreams like that? My record in baseball will be one thing I can leave. I also wanted something more concrete. That's how the foundation came along.

I've always thought you're better off giving money to one person to help change his or her life, rather than giving a few hundred dollars spread around. So my foundation concentrates on half a dozen youngsters at a time, but affects their life in very positive ways. We send kids through school, through the four years of college or prep school. We're talking about a commitment that can exceed fifty-thousand dollars to each youngster.

My friend and business adviser Carl Kiesler is a foundation director and he assesses the applicants, then talks it over with me. We make the final decision.

I met Carl through one of my oldest friends, Morty Rothschild, a Chrysler dealer in White Plains, New York. Carl is a C.P.A., and he helped get me back on the right track toward financial stability. I have gotten involved in real estate, for example, and I also have spread my investments so that they're not all tied up in one bundle. Once I was able to get my finances straightened, I was in a position to help others. Through the foundation we take care of a very interesting group of kids of all races: a pre-med student at Cornell, a young woman from The Bronx who was at the poverty level and is now enjoying a new life at Wilberforce University in Ohio. There are others, and we hear from them and we know we have made an impact on their lives. A significant portion of the foundation's funding comes from a golf tournament I run every year in Briarcliff Manor, New York, at Briar Hall Country Club. I also direct money to the foundation from such events as, say, a roast in my honor, or from contributions sent to Bally's. If a young person's financial need is real, we'll take care of it. No strings attached. Well, in a sense there are: This is very important to me—if we help a kid, and he's an athlete, and he goes through four years of college and then becomes a pro when he gets out, all I ask is that he put it back. Now he's able to help someone himself.

But I'd been helping kids long before the foundation started. With Bally's, I visited youngsters and told them about the dangers of drugs and the kind of life they'd been leading, and emphasized how important it was that they get an education. Afterward, some of them would hug and kiss me—and none of them had even seen me play, except in picture books or on old film clips. I visited hospitals, bringing gifts donated by Bally's.

Nothing prepared me, though, for one extremely emotional day I had. I would go to schools, colleges, everywhere in the Philadelphia and South Jersey area. I never talk about gambling. I'd gear the talk to the audience. If I was at a school where the kids were between the ages of five and ten, I'd talk about myself and playing ball. I also spoke at many drug centers. That was the hardest part for me, talking to youngsters who were locked up. There was one place where I was talking when I spotted this young black kid in a corner. He raised his hand and he just started to cry. I brought him up with me and I said, "Go ahead. Cry." So he cried and then he just started to talk. He talked about himself, and how he got there, how religious he is, but how he couldn't help himself. I guess the two of us started to cry at the same time because I had never been through this before. We both cried and talked for fifteen or twenty minutes, and then after that I got through to all of the other kids.

It was strange how I wound up doing something Joe Louis did, working for a casino. Poor Joe. Whenever he came to San Francisco he'd always stay at my home. I'd pick him and his wife, Martha, up at the airport. He'd always take my bedroom. He used to call me "little boy," and would say things like, "Little boy, you got any equipment in the house?" He meant ice cream. He always liked to have ice cream around.

I sneaked in some when I used to play, but for the most part I really tried to take care of myself and always was very conscious of getting enough rest. Maybe there was some luck involved in lasting as long as I did. Maybe I also helped lengthen my career by telling the Candlestick groundskeepers to put extra padding under the artificial turf in centerfield. I'm sure that helped keep my legs for another couple of years.

I had fun when I played. But today they don't allow pepper games, throwing and batting the ball around near home plate. I used to play that all the time with Leo and

Monte Irvin. Leo was the batter and I always played him for a Coke. We'd stand fifteen feet apart and he'd try to hit the ball past me. He'd really rip some of them. If he got the ball by me, or I bobbled it, I'd owe him a Coke.

That's the way I approached the game. I tried to have fun, but also at times to use some psychology. I liked to go up to bat talking. I'd tell the catcher I didn't have any idea what his pitcher was throwing. Then, after the catcher would get in his crouch, I'd peek between his legs to see what sign he was giving the pitcher. Johnny Bench of the Reds caught me good one day.

"When you stop looking, Willie," he said, "I'll be ready to call for the pitch."

Or I'd tell Sam Jones I couldn't hit his curve ball. Sure enough, with two strikes on me, Sam would try the curve as his "out" pitch and I was ready for it.

But the All-Star Games really were the most fun, because nothing was on the line except your talent. Still, once the game started, you played to win. I played in 24 games. I didn't miss one from 1954 to 1973, including the four years in between when we played two games a year. I hit .307 in the All-Star Games; but at one at bat in 1961 Whitey Ford got me to strike out on the craziest pitch I ever saw. It was an 0–2 count, and I waited for the curve ball. It started for my shoulders and I ducked away. All of a sudden the ball dropped across for a strike. I looked straight ahead past Ford and I saw Mantle in centerfield jumping up and down like a little boy.

What was that all about? I asked Whitey later. He told me that they had run up a big tab at Horace Stoneham's club, and that Horace had bet him double or nothing. If Whitey could strike me out, they didn't owe him a thing.

"I'm sorry, Willie," said Whitey, "but I had to throw you a spitter."

Can you imagine ballplayers today trying to beat someone for the price of a free meal? Well, maybe I can, because

we've always been known as cheapskates. But still, a good
ball player—I'm not even saying a great one—makes
enough in two or three years now to retire for life. That is,
if he doesn't just let it all slip away. If there's one thing I'd
tell today's ball player about money, it's that you've got to
do something with it right now. If you don't, it leaves you.
I didn't learn that when I was playing baseball. I found out
about that after I left. Do something now, while your name
is up here, not when it's down there. When your name's on
the ground, no one's going to do anything for you. I wish
someone had told me this when I was playing. Luckily, I
had Carl and other solid friends to give me advice once I
did stop playing.

   A lot of people got things wrong when they talked about
me and money when I was playing. One of the things I
heard some criticism about was that I charged a hundred
dollars to be interviewed on the air. Usually I'd be on radio
or television after a game if I was the star of that game.
What wasn't known was that the one hundred went to four
people. Those four were the 25th, 24th, 23rd and 22d players on the ball club. Those guys never played every day, but
they wanted to be part of the team. You see, when you're
the star of a ball club, and, say, you have a three-game series
and you hit two or three home runs in that series, you'll go
on a different radio or television show every night. They
used to pay twenty-five or fifty dollars, but I told them,
"Give me a hundred." They didn't have to know what I was
doing with it. But stories came out about that, and they
made it look as though I was grubbing for money. But
people didn't know what I really did with the money, that I
wasn't asking for me. I gave four guys twenty-five dollars
apiece. I made the 22d through 25th ball players happy.

   Twenty-five dollars today? Now, the 25th player probably is earning more than DiMaggio or Williams or Mays
ever did. What this does is mess with a man's incentive. I
came up in the era when your next year's salary was based

on what you did last year—not what you did three years ago, when you signed a five-year contract.

DiMaggio told me the best story I ever heard about the old days—about how you got paid for performance.

In 1940 he hit .352. He led the league. He had a .626 slugging average. He hit 31 homers and drove in 133 runs. But the team finished third. So when he went in to negotiate his 1941 contract, they actually offered him less money.

"They told me that I had hit .381 in 1939 and we had won the pennant," laughed Joe. "Since we didn't win the pennant in 1940, I obviously didn't contribute as much."

I don't think Joe was laughing then. But that's what it was all about—contributing, and winning. That was the bottom line. And raises, even in my time, were figured in the thousands, not tens of thousands or hundreds of thousands.

It makes no sense to me to give a twenty-two-year-old who has a big year a contract that sets him up for life. I don't say that we played only for the money. But we certainly understood that if we did well, and the team did well, we'd get paid more. We couldn't live off last year's stolen base or great catch. That is what incentive is all about. You have to have a reason to want to be better. You want to be rewarded for an outstanding season. Now, though, you hear so many stories of clubs that are saddled with a long-term contract for a player they no longer want. What does the club do? It trades the player and still pays part of his salary to the new team.

All of this came about within a few years of my retirement, when free agency became the law of baseball land. Oh, my. Can you imagine the stars of the '50s as free agents? Stan the Man, or Mickey, or Duke, or Warren Spahn? How much would we have been worth?

I'm not so sure that free agency benefited the game of baseball so much as it benefited the ball players. It used to be that a club owner had a pretty good idea where he was

headed down the road—what sort of players he had coming
up in his farm system, how much he could count on his
veterans. An owner, a manager, a coach, they knew who
they could count on. They could make plans. There was a
certain stability to the franchise.

Once the arbitrator ruled that a player was free to make
his own deal, many of the values that I treasured suddenly
went down the drain. I believed in a family atmosphere on
a club. That's one of the reasons I was so upset when I
found out the Giants were going to trade me. But it also
was a reason I was so proud and happy to become a Met.
Mrs. Payson had a genuine regard for me. Now, as soon as
there is the least bit of friction, ball players threaten to
leave. Many do. Rather than work out their problems with
the manager, they take their attitudes with them to their
new team.

While I didn't play under free agency, I started to see a
change in mutual respect. Oh, ball players always griped.
I'm not saying we didn't. But there was also a . . . what's
the word I want? . . . pride. Yes, pride, in being there, in
being one of a few hundred ball players out of the tens of
millions of Americans who dreamed one day of becoming a
big-leaguer. Maybe the changes were part of the 1960's
social upheaval, or the cynical 1970's. Of course, a lot of
the things that changed were good. Maybe you should question authority when the orders just don't make sense. Hey,
didn't I have my run-ins? But my overall attitude was that I
respected my manager and I paid attention to what he
wanted. I think I also respected the people who owned the
club. They were the ones who were saddled with the ex-
penses when the team was lousy and the fans stayed home.
Some ball players I played with never understood my attitude toward ownership. They thought I must be some kind
of traitor to be able to see the other side of baseball life.
And I must admit that I've been closer to ownership than
most players, in fact, probably closer than any of my con-

temporaries. That never stopped me from trying to be the best ball player Willie Mays could be. Because I had always tried so hard, I couldn't relate to many of the things I saw going on in the years after I left baseball. Still, with all the aggravation I had endured over the casino business, I wanted to get back into baseball. God, I still loved it.

By 1985, Peter Ueberroth was baseball's new commissioner. I had known him from his days in the travel agency business. He called me on the phone a few times and discussed the possibility of bringing me back into baseball. Finally he called me into his office.

"Why shouldn't you be back in baseball? You're not doing anything wrong," he said. He told me about all the people who had been in baseball and horse racing over the years, even reminding me that Mrs. Payson had been a horse owner.

"The world changes," announced Ueberroth, and he promptly brought me and Mickey back into baseball.

"I am bringing back two players who are more a part of baseball than perhaps anyone else," he said.

Funny how thirty-five years before we broke into baseball together, and now we were getting back in together.

Later that season, I appeared in an Old Timers game at Yankee Stadium. I was in centerfield and a blooper was hit to right center. Bobby Avila was the second baseman and he chased it a little. Larry Doby was the rightfielder and he sort of loped after it, too. I ran between them and I made a shoestring catch, then did a somersault on the grass.

"Why did you guys do that?" I asked them in the dugout. "I didn't have to run all the way to make that catch. Either one of you could have caught it."

"This is New York, Willie," said Doby. "They didn't come to see us, they came to see you."

In 1986 Al Rosen was starting his first full year as president and general manager of the Giants. He wanted to reestablish pride in the uniform. He said he could think of no better way to do it than by bringing back some people like Willie Mays.

He explained to me he needed help in bringing back that old tradition of winning. We had been losing so much, and there just wasn't any motivation to win. "Something's missing in this organization," he said.

I met him in his office to discuss what I'd do. But I don't think I knew more than three players on his ballclub. There were just a bunch of young kids on the club. Of course, I knew Roger Craig, the manager. After a week with the club, I felt very comfortable and I think I had a good impact on them.

When Al was asked what he was hoping to do by bringing me back, he explained, "From everything I ever witnessed, Mays was the finest player I ever saw. When I took over the club it had no direction, no central core, everybody was looking to try to get away from the Giants. I had to do something dramatic to get things done. Willie was happy to get back into the game. Being back in uniform was a return for him to a past that he really enjoyed.

"What did I want from him? Only to be in uniform in spring training and to be with the players. I wanted nothing more than for him to be there, to advise and help out. His presence is electric, and the reaction by the other ball players was exactly what I was looking for.

"I played against him for years, when I was with the Indians. And the thing I remember most about Willie Mays, believe it or not, was the pepper games that he used to get into with Leo Durocher. To watch him do the things he did . . . you know, baseball players are rather jaded about other ball players . . . but I used to watch him playing pepper before a ball game. I also remember, playing against him you always had the feeling you were playing against someone who was going to be the greatest of all time.

"When I came to San Francisco, I found that for the fans there the Giants began in 1958. But I wanted to bring back someone who could remind them that the Giants have a great history, that there are more people in the Hall of Fame who wore a Giants uniform than from any other team."

Look at how quickly good things happened to the Giants once Al took over. You're talking about a team that went from last place to winning their division and almost getting to the World Series, all in a span of about three years. The average person might look at the record and say, well, what did Willie have to do with it? But I feel a part of it. I think that my motivating the players had a lot to do with it.

I know that I got more excited watching the Giants' pennant race in 1987 than I did at any time while I was playing. On the field you have to show you're calm. At least I tried to show I was in control because I had to take care of a lot of people on the field. A doctor once told me that I had put so much into the game, my body needed a breather. That's the reason I had those periodic collapses. My body was wound too tightly.

I do a lot now and sometimes I get tired. But I look at Bob Hope and George Burns, working well into their eighties, and I say, geez, I can't really be tired. Travel knocks me out, though. I suppose if I wanted to, I could be appearing in a different place every day. Sometimes it seems like I am. I restrict my activities now to things I have fun doing. Like baseball-card shows. There are a lot of great ball players out there who draw fans. But there are only five or six of us whom the promoter really can count on to sell out— Hank Aaron, Mickey, me. Not that many. I get my kicks when kids bring me a card from 1952 and ask me to sign it. You know, Topps bubble gum never made a Willie Mays rookie card for 1951, and the rookie cards are the most valuable ones of all. After the '51 season started, they came out with one, but you couldn't get one of me in the spring. When I began to realize how valuable those cards were— someone told me my '51 and '52 cards were worth four thousand dollars each—I actually looked around my house for old cards. But like most people, I didn't have one. I had thrown them out years before.

Golf probably takes up more of my time than any other activity. I started to get interested when I knew my career was moving toward a close. I realized I could use a sport to keep me active once I hung up the glove. Golf is a game I work at and I'm about a 9 handicap. I approach it the same way I did baseball. I want to win. I've never seen a good loser. But you always see a good winner, laughing, enjoying what he's doing. When I first took it up, I wasn't a good player. But I kept at it. I wish I were a better player, but I've also got a problem with my right hand. Bursitis, because of baseball. At least I like to think it's because of baseball. A doctor I went to says it's because of old age.

Golf has enabled me to play with the greatest of my time. To me, Arnold Palmer was the most dignified. He had a sense of himself. I never played with Jack Nicklaus, but I did play behind him. He was all business. Lee Trevino, Chi Chi Rodriguez and Lee Elder—they all were fun guys. Fuzzy Zoeller was like that. Fun, enjoying himself. Remember, when I play with these guys it's not usually in a tourney for a lot of money. But you can tell how they react during the big-money events by the way they act during the pro-ams. It still bothers me when I hear that Palmer can't automatically enter some big tournament because he hasn't qualified. After all he's done for the game? It reminds me of the time I couldn't go to the ballpark. As long as Arnie wants to play, let him play.

For me, I confess I'd still like to be able to have a job in baseball that gives me a say in the operation. I don't mean managing. I don't think I've got the temperament to manage. I don't think I could sit in a dugout every day and make those decisions. But I think this: I'd be a pretty smart manager because I'd know enough to surround myself with people who could help me. You show me one manager who thinks he can do the whole job, I assure you he won't be there long. But I've always been able to evaluate talent. Sometimes people don't think you know what's going on because they just don't ask for your comments.

Of course, if you ask me what I'd really like to be doing, the answer is simple: All I ever wanted was to play baseball forever. Leo always thought I could.

Index

Tannenbaum, Charlie, 264
Tatum, Goose, 35
Taylor, Robert, 25
Terry, Bill, 71, 95, 114, 128
Terry, Ralph, 185–88
Thies, Jake, 114
Thompson, Hank, 44, 63, 66,
    67, 112, 116, 119, 120, 122,
    136, 148
Thomson, Bobby, 63, 72, 81, 86,
    87, 88, 89, 95, 97, 106, 129,
    143, 148
    pennant-winning home run of,
    14–15, 90–91, 105, 163,
    176, 180, 181, 248
Thurman, Bob, 125
Tiant, Luis, 239
Torre, Frank, 241
Tresh, Tom, 185, 186
Trevino, Lee, 276

Ueberroth, Peter, 273

Veeck, Bill, 34–35

Wagner, Honus, 261
Wagner, Leon, 148
Wagner, Robert F., 110
Waitkus, Eddie, 86
Walker, Moses Fleetwood, 33
Walker, Rube, 91
Walker, Welday, 33
Walls, Lee, 181
Warneke, Lon, 86

Washburn, Ray, 232
Weavil, Bo, 25
Wegener, Mike, 243
Weinberger, Bill, 264
Weiss, George, 95
Wendell, Marghuerite, 133–34,
    147, 152, 154, 200–2
Wertz, Vic, 117, 119, 120, 121,
    144
Westlake, Wally, 120
Westrum, Wes, 78, 82, 83, 97,
    116, 120, 143, 148, 163
White, Bill, 136, 139, 140, 148
White, Sammy, 152
Wilhelm, Hoyt, 116
Williams, Charlie, 250
Williams, Davey, 116, 118, 130
Williams, Dick, 65
Williams, Ted, 28, 100 166,
    184–85, 190, 211, 225,
    229–30, 232, 270
Willis, Charlie, 19–20, 21
Wills, Maury, 171, 178, 181,
    221
Wilson, Artie, 35, 40
Wood, Charlie, 37, 42
Woodling, Gene, 94, 95, 97
Wright, Taft, 58–59
Wynn, Early, 117, 120
Wynn, Jim, 225

Yvars, Sal, 97

Zimmer, Don, 125
Zoeller, Fuzzy, 276

Photo Credits